Explorer's Guide to the Semantic Web

Explorer's Guide to the Semantic Web

THOMAS B. PASSIN

MANNING

Greenwich
(74° w. long.)

For online information and ordering of this and other Manning books, go to
www.manning.com. The publisher offers discounts on this book when ordered in quantity.
For more information, please contact:

    Special Sales Department
    Manning Publications Co.
    209 Bruce Park Avenue   Fax: (203) 661-9018
    Greenwich, CT 06830   email: orders@manning.com

 Manning Publications Co.   Copyeditor: Tiffany Taylor
    209 Bruce Park Avenue   Typesetter: Denis Dalinnik
    Greenwich, CT 06830   Cover designer: Leslie Haimes

ISBN 1-932394-20-6

Printed in the United States of America
1 2 3 4 5 6 7 8 9 10 – VHG – 08 07 06 05 04

To my father, the late Herbert Passin,
and to my dear wife, Mary Ann

contents

preface

In the mid-1990s, I happened upon the topic of conceptual graphs (CGs), which are a way to represent formal logic statements using diagrams. I was accustomed to entity-relationship (ER) modeling, and I was immediately fascinated by CGs because they seemed so expressive and natural, a tremendously useful extension of ER diagrams. Also, they had grown out of efforts to represent expression in natural language, and because of this it was easy to read off the contents of a graph in English. In 1999 I discovered topic maps, which instantly struck me as a simplified implementation of CGs, one that was well suited to hooking into the Web.

I had no project at work that justified my spending much time on these subjects, but I began to study them when I could and to introduce them to others. A year or two later, I started to come across mentions of RDF and then of the Semantic Web; I began to fit them into my mental picture, which by now included distributed databases and web applications, markup languages such as HTML and XML, and of course CGs and topic maps.

I found the Semantic Web the hardest of all to get a handle on, because it seemed to range from obvious extensions of what I already knew on the one extreme, to extremely complex and advanced integrations of logic, semantics, and artificial intelligence on the other. I now know that I was not the only one to become bewildered, yet fascinated, by the Semantic Web.

One other such person was Marjan Bace, publisher of Manning. The Semantic Web came up by chance during a phone conversation we had, and before I quite knew how it had come about, Manning had a new book project and I was off and running. At the time, I had no idea how demanding the work would be (although I thought I did) nor how long it would take (although I thought I did). The Semantic Web hooks into an enormous number of technologies and disciplines, and they all have to work together in complex and nonlinear ways. It is too much for a single person to know intimately, yet the author's job is to make it clear and understandable to the reader. That's what this book attempts to do: make this fascinating and complex subject clear, concise, and accessible.

acknowledgments

Working on this book has brought me in contact with many, many talented people, some of whom have become friends. I have learned from all of them: from their carefully thought-out posts to online discussion groups; from personal discussions; or from their example. It would be impossible to name them all, but I'd like to mention a few, including Uche Ogbuji, Paul Prescod, Sean McGrath, Bill de hÓra, Steve Newcomb, and Sam Hunting. Others who would otherwise be named here were generous enough to become technical reviewers for this book.

The technical reviewers played an important role in shaping the book—especially the subjects it omits. Not every comment and suggestion appears directly (and some I didn't agree with), but I gave each one individual consideration and they all left their mark on the book in one way or another. I'm enormously grateful to each of the reviewers for the time and care they put into their task. I have done it myself and know what it takes. Of course, errors and misinformation that remain are my doing alone.

Here are the reviewers whose names were passed on to me (two others wished their names to remain private): Michel Biezunski, Jim Davis, Duane Degler, Andy Dingley, Bob DuCharme, Erik D. Freese, Aron K. Insinga, Rick Jelliffe, Alexander Johannesen, Jeffrey Lowery, Bradford Miller, Erik Naggum, Uche Ogbuji, Neil W. Rickert, Joshua Stern, and Danny Vint.

Many developmental editors participated during the slow evolution of the manuscript, of whom Marilyn Smith was the most prominent. Alexander

Johannesen, also one of the reviewers, was good enough to agree to be the technical editor during production. Tiffany Taylor, the production editor, stunned me with the thoughtfulness and sheer volume of her copy-editorial markup (a result of her diligence and skill).

And without Marjan Bace and those long phone calls, there would be no *Explorer's Guide to the Semnatic Web*.

Finally, and most important, I've had the constant support and encouragement provided by my dear wife, Mary Ann. Little did she know what she was getting into when I agreed to write this book!

about this book

The *Semantic Web*—the phrase brings an outburst of enthusiasm from some, while putting a frown on the faces of others who suggest that it means little, if anything. Opinions vary wildly: The Semantic Web will give you software agents that will tackle your daily needs quietly, effectively, even with common sense, finding the information they need and negotiating with other agents on your behalf. Or, the Semantic Web will be a little more of what we have now—a little faster, a little smarter, with more complex software. Or, the Semantic Web is all hype. It all depends on whom you talk to.

This book claims that there is a degree of overlap between the views of various proponents: a commonality that goes beyond hype. If anything like these visions comes to pass, certain developments, infrastructure, and technology will be needed. Some are here now, some are almost here, some have barely begun. We'll look at the notion of the Semantic Web, what it might be, what it might do for people, and some of the base technologies that would support it. This book intends to bring you two kinds of understanding. First, you'll get a look at a number of these key ideas and how they might work together. This involves a degree of judicious guessing, since we can't know for sure which of them will turn out to be the most important. Second, the book will give you some background about the technical issues—enough to help you get started, should you be interested in going further. It can't go deeply into any one subject, for the work would expand like an accordion to an unwieldy size. Also, some of the areas are too undeveloped to reduce to standard practice.

The book concentrates on concepts and design rather than straight programming and code, but it includes markup examples to illustrate ideas and some basics of the technologies. It attempts to bring simplicity and clarity to the ideas, even though there is an inherent complexity that can't be totally disguised. To support these goals, the book uses non-mainstream techniques to enhance clarity. They include placing mind maps at the start of chapters and using a simplified format instead of the standard RDF/XML format for some RDF and OWL examples.

Think of this book as a field guide. In a field guide to birds, you would get a picture of their plumage and some facts about their environments, lives, and habits. To learn more, you would have to consult specialized material. So too with this work.

Roadmap

The first part of the book sets the stage with potential scenarios for the Semantic Web and highlights important technological features of the World Wide Web as we know it. It also shows the great range of ideas people have about what the Semantic Web is. The bulk of the book covers technologies and areas of interest or significance to the Semantic Web in an order that roughly represents both the current state of their development and the degree to which they will be built on by later, more complex developments.

The book starts with the representation of knowledge, represented by topic maps and RDF (chapters 1 through 3), moves to application areas like search and annotation (chapters 4 and 5), and proceeds to technologies and disciplines like logic and ontology that are being layered over the more developed technologies (chapters 6 and 7). Then the book examines web services and how they fit into the Semantic Web picture (chapter 8). Next come intelligent agents and then the difficult and complex areas of distributed trust and belief (chapters 9 and 10). The book ends with an attempt to put all the previous material into a useful perspective. How much is practical now, how much will be in the near or mid future, and what parts may be asking too much? I provide suggestions and guidelines for possible use in your upcoming projects that can assist in orienting your work more toward the Semantic Web as it starts to materialize and evolve (chapter 11).

Who should read this book?

Who will find this book useful? Essentially, anyone with a software-related interest in the future World Wide Web, from programmers to designers, requirements engineers, and managers. This book is not a programming manual, but focuses on foundations and concepts. Markup examples are included to illustrate certain key points and to give some sense of how the technologies work. Clarity, simplicity, and readability are emphasized above technical completeness.

Because Extensible Markup Language (XML) plays a prominent role in some of the important technologies such as RDF, Topic Maps, and OWL, a reading acquaintance with XML will be useful. If you've written a little HTML, that should be enough to read the examples. If you haven't encountered either XML or HTML before, a basic introduction to XML would be helpful (you won't need any of the more esoteric parts).

Typographical conventions

There is no code, in the sense of programming language fragments, in this book. However, there are a number of examples of markup language. These are typeset in a fixed width font. Lines that are too long to fit on the page have been wrapped. Whenever possible, these lines have been broken in a manner that is acceptable for the markup. Many of the markup listings have been annotated with numbered bullets that link to explanations following the listings. In a few cases, comments have been inserted into the markup at strategic locations.

About the mind maps

Each chapter in this book starts with a mind map that captures the essential pieces of the material presented in the chapter and their interrelations. For example, here's the mind map from chapter 3.

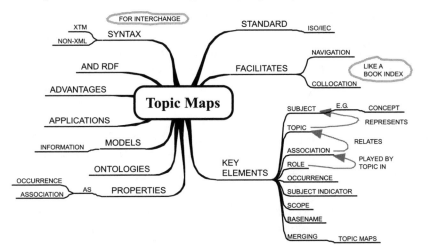

Mind-mapping is an informal way to capture ideas and associations between them. Tony Buzan invented the technique; his book (*The Mind Map Book: How to Use Radiant Thinking to Maximize Your Brain's Untapped Potential*) is well worth reading. Among other uses, mind maps are excellent for notes and lecture plans. They can be helpful in stimulating creativity. They aren't well known, though, so they merit a few words of explanation.

Mind maps have a central focal topic and branches on which ride keywords. The branching pattern connects associated concepts, thoughts, ideas, or facts—whatever is important or notable to the map's creator. It's also possible to use color, graphic images, cross links, and other features to enhance your mind maps and to make them more effective. The branches of a mind map aren't usually ordered, although you can order them if you like.

Author Online

Purchase of *Explorer's Guide to the Semantic Web* includes free access to a private web forum run by Manning Publications where you can make comments about the book, ask technical questions, and receive help from the author and from other users. To access the forum and subscribe to it, point your web browser to www.manning.com/passin. This page provides information on how to get on the forum once you are registered, what kind of help is available, and the rules of conduct on the forum.

Manning's commitment to our readers is to provide a venue where a meaningful dialog between individual readers and between readers and the authors can take place. It is not a commitment to any specific amount of participation on the part of the author, whose contribution to the AO remains voluntary (and unpaid). We suggest you try asking the author some challenging questions lest his interest stray! The Author Online forum and the archives of previous discussions will be accessible from the publisher's web site as long as the book is in print.

About the author

Thomas Passin is Principal Systems Engineer with Mitretek Systems, a non-profit systems and information engineering company. He has been involved in data modeling and a variety of XML-related projects. He has created several complex database-backed web sites and has also been engaged in a range of conceptual modeling approaches and graphical modeling technologies. He was a key member of a team that developed several demonstration XML-based web service applications and he worked on creating XML versions of draft message standards originally written in ASN.1.

He graduated with a B.S. in physics from the Massachusetts Institute of Technology, then studied graduate-level physics at the University of Chicago. He became involved with XML-related work in 1998 and with Topic Maps in 1999 and developed the open-source TM4JScript Javascript topic map engine. Thomas Passin is also coauthor of the book *Signal Processing in C*. He lives in Reston, Virginia.

About the cover illustration

The figure on the cover of *Explorer's Guide to the Semantic Web* is a "Muger Arabe del desierto de Zara," an Arab woman who lives in the Sahara Desert. At 3.5 million square miles, the Sahara Desert in northern Africa is the world's largest desert. In spite of the inhospitable climate, it is home to over two million people. The illustration is taken from a Spanish compendium of regional dress customs first published in Madrid in 1799. The book's title page states:

> *Coleccion general de los Trages que usan actualmente todas las Nacionas del Mundo desubierto, dibujados y grabados con la mayor exactitud por R.M.V.A.R. Obra muy util y en special para los que tienen la del viajero universal*

which we translate, as literally as possible, thus:

> *General collection of costumes currently used in the nations of the known world, designed and printed with great exactitude by R.M.V.A.R. This work is very useful especially for those who hold themselves to be universal travelers*

Although nothing is known of the designers, engravers, and workers who colored this illustration by hand, the "exactitude" of their execution is evident in this drawing. The Muger Arabe del desierto de Zara is just one of many figures in this colorful collection. Their diversity speaks vividly of the uniqueness and individuality of the world's towns and regions just 200 years ago. This was a time when the dress codes of two regions separated by a few dozen miles identified people uniquely as belonging to one or the other. The collection brings to life a sense of isolation and distance of that period—and of every other historic period except our own hyperkinetic present.

Dress codes have changed since then and the diversity by region, so rich at the time, has faded away. It is now often hard to tell the inhabitant of one continent from another. Perhaps, trying to view it optimistically, we have traded a cultural and visual diversity for a more varied personal life. Or a more varied and interesting intellectual and technical life.

We at Manning celebrate the inventiveness, the initiative, and, yes, the fun of the computer business with book covers based on the rich diversity of regional life of two centuries ago, brought back to life by the pictures from this collection.

1

The Semantic Web

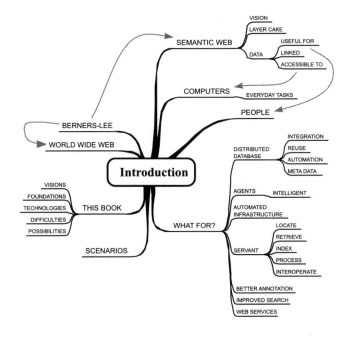

So he went down to the agora, or marketplace, where there were a lot of unemployed philosophers—which means philosophers which were not thinking at that time.

Thought—in other words, philosophers can tell you millions of things that thought isn't, and they can't tell you what it is—and this bugs them!

—Severn Darden, *Lecture on Metaphysics*

In the beginning, there was no Web. The Web began as a concept of Tim Berners-Lee, who worked for CERN, the European organization for physics research. CERN's technical staff urgently needed to share documents located on their many computers. Berners-Lee had previously built several systems to do that, and with this background he conceived the World Wide Web. The design had a relatively simple technical basis, which helped the technology take hold and gain critical mass.

Berners-Lee wanted anyone to be able to put information on a computer and make that information accessible to anyone else, anywhere. He hoped that eventually, machines would also be able to use information on the Web. Ultimately, he thought, this would allow powerful and effective human-computer-human collaboration:

I have always imagined the information space as something to which everyone has immediate and intuitive access, and not just to browse but to create... Machines become capable of analyzing all the data on the Web—the content, links, and transactions between people and computers.

...when [the Semantic Web] does [emerge], the day-to-day mechanisms of trade, bureaucracy, and our daily lives will be handled by machines talking to machines, leaving people to provide the inspiration and intuition. (Berners-Lee 2000)

I find this vision inspiring, and the means to get there intriguing.

The Semantic Web has, in a way, become almost a celebrity—*Scientific American* has even published an article on it (Berners-Lee, Hendler, and Lassila 2001)—although most people don't know what it is, and although there really isn't a Semantic Web yet. There are many different ideas of what it is, not just one. In this chapter, we examine a range of ideas about what the Semantic Web should be. Some of them may seem futuristic or impractical, but a great deal of work is going on in all the areas we'll examine.

1.1 What is the Semantic Web?

The word *semantic* implies meaning or, as WordNet defines it, "of or relating to the study of meaning and changes of meaning." For the Semantic Web, *semantic* indicates that the meaning of data on the Web can be discovered—not just by people, but also by computers. In contrast, most meaning on the Web today is inferred by people who read web pages and the labels of hyperlinks, and by other people who write specialized software to work with the data. The phrase *the Semantic Web* stands for a vision in which computers—software—as well as people can find, read, understand, and use data over the World Wide Web to accomplish useful goals for users.

Of course, we already use software to accomplish things on the Web, but the distinction lies in the words *we use*. *People* surf the Web, buy things on web sites, work their way through search pages, read the labels on hyperlinks, and decide which links to follow. It would be much more efficient and less time-consuming if a person could launch a process that would then proceed on its own, perhaps checking with the person from time to time as the work progressed. The business of the Semantic Web is to bring such capabilities into widespread use.

In brief, the Semantic Web is supposed to make data located anywhere on the Web accessible and understandable, both to people and to machines. This is more a vision than a technology. In this book, we'll explore the technologies that will play roles in bringing the vision to life.

As you might expect, there are many different ideas about what this general vision encompasses. An almost overwhelming number of different ideas exists about the supposed nature of the Semantic Web, and that's the first lesson to learn: The Semantic Web is a fluid, evolving, informally defined concept rather than an integrated, working system. To give you a feel for this range of ideas, here are some representative quotations about the nature of the Semantic Web:

- *The machine-readable-data view*—"The Semantic Web is a vision: the idea of having data on the Web defined and linked in a way that it can be used by machines not just for display purposes, but for automation, integration and reuse of data across various applications." (W3C 2003)

- *The intelligent agents view*—"The aim of the Semantic Web is to make the present Web more machine-readable, in order to allow intelligent agents to retrieve and manipulate pertinent information." (Cost et al 2001)

- *The distributed database view*—"The Semantic Web concept is to do for data what HTML did for textual information systems: to provide sufficient flexibility to be able to represent all databases and logic rules to link them together to great added value." (W3C 2000) "A simple description of the Semantic Web is that it is an attempt to do for machine processable data what the World Wide Web did for human readable documents. Namely, to transform information processing by providing a common way that data can be accessed, linked together and understood. To turn the Web from a large hyperlinked book into a large interlinked database." (SWAD-E)

- *The automated infrastructure view*—"In his recent *Scientific American* article Berners-Lee argues that the Semantic Web is infrastructure and not an application. We couldn't agree more." (Tuttle et al 2001) "Therefore, the real problem is the lack of an easy automation framework in the current Web…" (Garcia and Delgado 2001)

- *The servant-of-humanity view*—"The vision of the Semantic Web is to let computer software relieve us of much of the burden of locating resources on the Web that are relevant to our needs and extracting, integrating, and indexing the information contained within." (Cranefield 2001) "*The Semantic Web* is a vision of the next-generation web, which enables web applications to automatically collect web documents from diverse sources, integrate and process information, and interoperate with other applications in order to execute sophisticated tasks for humans." (Anutariya et al 2001)

- *The better-annotation view*—"The idea of a 'Semantic Web' [Berners-Lee 2001] supplies the (informal) web as we know it with annotations expressed in a machine-processable form and linked together." (Euzenat 2001)

- *The improved-searching view*—"Soon it will be possible to access Web resources by content rather than just by keywords." (Anutariya et al 2001) "The main goal [of the technology described in the paper] is to build a structured index of the Web site." (Desmontils and Jacquin 2001)

- *The web services view*—"Increasingly, the Semantic Web will be called upon to provide access not just to static documents that collect useful *information*, but also to *services* that provide useful *behavior*." (Klein and Bernstein 2001) "The Semantic Web promises to expand the services for the existing web by enabling software agents to automate procedures currently performed manually and by introducing new applications that are infeasible today." (Tallis, Goldman, and Balzer 2001)

It's clear that this notion of the Semantic Web covers a lot of ground, and perhaps no two people have quite the same idea about it. Still, several themes are expressed time and again:

- Indexing and retrieving information
- Meta data
- Annotation
- The Web as a large, interoperable database
- Machine retrieval of data
- Web-based services
- Discovery of services
- Intelligent software agents

Let's look more closely at these themes.

1.1.1 Indexing and retrieving information

Everyone wrestles with how to find information. Libraries have card catalogs, and now many have electronic indexes. Search engines are vital components of the Web. Yet at some point, everyone has been frustrated and annoyed by how hard it is to locate things, especially when you aren't sure what to ask for. To find information, a Semantic Web approach would expect to go beyond keyword and alphabetical indexes to let users search by concepts and categories.

The *Web* part brings in a persistent theme, in which information is distributed—spread throughout the Web—rather than concentrated in a few repositories. Most systems that use concept identification to retrieve information maintain their own concept hierarchies and attempt to identify those concepts in the documents they index. Sometimes concepts in a document collection are identified automatically, with varying success. To go further requires that documents be able to declare their own vocabularies and sets of concepts and to identify where they're used.

1.1.2 Meta data

Card catalogs and electronic indexes contain data about the works that are cataloged and indexed. Data about other data is often called *meta data*. For example, the ISBN number and the author's name are meta data about a novel. The data types describing the data in a database also fall into the category of meta data. It's even possible to have meta meta data (a statement about the origin of a piece of meta data could be considered to be meta data about meta data, or meta meta data).

In one sense, meta data is still data; the distinction lies in the intended use of the data and in the subject of the meta data. It's meta data that will be used for searches and for discovery of information. Annotation can also be thought of as meta data.

1.1.3 Annotation

In the world of physical documents (such as books), people write margin notes and comments, they underline and highlight passages, they staple new items to reports, and they add thoughts and ideas to those of the original authors. Markup languages like XML should, you'd think, be able to add such annotations; but today it's hard to do this in a simple way that lets other people share your annotations and lets you move your annotations to other applications and computers. *Wiki*-style web sites attempt to let many people comment on and modify web pages, but this process covers only a little of what people would like to do.

Because annotations should be shareable, and because the meaning of different types of annotations should be widely understood, support for extensive annotation capabilities is often seen as part of the Semantic Web.

1.1.4 A huge interoperable database

Today it's common to get data from a database over the Web. These databases are generally separate and not easily used as merged data sources, and a great deal of data exists outside of databases. This part of the Semantic Web vision sees ways to unify the description and retrieval of stored data, allowing much of the Web to be considered part of a large virtual database.

Consider a sports researcher looking for baseball data. There are various online baseball databases: The Major League Baseball web site is but one of many. But if our researcher wants to find performance statistics for Stan Musial, whose career lasted from the 1940s to the 1960s, she can't get data for the whole period in a mutually compatible format. At least for baseball statistics, there is some common agreement on the definitions of the most important statistics, so that a batting average is always computed the same way—this is more than can be said for most separate collections of data.

If the Web functioned as an interoperable database, the researcher could get the data from all the important sites, and the researcher's software would be able to either display all the data together or automatically combine data from, say, the Major League Baseball site and the Baseball Almanac.

1.1.5 Machine retrieval of data

This part of the vision focuses on automatic acquisition of data. This means that a piece of software, in pursuit of its assignment, determines what data it needs and where and how to get it, and then goes out and gets the data. Using the baseball example from the previous section, suppose our researcher has to find the right web pages, load them, and then figure out a way to get the data and organize it. This is hard to do and often takes a lot of time. Under the Semantic Web, the data format and its manner of access would be described in a way that would allow the researcher's computer to get and use the data automatically.

1.1.6 Services

A *service* is a behavior that provides a benefit. Examples include making reservations, arranging schedules, providing prices, placing orders, and so forth. Think of ordering, say, a perishable item like flowers or food. Once you've selected a product to buy, you have to make sure that its delivery will fit into your schedule. The price, buying conditions, delivery options, and your schedule can all be thought of as services that must be activated and coordinated. In the "Semantic Web as web services" view, all these services would publish machine-readable data that would allow a computer to do all the activation and coordination for you.

1.1.7 Discovery

To use services, you (and especially your software) must be able to find them, discover what they do, and learn how to invoke them. This is the realm of *discovery of services*. The most obvious approach would be to create directories of services with standard access methods. The services would be described in standard terms, and information about how to access them and the available information would be encoded in standard ways.

Consider an analogy with a physical library. Most libraries in the United States use either the Dewey Decimal System or the Library of Congress method to catalog their books. After using the card catalog or its electronic version, a person becomes familiar with the classifications and learns how to find books on the shelves. Here, the standard access methods are the familiar classification system and the physical arrangement of books in the library.

A more advanced approach would be to send out discovery requests based on the services required, and for candidate services to describe their capabilities in such a way that the would-be user could deduce their capabilities and instigate a conversation to find any missing or uncertain information. Returning to the library example, this would be like getting an experienced research librarian to tell you which reference books to look at and how to understand the information in them.

1.1.8 Intelligent agents

An *agent* is someone or something that acts on your behalf. A software agent would act in a somewhat autonomous way, communicating with other software agents (which might be specialized) to discover services, products, or information for you. For instance, one of those specialized agents might know how to purchase airline tickets and make reservations. Another agent might perform the required services, passing the results back to your own agent, which would notify you of the outcome.

It's clear that a network of interacting agents would have to be able to describe its goals using established vocabularies, to discover services and information resources, and to use many of the capabilities described in the previous sections.

1.2 Two Semantic Web scenarios

To give you a feel for the way these areas might interact and how the Semantic Web could provide great value, here are two scenarios that were developed during the workshop "Research Challenges and Perspectives of the Semantic Web."[1] Both scenarios illustrate what might be called *personal services*. Of course, similar scenarios could be constructed for many other areas, such as business-to-business transactions. Note that the language is taken directly from the report without corrections for grammatical and spelling errors.

Scenario 1: A research assistant

During her stay at Honolulu, Clara ran into several interesting people with whom she exchanged vCards. When time to rest came in the evening, she had a look at her digital assistant summarizing the events of the day and recalling the events to come (and especially her keynote talk of the next day). The assistant popped up a note with a link to a vCard that reads: "This guy's profile seems to match the position advertisement that Bill put on our intranet. Can I notify Bill's assistant?"

Clara hit the "explain!" button. "I used his company directory for finding his DAML[2] enhanced vita: he's got the required skills as a statistician who led the data mining group of the database department at Montana U. for the requirement of a researcher who worked on machine learning." Clara hit then the "evidence!" button. The assistant started displaying "I checked his affiliation with university

---

[1] This workshop was organized by the European Consortium in Informatics and Mathematics (ERCIM) for the European Union Future Emergent Technology program (EU-FET) and the US National Science Foundation (NSF). It was held in Sophia-Antipolis, France, in October 2001.

[2] DARPA Agent Markup Language; see chapter 7.

of Montana, he is cited several times in their web pages: reasonably trusted; I checked his publication records from publishers' DAML sources and asked bill assistant a rating of the journals: highly trusted. More details?"

Clara had enough and let her assistant inform Bill's.

Scenario 2: Negotiating a date

Bill's and Peter's assistants arranged a meeting in Paris, just before ISWC[3] in Sardinia. Thanks to Peter's assistant knowing he was vegetarian, they avoided a faux pas. Bill was surprised that Peter was able to cope with French (his assistant was not authorized to unveil that he married a woman from Québec). Bill and Peter had a fruitful meeting and Bill will certainly be able to send Peter an offer before he came back to the US.

Before dinner, Peter investigated a point that bothered him: Bill used the term "Service" in an unusual way. He wrote: "Acme computing will run the trust rating service for semanticweb.org" (a sentence from Bill). His assistant found no problem so he hit: "service," the assistant displayed "service in {database} equivalent To: infrastructure." Peter asked for "metainfo," which raised "Updated today by negotiating with Bill's assistant."

Peter again asked for "Arguments!": "Service in {database} conflicts with service in {web}." "Explain!" "In operating system and database, the term services covers features like fault-tolerance, cache, security, that we are used to putting in the infrastructure. More evidence?"

Peter was glad he had not to search the whole Web for an explanation of this. The two assistants detected the issue and negotiated silently a solution to this problem. He had some time left before getting to the théatre de la ville. His assistant made the miracle to book him a place for a rare show of Anne-Theresa De Keermaeker's troupe in Paris. It had to resort to a particular web service that it found through a dance-related common interest pool of assistants.

In these scenarios, you can see quite a few Semantic Web areas in operation at the same time. Software agents (the digital assistants) are discovering meta data and information and processing it. Logical reasoning is not only used to make inferences, it's also explained to the human user. Assessments of trust and reliability are deduced through networks of interacting information. We see the discovery of web services. It all seems so plausible and so useful.

---

[3] Presumably the International Semantic Web Conference.

1.2.1 Can the Semantic Web work this way?

What needs to be developed, what needs to be in place, for the Semantic Web to work as envisioned in the previous scenarios? The keys are the widespread interchange of data and ways to mark, indicate, or describe what that data is, how it's structured, how it can be retrieved, and what it means. Each of these areas is a large undertaking in itself. But the Semantic Web will be a sociological development, too. Companies must cooperate where they might normally compete; academic research must be translated into practical systems; individuals must discover how they can contribute; and issues of for-profit versus free, of closed versus open systems, and of trust need to be worked out.

The task is much bigger than the building of the original World Wide Web. At that time, few people realized how many new capabilities the Web would unleash. Today, some of the basic infrastructure is already in place. There are organizations like the World Wide Web Consortium (W3C; www.w3c.org), whose purpose includes developing and advancing standards of importance to the Internet as a whole, including the Semantic Web. So the task is bigger, but the starting point is more advanced.

Can the visions be realized? Opinions vary—mine is that many of them will come to pass (some are already beginning to operate) and make a real difference in the lives of people who use the Web.

1.3 The Semantic Web's foundation

The World Wide Web has certain design features that make it different from earlier hyperlink experiments. These features will play an important role in the design of the Semantic Web. The Web is not the whole Internet, and it would be possible to develop many capabilities of the Semantic Web using other means besides the World Wide Web. But because the Web is so widespread, and because its basic operations are relatively simple, most of the technologies being contemplated for the Semantic Web are based on the current Web, sometimes with extensions. However, web services (chapter 8) and agents (chapter 9) may step outside the architecture of the current Web, as you'll see.[4]

The Web is designed around resources, standardized addressing of those resources (Uniform Resource Locators and Uniform Resource Indicators), and a

---

[4] I'm referring in part to the so-called REST (Representation State Transfer) architecture and the controversy over whether current SOAP-based web services that don't use this model would be better suited to the Web if they did.

small, widely understood set of commands. It's also designed to operate over very large and complex networks in a decentralized way. Let's look at each of these design features.

1.3.1 Resources

The Web addresses, retrieves, links to, and modifies *resources*. A resource is intended to represent any idea that can be referred to. Usually we think of these resources as being tangible packages of data (documents or pages), but the notion of a resource is more general in two ways. First, a resource can change over time and still be considered the same resource, addressed by the same Uniform Resource Identifier (URI). Thus, a series of drafts of a manuscript could be addressed by the same URI. Alternatively, a URI could denote one specific, unchanging version of the same document. The notion of *resource* is flexible enough to encompass both varying and fixed resources.

Strictly speaking, a resource itself is not retrieved, but only a representation of the resource. For some protocols, like File Transfer Protocol (FTP), the representation is normally a copy of a file. For others, like HTTP, the representation may or may not be a copy of a file. A resource can even be represented by different forms—a PDF file, an HTML page, a voice recording, and so on.

Second, and perhaps harder to grasp, a resource can be something that doesn't yet exist, and that may never exist. A resource can be a concept or a reference to a real or fictitious person—something that can't be addressed and transferred over a network, but that can be talked about, thought about. For the purposes of the Semantic Web, such a resource can be referred to or identified by a URI.[5]

1.3.2 Standardized addressing

All resources on the Web are referred to by URIs. The most familiar URIs are those that address resources that can be addressed and retrieved; these are called URLs, for Uniform Resource Locators. These URIs have a uniform structure that can refer to the use of other protocols besides HTTP (like FTP), and they are easy to type and copy. They can be inserted into hyperlinks so that any addressable information can be easily linked.

---

[5] For example, RFC 1737, "Functional Requirements for Uniform Resource Names" (a subset of URIs), says, "The purpose or function of a URN is to provide a globally unique, persistent **identifier** used for **recognition**, for access to characteristics of the resource or for access to the resource itself." (Emphasis added.)

1.3.3 *Small set of commands*

The HTTP protocol (the protocol used to send messages back and forth over the Web) uses a small set of commands. These commands are universally understood by web servers, clients (like browsers), and intermediate components like caches, which can reduce network traffic by storing copies of documents that were previously sent. With this limited set of commands, there is no question about what is being requested of the server and network, and no visibility into how the server may choose to carry out the requests. This model doesn't provide security or personal privacy for the information being sent or requested; but, since it is simple and well understood, the model lends itself to the provision of additional layers of security.[6]

However, some architectures use complex messages or need to restrict the visibility of message contents, and they use an approach that's more involved than basic HTTP. Other Internet protocols can be used, and additional messaging layers can be carried over HTTP as well (such as SOAP, whose name no longer stands for anything). There is some controversy over what methods should be used for the Web—as distinct from the Internet, which includes much more than the World Wide Web—and whether the Semantic Web architecture should restrict itself to the simpler architecture of the current Web.

1.3.4 *Scalability and large networks*

The Web has to operate over a very large network with an enormous number of web sites and to continue to work as the network's size increases. It accomplishes this thanks to two main design features. First, the Web is decentralized. If you have a computer on the network, you can put a web server on it; and if you have a server, you can add resources to it without registering them anywhere else.

Second, each transaction on the Web (that is, a request and the subsequent response) contains all the information needed to handle the request. No data needs to be stored by the server from one request to another. However, many practical uses of the Web do require that some data be saved for a period of time. If you reserve a ticket and then order it on another web page, the system must store your ticket reservation and be able to connect it to your request to purchase. Since any web transaction is separate from all others, it's harder to arrange to maintain data across a connected series of transactions. Independent interactions

---

[6] There is some controversy over whether the web model supports security provisions better than other network architectures, such as Remote Procedure Call (RPC) systems.

make possible a large, decentralized system where responses can be cached to allow faster responses and reduce network traffic.

Data that maintains some history of transactions is sometimes called *state*, as in "the state of the system." Web transactions are stateless.[7] If there is a business need to store information across several interactions, the server must provide special arrangements to make it happen.

1.3.5 Openness, completeness, and consistency

The Web is *open*, meaning that web sites and web resources can be added freely and without central controls. The assignment of domain names to servers does need some central authority to avoid duplicate names,[8] but this in no way restricts your ability to establish web servers and the information they provide.

The Web is *incomplete*, meaning there can be no guarantee that every link will work or that all possible information will be available. It can be *inconsistent*: Anyone can say anything on a web page, so different web pages can easily contradict each other. Information on the Web will never be fully consistent, and it also changes constantly. Just think of all the web pages you've returned to that changed since you last visited them, or that don't even exist anymore. Software that wishes to draw logical conclusions from data on the Web must work with reasonable reliability in the face of all this change, potential inconsistency, and incompleteness.

1.3.6 The Web and the Semantic Web

For the Semantic Web to follow the current web model, then, it should use key aspects of the current World Wide Web:

- Use URI-style addressing
- Have notions of addressable and non-addressable resources (a *non-addressable* resource is something that can be talked about—like a car or a concept— but can't be retrieved over a communications network)
- Use protocols with a small and universally understood set of commands (likely to include extensions to the current command set)
- Maintain little or, preferably, no state information

---

[7] When a cookie is stored on your computer, the cookie stores some state information. Unfortunately, this state doesn't fit the web model well, so it can sometimes cause confusion between browser, server, and user.

[8] The domain name is the general part of the server's name—usually, many servers share a domain name. For example, in the URL www.cnn.com, the domain name is cnn.com.

- Be as decentralized as possible
- Function on a large scale
- Allow local caching of information to speed access and reduce network loads
- Be able to operate with missing links and with incomplete and inconsistent information.

It's an open question whether services and agents will be designed to—or will be able to—follow these prescriptions.

1.4 *The Semantic Web layer cake*

The W3C has been a leader in developing technologies for the Web. The organization is headed by Tim Berners-Lee, who, not resting on his earlier accomplishments in relation to the Web, has also been promoting the development of the Semantic Web. Many of the apparently foundational technologies, such as XML and RDF, have been developed by the W3C. So the W3C approach to the evolution of the Semantic Web is worth looking at.

The W3C web pages on the Semantic Web include a diagram labeled *Architecture*. This diagram, sometimes called the "Semantic Web layer cake," has been reproduced often, and our own version of it is depicted in figure 1.1. Descriptions of the layers are as follows:

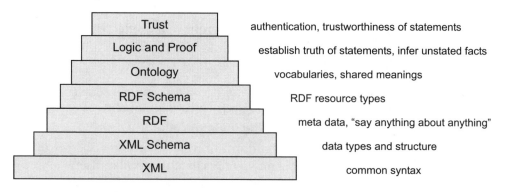

(adapted with changes from Berners-Lee,
http://www.w3.org/2000/Talks/1206-xml2k-tbl/slide10-0.html)

Figure 1.1   The layered technologies of the Semantic Web, according to Tim Berners-Lee and the W3C. Each layer is seen as building on—and requiring—the ones below it. The W3C has developed, or is in the process of developing, standards and recommendations for all but the top two layers, and the W3C recommendations for digital signatures and managing encryption keys will also play roles in the Trust layer.

- *XML*—Extensible Markup Language. The language framework that, since 1998, has been used to define nearly all new languages that are used to interchange data over the Web.

- *XML Schema*—A language used to define the structure of specific XML languages.

- *RDF*—Resource Description Framework. A flexible language capable of describing all sorts of information and meta data. RDF is covered in chapter 2. Topic maps, a non-W3C alternative standard, are discussed in chapter 3.

- *RDF Schema*—A framework that provides a means to specify basic vocabularies for specific RDF application languages to use. RDF Schema is covered in chapter 7.

- *Ontology*—Languages used to define vocabularies and establish the usage of words and terms in the context of a specific vocabulary. RDF Schema is a framework for constructing ontologies and is used by many more advanced ontology frameworks. OWL is an ontology language designed for the Semantic Web. Chapter 7 discusses ontologies, including OWL.

- *Logic and Proof*—Logical reasoning is used to establish the consistency and correctness of data sets and to infer conclusions that aren't explicitly stated but are required by or consistent with a known set of data. Proofs trace or explain the steps of logical reasoning. Chapter 6 covers some issues relating to logic in the Semantic Web.

- *Trust*—A means of providing authentication of identity and evidence of the trustworthiness of data, services, and agents. Chapter 10 covers issues of trust with regards to the Semantic Web.

Each layer is seen as building on the layer below. At the base, most data is expected to be created in XML formats. Each layer is progressively more specialized and also tends to be more complex than the layers below it. A lower layer doesn't depend on any higher layers. Thus the layers can be developed and made operational relatively independently. XML is in place now, and XML Schema has recently become standardized. RDF has been released as a W3C Recommendation,[9] (and has just been re-released with changes). The other layers

---

[9] The W3C publishes technology standards like HTML, the common Hypertext Markup Language. It calls them *Recommendations*, even though many people informally call them *standards* or *specifications*. In the W3C process, a document proceeds through a series of draft stages, moving from *Working Draft* through *Candidate Recommendation* before it gets released as an approved Recommendation.

are under development, and their form and direction are progressively uncertain according to their altitude in the layer cake.

You should realize that this diagram represents the W3C view, and most of the technologies depicted in the diagram are W3C developed or endorsed. There are potential alternatives for some of the layers. Among others, alternative schemas exist for XML documents, and there are quite a few alternative efforts to develop ontology systems.

If you noticed that there is no layer labeled *Web Services*, it's true that services don't fit neatly into this layer cake. Such technologies make use of several layers, such as XML and XML Schemas—and perhaps, in the future, RDF and Ontology. This book also discusses other technologies and subjects that don't appear in the layer-cake diagram.

1.4.1 *The base*

The Web holds an enormous amount of information, and most of it is in HTML format—the language used to describe the content of ordinary web pages. This works because HTML is so widely understood (by browsers) and also because HTML is simple for page creators to understand. HTML does describe the information it contains, but it does so in terms of generic units that apply to most ordinary documents—paragraphs, headings, images, tables, and so on. An HTML page can't label a chunk of the page to say, "This is employee information from database 'X';" it can only say (in terms that a computer can use), "This is a table, and here are its rows and columns."

The HTML for a page describes these generic document units and their order, and it's the browser's job to decide how to display them. You can give browsers suggestions, which they will normally try to honor as best they can. This approach has been wildly successful when the information is intended for people to read.

With XML, you can describe the structure of the information in other ways, not just in terms of generic document units. You can choose the kind of structure that's most suitable for the particular information and anticipated use. Thus, XML is seen as the foundation layer of the Semantic Web.

The XML Schema layer provides the ability to specify structures and data types to be used by a particular XML document. The XML and XML Schema layers aren't covered in this book, because they're general-purpose technologies that aren't specially related to the Semantic Web.

1.4.2 *Properties and relationships*

To a browser, the "meaning" of an HTML page lies in the widely shared understanding of how to display the different kinds of generic units that appear on a web page. For a general-purpose structure, there likewise needs to be a means of indicating the meaning of the different structural units, and this should also be widely shared. This is the role of RDF. However, the idea of *meaning* is complicated and has many levels, and RDF deals with only two of them: assigning properties to things and relating one thing to another.

The RDF Schema layer describes those properties—what they are, which resources they can be assigned to, and so on. The Ontology layer takes this a step further: Not only does it describe the properties and terms that can be used, but it also can describe relationships between them.

These layers are used to describe, or represent, knowledge. Although the W3C version of the layer cake shows only RDF and RDF Schema, this book also discusses another candidate for representing knowledge: topic maps.

1.4.3 *Analysis, verification, and trust*

Once the relationships between resources, terms, and properties have been established, the statements that RDF expresses can be analyzed for consistency and inferences can be made. By this means, facts that aren't explicitly stated can be discovered, and inconsistent facts can (sometimes) be reconciled. The Logic and Proof layer provides these capabilities.

When I purchase a book and give my credit card number, the bookseller wants to know if the card is mine. If I'm there in person, I can show my driver's license to give a kind of credence to my claim of identity. In essence, I'm saying, "If you don't believe me, then trust the licensing authority." This is acceptable as long as the seller believes that the identity card is not counterfeit. The seller might assess the validity of the card by its visual appearance, the match between the picture and my face, the degree of agreement between the age on the card and my apparent age, and any number of other clues. Here you see several principles in play: an appeal to authority, the trustworthiness of that authority, an inference of validity based on a set of facts, and beliefs about those facts.

When I buy the same book online, the seller likewise needs to have some assurance that the credit card is valid and that I'm authorized to use it. I need assurance that the web page really belongs to the bookseller and not to a criminal who wants to get access to my card. When software programs work with data they get over the Web, they face the same problems. The Trust layer will attempt to handle these issues. You can see how it will use all the other layers. The Trust machinery has to call on the Logic and Proof layer to analyze claims, make inferences, and draw conclusions. The Logic and Proof layer needs to know how the terms and properties relate to each other and whether they're used correctly, which is the business of the Ontology layer. The Ontology layer needs to use the data structures defined and created by the RDF and XML Schema layers. These dependencies can also be viewed in the other direction: the RDF layer uses RDF Schema and Ontology as it assigns its properties, and the XML layer provides transportable data structures for the RDF information.

This layer cake structure sounds complicated, and it is. But it doesn't all have to be in place before anything can be done. The important thing is to get widespread acceptance of relevant bits. That's how the Web spread in the first place.

1.5 Summary

The Semantic Web is not a cut-and-dried, integrated technology. It's a concept of how computers, people, and the Web can work together more effectively than is possible now. Because it's visionary, it has no one definition. In fact, you saw a staggering array of notions earlier in this chapter, such as the machine-readable-data view, the intelligent agents view, and many more. However, these overlapping views have some aspects in common, and this book deals with these commonalities.

Basically, all the views assume that computers will be able to read and use data that today is mainly accessible to people. All views see computers as being able to use this data to perform tasks that help people. Within this broad range, certain themes show up repeatedly, as we've discussed in this chapter. The rest of this book covers each of these themes as they relate to the Semantic Web.

The current Web is the one success story we have of a very large, distributed, loosely connected, inconsistent system. It seems reasonable, therefore, that the Semantic Web should use the strengths of the current Web, especially key design patterns that have made it a success. In fact, it should be an extension of the current Web.

2

Describing data with RDF

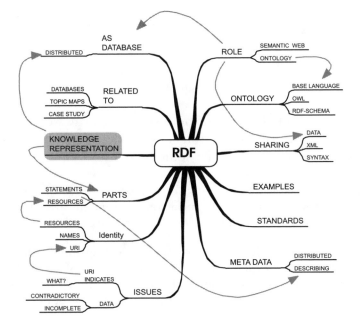

...quoted Heraclitus incorrectly as saying that time was "a river that flows endlessly through the universe." He didn't say this at all. He said that time was "LIKE a river that flows endlessly through the universe." Aha, there you are, Benedetti!

—Severn Darden, *Lecture on Metaphysics*

Oni tu handrid poati da salari.
[The salary (was) only 240 (pesos).]

—Derek Bickerton and Carol Odo,
Change and Variation in Hawaiian English, vol. 1

With the lay of the land sketched out in chapter 1, we move into the terrain of modeling or representing knowledge. This serves as a foundation for the Semantic Web; however, without some way to describe knowledge (or information, or data), we'll have nothing for the Semantic Web to work with. But what kind of knowledge? Let's try this:

The melons
I scolded him about last year,
I now offer to his spirit

—Oemaru (Blyth 1982)

Well, perhaps not. This spare and lovely haiku, can we even say for sure what it tells us? So evocative to a person, surely an eternity will pass before a computer can extract its essence. Let's try something else.

This haiku was written by Oemaru (a Japanese person), was translated by R. H. Blyth (a British person), and appears on page 763 in Blyth (1982), which is volume three of a set of books entitled *Haiku*. Blyth makes this commentary on the verse:

Only last year he scolded his son for eating the melons. This year he offers them at the family altar for the repose of his soul. Everything is usable in every way. Good or bad, holy or unholy, profitable or unprofitable—these qualities do not even in the slightest degree inhere in the things themselves.

Yes, this is more like it. We can represent this kind of information to a computer—specific bits and pieces about something definite. At the base of the Semantic Web are technologies that can capture data like this. Perhaps in the future there will be a need to represent more complex and textured information, but for now, the

Resource Description Framework (RDF) is designed for specific data about specific subjects. The essence of the haiku will have to come later, if ever.

In this example, the data are all about the poem—its author, where it was published, and so forth. Data like this are usually called *meta data*, as you saw in section 1.1.2. On the other hand, information such as a person's name and address is usually thought of as plain data, even though it too is "about" its subject. RDF and similar technologies can represent data and meta data equally well—they make no distinction between them.

Databases all over the world contain billions of items of meta data just like our haiku's and billions of bits of data just like our person's name and address; so do paper catalogs and web sites. The data is there, but some of it is stored in proprietary database formats, and some is available only in human-readable form. To make all this data accessible to computers, we must do it with a language they can understand. We'll also have to make it addressable over networks like the Internet.

It won't do a computer much good to find out that a book has a publisher named University of Chicago Press unless it knows the relationships that exist between a book, a publisher, and the names of the book and publisher. In the past, this knowledge has been built into specialized software for particular applications. But if we expect a computer to use someone else's data (and meta data), we must give the computer a way to find and use the concepts, vocabulary, and relationships that define the structure of that data. We also need a standard way to refer to any particular bit of information, just as a URL refers to a particular web page (or other resource on the Web).

Note that these concepts, vocabularies, and relationships form a kind of meta data about the data sets they apply to. Ontology, the subject of chapter 7, is about such concepts and vocabularies and the logical relationships between them. The Semantic Web will need a widely used and simple language that can convey both data and meta data of varying structures.

RDF is the W3C's candidate for a language to fill this role (W3C 1999). RDF was developed to provide a standard way to model, describe, and exchange information about "resources"—that is to say, practically anything about practically anything—as long as it is specific data about a specific subject. RDF also serves as a base for higher-level languages that describe ontologies. These capabilities for modeling and exchanging information, and for constructing the vocabularies and rules used to describe that information, explain why RDF figures prominently in the W3C's plans for the Semantic Web.

This chapter covers basic features of RDF, and chapter 7 shows how RDF can be used to model and exchange ontologies. This chapter is more detailed and has more technical information than most of the others because the technology is more developed, and also because RDF is likely to be used by some of the other Semantic Web technologies as they evolve.

2.1 *Introducing RDF*

To play its role of describing data and meta data, RDF (and other potential languages for the role) needs to include the following capabilities:

- Able to describe most kinds of data that will be available
- Able to describe the structural design of data sets
- Able to describe relationships between bits of data

Toward these ends, RDF uses a simple data model. Basically, there are things called *resources*, and there are *statements* that can be made about those resources. A single statement links two resources. These statements are like simple sentences that have a subject-verb-object structure, such as "Billy lives in Chicago." *Billy* is the subject, *lives in* is the verb, and *Chicago* is the object. That, in a nutshell, is the data model. Naturally, complications arise as the model is adapted to practical applications, but fundamentally RDF is about simple statements that describe information about specific subjects.

2.1.1 *Some terminology*

In RDF, a statement is sometimes called a *triple* because it has three parts. The subject of a statement is in fact called the *subject*. The equivalent of a verb is called the *predicate*, and the remaining part is called the *object*. Other terms are also in common use: *property* instead of predicate, and *value* instead of object (because many RDF statements assign property values to their subjects).

The following diagram depicts the structure of an RDF triple:

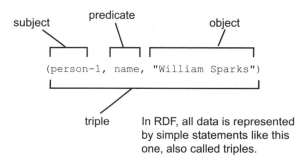

In RDF, all data is represented by simple statements like this one, also called triples.

The value of a property can be a simple value, like an ordinary number or a string of characters such as *William Sparks* in the diagram. Such values are called *literals*. The value of a property can be either a literal or another resource, as appropriate. RDF has a way of indicating whether a literal value has a data type, meaning that it is intended to be, for example, an integer or a chunk of XML. A literal can't be the subject of a statement

A collection of RDF data has no standard name. It's sometimes called an *RDF store*, an *RDF data set*, a *knowledge base*, or even a *database*.

2.1.2 *Identifying resources*

To be widely usable over the Web, RDF needs to be able to identify the things it describes in a standard, widely used manner so that a host of systems on the Web can also refer to them. Older systems, such as conventional databases, have no standard way to identify their (equivalent of) subjects across systems and networks.

To identify resources—that is, what RDF makes statements about—RDF uses *URI* (Uniform Resource Identifier) *references*. A URI can be used to identify a concept, a tangible thing that can't be downloaded, or a chunk of data that can be retrieved over a network. A URI reference is a URI plus optional characters, such as the so-called *fragment identifier* (the part that follows the # sign after a URI, if any). RDF has rules about how to construct related URIs so that they can be used conveniently when RDF data is exchanged.

The general problem of identifying things is complicated, and there probably will never be a general solution. Names aren't normally unique—many Robert Smith individuals live in the United States, but they aren't the same person just because they have the same name. Conversely, a given thing may have many names. To identify a resource, a URI is paired or associated with the resource, and not with any other resource. How this is accomplished isn't specified and probably can't be specified in general. One way is to write the association into a document, such as a specification. However, there is always the possibility that the description in the document may not be sufficiently clear or unambiguous enough to fully identify the thing described. And if the target is a concept instead of a tangible thing, the meaning of the concept may not be made sufficiently clear. Of course, this problem isn't unique to RDF or the Semantic Web.

Another way to identify a resource is to say (preferably in RDF) that it's the same as some other, presumably well-known, resource. This can be done in RDF by using the right predicate (more on this topic when we discuss the Web Ontology Language in chapter 7).

You can also identify a resource by its properties and relationships with other resources. The New York Yankees baseball team had only one general manager during the 2003 playing season. If it were known that a person had been the general manager of the Yankees during that time, that individual would be uniquely identified even if his name were not mentioned. Obviously, some properties and relationships are more useful for establishing identity than others.

However the identity of a resource is established, RDF uses the identifying URI reference as a unique string. If the string is also easy for a person to read, that's fine, but RDF doesn't care.

When the pairing of a URI with its identified resource is described in a document, whether by prose, RDF, or some other form, a question naturally arises: How can that defining document be found? RDF provides no standard method.[1] Some practitioners use an informal convention that the URI should be in the form of an HTTP URL that can be used to retrieve the defining document from a web site. When this is done, it's important to be clear that the fact that the URL is used to identify a resource *does not* indicate that the descriptive document itself is the identified resource. The URI as an identifier is just an arbitrary string, and any utility it may have for obtaining a document is a bonus that isn't prescribed by RDF.

Here's an example to make this discussion more concrete. The RDF Recommendation contains a concept called a statement, discussed later in this chapter. The type of a resource that is an RDF statement is identified using its URI:

```
http://www.w3.org/1999/02/22-rdf-syntax-ns#Statement
```

There happens to be an RDF document at that URI. It contains the following RDF fragment, among others:

```
<!--
   This is the RDF Schema for the RDF data model as described in
   The Resource Description Framework (RDF) Model and Syntax
   Specification http://www.w3.org/TR/REC-rdf-syntax -->

<s:Class rdf:ID="Statement"
   s:comment="A triple consisting of a predicate, a subject,
   and an object." />

<s:Class rdf:ID="Property"
   s:comment="A name of a property, defining specific meaning
   for the property" />
```

---

[1] Topic maps provide more clarity about what is identified, and when a URL is (or is not) the same as the subject of interest. See chapter 3.

The URI in question isn't required to point to a document. The fact that it does is useful (in this case, the fragment identifier, or `"#Statement"`, would cause the bold-faced portion to be displayed in a browser that understands XML).

2.1.3 Anonymous resources

RDF doesn't require that every resource in a statement be identified with a URI reference. A resource without an identifying URI reference is analogous to referring to a person as "that man" or "a woman with a red car." As you'll see, it would be awkward to model complex data sets with RDF's simple triples without the use of anonymous resources, because we'd be forced to invent unnecessary identifiers for them. Most computer programs make up their own internal identifiers for these resources anyway, but these don't have to be known outside the application. Anonymous resources are also called *blank nodes* or b-nodes.

2.1.4 RDF and conventional databases

The RDF model of resources and triples may seem very different from the model found in conventional relational databases, but the difference isn't as great as it first appears. In conventional databases, data is usually organized into tables like that illustrated in table 2.1.

Table 2.1 Table fragment from an imaginary database.

Name	Phone	Email	City	State
William Sparks	435 555-6789	wsparks@mailto.com	Springfield	MA
Constance Sim	312 555-2238	csim@coldmail.com	Chicago	IL

Each row of the table has the same structure as every other, and the row represents a particular relationship between all the cells of that row. In table 2.1, each column contains a fact about a particular person, and each row represents one of those people.

A collection of items that belong together is often called a *tuple*. More exactly, a tuple is an ordered list of values. Although the items in a row of a relational database aren't ordered in principle, in practice they're ordered so that you can know which item corresponds to which column. In other words, the first row of table 2.1 can be represented by the tuple (`"William Sparks"`, `"435 555-6789"`, `"wsparks@mailto.com"`, `"Springfield"`, `"MA"`), as long as we know that the first item in the tuple is the name, the second is the phone number, and so forth.

In a well-designed table, all the facts in a row depend on one cell, called the *primary key*, which should be unique within a table. The obvious candidate here is the person's name. If we were to put this data into words, it would read something like this:

> There is a person whose name is William Sparks, whose phone number is 435 555-6789, whose email address is wsparks@mailto.com, who lives in Springfield, and whose state code is MA.

Purely from a data modeling point of view, a few things here aren't quite what they should be. For one, we said that each table cell should depend only on the primary key, but the city and state fields aren't completely independent. In fact, there should probably be an address field, which would include the city and state. These details, although important to database design, don't matter here. Let's consider another point. A person's name can change, and there can be different versions of a name—and, of course, more than one person can have the same name. So, it would be better to identify a person using something more definitive, like an arbitrary but unique ID number, or a national identification number. This number would represent the person, and the person's name would be just one more fact. Table 2.2 shows this change.

Table 2.2   Improving the design by adding a column for a unique ID.

Person ID	Name	Phone	Email	City	State
person-1	William Sparks	435 555-6789	wsparks@mailto.com	Springfield	MA
person-2	Constance Sim	312 555-2238	csim@coldmail.com	Chicago	IL

In words, the new version reads like this:

> Person-1 has the name William Sparks, a phone number 435 555-6789,...

The difference between the two versions lies in the identity of the person. Version 1 lists data about some person who happens to have the name William Sparks. Version 2 lists data specifically about person-1. In version 1, we'll have trouble if the person's name changes, since any other data that refers to the original name will become orphaned. You'll see that both versions can be represented in RDF.

Remember that RDF only has resources and triples. To get this data into triples, we need to simplify the table into the smallest pieces possible. A row of a two-column table can be seen as a triple. We can turn our table into a set of two-column tables, as shown in table 2.3.

Table 2.3 Splitting up the tables leads to maximum simplification of the database table, suitable for description by RDF triples.

Person ID	Name
person-1	William Sparks
person-2	Constance Sim

Person ID	Phone
person-1	435 555-6789
person-2	312 555-2238

This is legitimate as long as the facts (the columns of the original table) are truly independent of each other. Notice the regular pattern: (`person`)-(`type of fact`)-(`value of fact`). In this case, the `type of fact` is "Name" for the first table and "Phone" for the second.

In general, of course, the left-hand item can be anything, not just a person. In RDF, as we've mentioned, things that can be talked about are called resources. So, we can write an RDF triple as (`resource`)-(`type of fact`)-(`value of fact`). This is exactly what a row of our two-column table represents. It takes a collection of them to represent the contents of a database.

The facts in any well-designed set of tables can be rewritten in the form of RDF triples. We'd like to convert the primary key into a URI reference, in order for it to identify the subject in the RDF manner, although in some cases it might be feasible to use anonymous nodes to represent the rows.

If this is the case—if RDF and relational tables are in some sense equivalent—then why bother with RDF? The database will probably have better performance if the data is perfectly regular, but with RDF, the data doesn't have to be regular. You can always add new triples representing new information. If the triples have a different predicate (the data type represented by the column name), they won't fit into an existing table. This would cause some problems for a conventional database but none for an RDF data store. So, an RDF data store has the advantage of flexibility. In addition, you can make statements about the predicates as well as statements about property values, because predicate types are also resources in RDF. In other words, RDF can describe many of the properties of its own data structures.

MORE ABOUT TRIPLES Is a triple enough to represent all the data you might be interested in? Consider the case of a conventional database, as set forth in the preceding section. All the items in a row normally belong together, whereas the dismemberment into a collection of triples seems to lose that connection. After all, a resource might have hundreds of facts related to it, only five of which may belong to a given row of a given table. Some programming languages, including Prolog, which is especially designed for logical programming, can use tuples of any length to capture facts and properties. Why restrict RDF to triples, which amount to tuples of length three?

The reason is simplicity: Triples are smaller and simpler than anything bigger. Data structures within programs can be simpler, because their size will always be the same. The data structures are relatively easy to access and work with. The result, ironically, can sometimes be additional complexity. To capture the essence of a row in a database table, you need a resource to collect all the individual triples and state that all these (and only these) triples belong to the row. This process can be cumbersome. Fortunately, it isn't always necessary to identify the rows that originally contained the facts that have been decomposed into individual triples.

2.2 Working with RDF properties

In RDF, a statement associates a resource with a property value—the predicate, or property type, denotes the type of association, and the object represents the value assigned. Predicates in RDF are interesting because they too are resources and can be the subject of statements.

2.2.1 Properties as resources

Since an RDF predicate (or property) is also a kind of resource, it's identified by a URI reference. Here's a standard RDF property, defined in the RDF Model and Syntax Recommendation (W3C 1999):

```
http://www.w3.org/1999/02/22-rdf-syntax-ns#type
```

A property identified by this URI reference is used to state the type of a resource. The Recommendation includes an example where the subject is a person, which is to say, the subject has a `type` property whose value is `http://description.org/ schema/Person`. We know that the property in the statement is the `type` property because its identifier is given as `http://www.w3.org/1999/02/22-rdf-syntax-ns# type`. Now, since a property is a resource, it can also be the subject of statements.

Typically such statements specify how the predicate is to be used, or impose other constraints on it.

2.2.2 *Names, labels, and identifiers*

When triples are written for the purpose of illustration, the URIs can be hard to read, which defeats the purpose of the illustration. It's common for names or labels to be substituted (not in the real triples stored by an RDF application, but for illustration purposes) with self-explanatory names (like `Person` instead of `http://description.org/schema/Person`). There are also other ways to make triples more readable (see section 2.6).

You could build an entire database using the RDF model of triples without using URIs—just common names.[2] This is what you'd get if you mechanically translated a database table, as you saw earlier. It would work well as long as your database was a closed system that only you used. But if you wanted to share your data, other systems wouldn't understand your names and properties. Then you'd need to use properties and identifiers that were more general, which is where the URI references come in.

Creating shareable vocabularies and identifiers is the domain of ontology, and most ontologies intended for use on the Web use URIs, just as RDF does. For the purpose of clear explanations, we'll mostly use ordinary words and names (because long URIs are hard to read); but remember that in actual practice URI references are used to identify resources. Using shared URI references to identify resources is one way to make it possible for RDF data to be distributed across the Web, which is necessary for the Semantic Web.

If a resource is identified by a URI reference, what should an application display to represent it? Typical URI references aren't very readable. It's better to use a readable label, which is generally the ordinary name for the resource, if it has one. The label itself is yet another RDF property of the resource. The RDF Schema Recommendation (W3C 2004b) defines a standard label property. Its full URI is `http://www.w3.org/2000/01/rdf-schema#label`, or `rdfs:label` for short (using prefixes like `rdfs:` to stand for the common part of a URI is another way to make a URI more readable, a practice closely related to the use of namespaces in XML). Notice that the resource isn't identified by its name, although the right software could perform a query and retrieve all the resources

---

[2] The Sentences database (www.lazysoft.com) does this, but predicates can't be subjects of statements.

that had the given label. Naturally, you could also define a Name property to supplement the label.

2.2.3 *Properties of statements*

You might want to talk about a statement itself. You might want to say who published it and where, or to state that you disagree with it. In other words, we think of statements as having their own properties. But this isn't straightforward in RDF, because a statement has no inherent identity in the RDF model. A statement isn't a resource and so can't be the subject of another statement. RDF gets around this limitation in a slightly odd way. There is a particular type of resource with this identifier:

```
http://www.w3.org/1999/02/22-rdf-syntax-ns#Statement
```

Such a resource is called rdf:Statement for short and has four properties: rdf:subject, rdf:predicate, rdf:object, and rdf:type (whose value is rdf:Statement).

An rdf:Statement declares that there is a statement with the given subject, predicate, and object. The strange thing is that such an rdf:Statement can't be identified with any triple, *even if one exists that has the same subject, predicate, and object*. You can't make statements about any actual triple, but you can make statements about something of type rdf:Statement that has the same values for each of the three parts of the statement in question.

This is easier to make clear using a diagram of the kind introduced in the next section; section 2.3.5 presents a graphical view of an rdf:Statement.

2.3 *Visualizing statements with RDF graphs*

Many kinds of notations can be used to display RDF data; some of the more important are discussed in section 2.6. It turns out that directed, labeled graphs (see, for example, Weisstein) are excellent for representing RDF statements. A *graph* is a collection of *nodes* or vertices connected by *edges* (sometimes called *arcs*). In a *labeled* graph, the edges carry labels; in a *directed* graph, the edges point from one node to another. Graphs can naturally be illustrated by diagrams.

In graphs that represent a collection of RDF statements, a node represents a resource or literal value, and an arrow represents a predicate. Figure 2.1 shows a labeled graph for the color of a shoe.

This graph is extremely simple, but even so it's easy to notice that the label "shoe" is ambiguous. Are we talking about a generic shoe, or one specific shoe?

Figure 2.1
A graph stating that a shoe has a color whose value is "red." The arrow always points from the subject to the object of the statement.

In RDF, we can't talk about all shoes, just about particular resources. We can make statements about the class of shoes, which represents a collection of objects that share properties that make them "shoes," but this isn't the same as making statements about a generic shoe. Let's give this shoe an identifier instead of a generic name, as shown in figure 2.2 (remember that in practice, the identifiers for the shoe and for the property `color` would be URI references).

Figure 2.2
Asserting the color of a specific shoe.

In depicting RDF graphs, it's conventional to use a circle or oval to represent a resource and a rectangle to represent a literal value, such as a string. In this example, the value of the property is a literal—a simple string consisting of the characters *r, e, d*. The figures in the next section show both literals and resources as values of statements.

2.3.1 Resources with many statements

Next, let's look at a graph depicting several statements about the same resource (see figure 2.3). For this, we return to the database row from section 2.1.

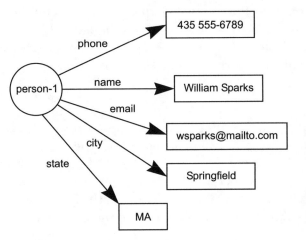

Figure 2.3
A resource that has many properties. This graph is equivalent to a row in the database table from section 2.1. Note that each arrow/property represents a separate statement. The subject of all these statements is person-1.

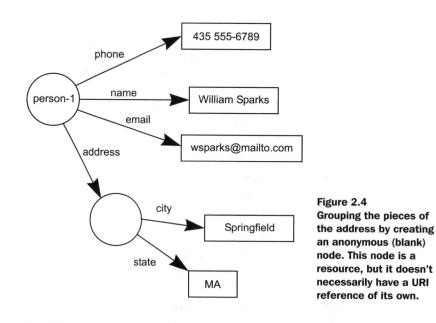

Figure 2.4
Grouping the pieces of the address by creating an anonymous (blank) node. This node is a resource, but it doesn't necessarily have a URI reference of its own.

Notice that the city and state aren't related to each other here, although we know that in reality, the state gives the location of the city. This was a weakness in the original data table that we noted but ignored in section 2.1. In figure 2.4 this problem is fixed, in a way that illustrates another important feature of RDF: the anonymous node (discussed in the next section).

Now our person has an address, which is associated with a city and state. But how do we know that the new node is a resource of type address? Either we could infer it, if we knew that the object of an address property must be an address type (a schema or ontology can tell us—see chapter 7), or we could explicitly state it by asserting the type of the new node, as shown in figure 2.5.

Notice that the object of the type property is an oval—a resource instead of just a text label. The type of a resource is itself a kind of resource.

2.3.2 *Anonymous nodes*

What is the identifier for the new node? There isn't one. In words, the graph says, "person-1 has an address that is something whose type is address, whose city is 'Springfield', and whose state is 'MA'." This "something" is known by its properties, but not by an intrinsic identity. The node is an artifact of the way we decided to group the facts. There's nothing wrong with this approach, and there's also no reason to assign a universal identifier to such a node.

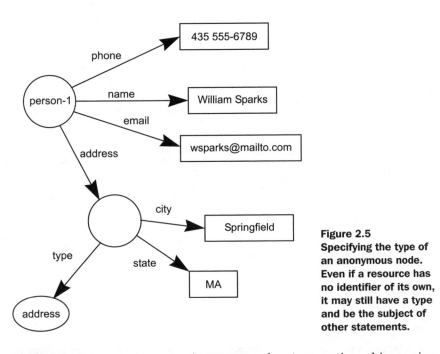

Figure 2.5
Specifying the type of
an anonymous node.
Even if a resource has
no identifier of its own,
it may still have a type
and be the subject of
other statements.

Such situations are common in RDF graphs. As mentioned in section 2.1.3, such nodes are called *anonymous* nodes, or sometimes *blank nodes* or *b-nodes*. A relational database includes dependent and independent tables. A dependent table depends on one or more other tables for its existence and meaning. An anonymous RDF node is somewhat analogous. The RDF processing program may assign an internal node identifier to the node for practical purposes, but that identifier has no utility to another processor that receives the graph. The node's situation in the graph gives it its fundamental identity.

2.3.3 *Resources as objects of statements*

Next, suppose we want to make a statement about person-1's email account. Perhaps it was opened on August 1, 2001. We'd like to create a triple with the email address as the subject, but we can't because the subject has to be a resource, not a literal.

We can work around this limitation either by using an anonymous node or by creating a new resource. The approach we choose may depend on how the information is organized when we receive it. Figure 2.6 shows a graph for the second approach.

This seems simple enough, but it exposes a new aspect of RDF processing. In figure 2.5, you can find the email address in a straightforward manner if you

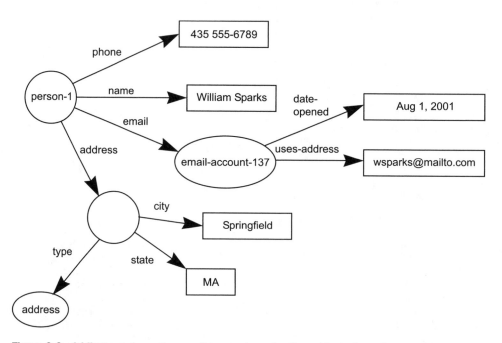

Figure 2.6 Adding a node so the email account can be the subject of another statement.

understand the meaning of the property called email. But in figure 2.6, there is no email address—at least, not one labeled as such. To locate the actual email address, you must find a resource of type email-account (to keep the graph simple, we did not include a type statement for the account resource), look for a property called uses-address, and then get its value.

Although this process may seem obvious, that's because you infer what the entities mean from their labels. A computer will see the labels and types as arbitrary strings. The computer has to infer from the predicate and object types how to get the email address. In order for it to do this, rules must be in place about those types, along with rules for making the inferences. Rules about the types are the business of RDF schema and data types, and of the ontology in use (if any). The rules for making inferences are mainly the business of logic.

2.3.4 *Container nodes*

It often happens that we want to talk about a collection of things, like items in a list, or a collection of cars in a garage. RDF defines three special resource types to hold such collections, and a set of special properties to relate the collection to its members:

- *Bag*—Contains any number of resources without any order (duplicates are allowed)

- *Sequence*—Contains an ordered collection of resources

- *Alternative*—Specifies that any one of the members can be selected (for example, a light can be on or off)

The arcs from a collection node to its members are given the special labels rdf:_1, rdf:_2, and so on.

Figure 2.7 illustrates the alternative container. In figure 2.8, the labels say "Truck" and "Car" for simplicity; in practice, they would represent a specific car and a specific truck.

The latest RDF Recommendations also provide for a *collection* type. This type has an interesting behavior that is different from the previous three container types. A sequence, bag, or alternative container is open-ended because anyone can add another item by adding the corresponding triple to the container. But a collection is closed—once constructed, it can't accept any more members. Consult the RDF Recommendations for more information about these details.

2.3.5 *Graphing properties of statements*

To round out this section, we return to rdf:Statement, which we introduced in section 2.2.3. It's a special kind of resource that can be used to say things about triples. In the RDF model, an ordinary triple isn't a resource, so it can't be the subject of another statement. But we can make the set of coordinated statements shown in figure 2.9.

In words, this graph says that "There is something whose type is RDF:Statement. It has 'person-1' as a subject, 'name' as a predicate, and 'William Sparks' as an

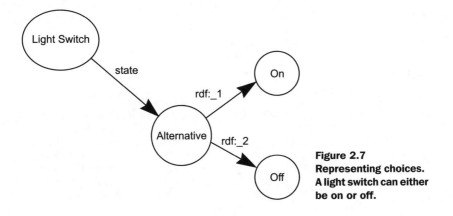

Figure 2.7
Representing choices.
A light switch can either
be on or off.

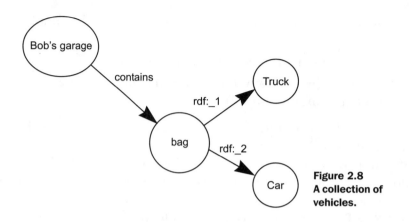

Figure 2.8
A collection of vehicles.

object" (recall that our use of RDF: here is a shorthand for a much longer URI—the fact that we use uppercase letters instead of lowercase highlights the fact that these prefixes are arbitrary as long as they're used consistently). We could give this node, whose type is RDF:Statement, a URI if we wanted to, but chances are we'll leave it blank. We can use this new node as the subject of other statements. An RDF processor can infer that those statements apply to the original triple by matching the subject, object, and predicate.

This procedure is called *reifying* the original statement. To *reify* is to make a "thing" out of something. In this case, we've made a resource out of a statement, in a manner of speaking. The rdf:Statement resource doesn't assert the fact asserted by the original statement—only the original statement can do that. In fact, the statement described by the rdf:Statement doesn't have to exist. This situation is like saying, "I'm thinking about saying that I want to go to a restaurant."

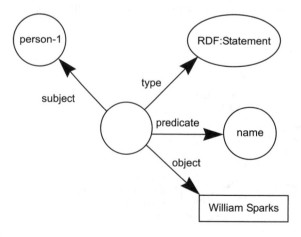

Figure 2.9
Reifying a statement so that things may be said about it. This graph says in effect that "There is a Statement whose subject is 'person-1', and the statement says that person-1's name is 'William Sparks'."

You can say it even if you never actually say that you want to go to a restaurant. The reified statement may not replace the statement it represents, but it provides a limited way to talk about that statement (strictly, a statement with the same properties, since we can't identify any specific statement).

2.4 *Six RDF applications*

At the beginning of the chapter, you saw that RDF represents data and meta data the same way. There is no difference, as far as RDF is concerned. In this section, we'll look at a few current applications of RDF that are designed to work with meta data. The FOAF case study in the appendix also falls into this category.

2.4.1 *RDF in Mozilla*

The Mozilla browser (www.mozilla.org) has an extremely flexible, configurable system that is used to build special user interfaces. The detailed instructions are contained in XML files using the XUL (Extensible User interface Language) format. Mozilla uses RDF as the source for listings and other control information that defines which XUL files to use for the specific XUL interfaces. All the applets in the sidebar within the Mozilla application are described this way using RDF.

Mozilla uses RDF to describe email and news items stored by the mail and news reader. This RDF meta data is used to build the trees that display available items. Much data about user preferences, such as the "skin" in use, is stored as RDF. Any data that you can turn into RDF can be displayed using a customized user interface, as described at the Mozilla web site:

> The entire Mozilla UI is built from "XUL" files, Javascript snippets and calls to XP-COM interfaces for services such as RDF query and aggregation.... XUL is an XML application that allows interfaces to be built using XML, HTML, Javascript and RDF.

The XUL Template Reference describes in some detail how XUL widgets (trees, menus) are populated by querying RDF data graphs.

2.4.2 *RSS*

Blogging—web logging—is becoming increasingly popular. The RSS technology is making blogging more widely known by letting people distribute summaries of new blog stories efficiently and cheaply. (The RSS acronym originally stood for Rich Site Summary, then transformed to Really Simple Syndication, and now has several different meanings.) An RSS file describes a site (a blog or other kind of site) with meta data, including its name, its URL, and its channels. Then each channel is described, including summaries of the newest stories on the site, with URLs to each of them. Many free or inexpensive reader applications are available.

There are several versions of the RSS format, all of which are small, XML-based languages. Two versions use RDF's XML exchange format. All the versions contain substantially the same information, but the RDF news feeds could be collected by an RDF processor and stored in an RDF database. Blogs link to each other, and with the RDF available for analysis, it would be possible to do a number of interesting things. You could derive a set of worldwide threaded conversations on a subject, or investigate how influence spreads across the blogging communities, or connect the blog data to other data published by the blog authors.

Some of these same things could be done without RDF (and some are being done), but in each case special programming machinery must be invented and the results wouldn't be readily useful for further analysis by other software. On the other hand, many writers of RSS software prefer to work with the non-RDF formats, which they find easier to read and create during software development.

The example of RSS suggests that some non-RDF data formats could coexist with RDF in the future by converting them into RDF. Doing so would make a lot of non-RDF data immediately accessible to RDF systems. The drawback is that a different custom transformation would be required for each format.

RSS, in its RDF versions, is a particularly interesting case because it's one of the few current RDF applications that is distributed over the Web rather than being used locally, the way Mozilla uses its RDF data. Thus, RSS can be seen as an early—some might say primitive—Semantic Web application.

2.4.3 RDF for annotations: Annotea

Annotea (http://annotest.w3.org/) is an experimental scheme by the W3C for annotating web pages. It uses RDF to point to the place in the page that is to be annotated, and it captures the date, time, location in the text, author of the annotation, and the text of the note. When an Annotea-capable browser loads a page, it checks its list of Annotea servers to see if they have any notes against the page. If they do, the browser loads them and puts visible indicators in the displayed page to show where the notes are. Annotea has spread beyond the Amaya browser where it got its start; several other browsers and applications provide Annotea capability.[3]

---

[3] At the time of writing, there is a third-party Annotea extension for Mozilla (Annozilla, at http://annozilla.mozdev.org/) as well as several extensions for Internet Explorer.

2.4.4 *Bibliographic meta data: Dublin Core*

Dublin Core (http://dublincore.org) is a system for describing bibliographic meta data. Its use has been spreading, because it provides practical standard terms applicable to nearly any published work (terms like *Title*, *Creator*, and *Subject*). Dublin Core can be expressed in several different ways, of which RDF is one.

2.4.5 *WebScripter: fusing information*

WebScripter (www.isi.edu/webscripter) is a system developed at the University of Southern California that uses DAML (DARPA Agent Markup Language) to mark up web pages so that information about the web page can be extracted in a uniform way and combined with information from other web pages. DAML, discussed further in chapter 7, is a language that uses RDF to define ontologies, or vocabularies. To quote from the WebScripter web site:

> WebScripter is a tool that enables ordinary users to easily and quickly assemble reports, extracting and fusing information from multiple, heterogeneous DAMLized Web sources.

Here is a fragment of WebScripter markup from an example web page (the name and phone number have been changed). Section 2.6 shows how to represent RDF data in XML format; this particular example should be fairly self-explanatory even without that discussion. The meta data (`First`, `Project Nicknames`, and so on) should be clear:

```
<WebScripterReportRow rdf:ID="5">
  <First>William</First>
  <Last>Sparks</Last>
  <Role>researcher</Role>
  <Role_No>5</Role_No>
  <Role_Label>Researcher</Role_Label>
  <Prefix>sparks</Prefix>
  <Office>1231</Office>
  <Phone>435-555-6789</Phone>
  <Addendum>http://www.isi.edu/~sparks/sparks.daml</Addendum>
  <Interests>user interfaces development, XML/Database
    application, Distributed Resource Allocation and
    scheduling</Interests>
  <Home_Page>http://www.isi.edu/~sparks</Home_Page>
  <Project_Nicknames>CAMERA</Project_Nicknames>
  <Project_Nicknames>CACE-UI-IPT</Project_Nicknames>
  <Project_Pages>http://www.isi.edu/camera</Project_Pages>
  <Project_Pages>
  http://www.xfaster.com/xfast.nsf/pages/useript?opendocument
```

```
    </Project_Pages>
    <Thumbnail>
    http://www.isi.edu/webscripter/sparks-thumb-2001-02-27.jpg
    </Thumbnail>
    <Medium>
    http://www.isi.edu/webscripter/sparks-medium-2001-02-27.jpg
    </Medium>
    <Full>
    http://www.isi.edu/webscripter/sparks-full-2001-02-27.jpg
    </Full>
</WebScripterReportRow>
```

All the element names, such as First, Last, and Role, have been defined using DAML and are available to any WebScripter application.

An application that can parse RDF and understand DAML can use this information in many ways. For example, if the owner of this page, William Sparks, included the WebScripter markup on his page, an application could extract it and use it to build a table of faculty members with their professional and personal interests.

2.4.6 *Haystack: personal information management*

Haystack (http://haystack.lcs.mit.edu/index.html) is a project of the Laboratory for Computer Sciences at the Massachusetts Institute of Technology. It aims to unify the management of personal information including email, web pages, documents in the filesystem, and calendars, to allow people to create collections from their digitized information, to categorize their information in flexible ways, and to help them find what they need effectively.

To quote a bit of the project overview (italics added):

> **Flexibility**. The data types Haystack understands aren't hard-wired; any additional types of information that a user wants to work with can be easily incorporated. The user can readily define new object attributes that help them categorize and retrieve information, and new relationships between objects. *Rather than being tacked-on afterthoughts, user-defined attributes and relationships are given the same centrality in the interface as built-in relationships such as "author" and "date."*

From this description, RDF would seem to be a natural choice for representing the data, and RDF is what the designers chose. This choice allowed them to use several open-source RDF processing libraries.

This is obviously a complex system, and the first release has a confusing interface and very slow performance. But that isn't unusual for a new system, and no doubt Haystack will continue to improve.

2.5 *Meshing data and meta data*

To illustrate how meta data and data mesh smoothly in a collection of RDF statements, let's use RDF to store data that might originally have been in a relational database. Sections 2.1 and 2.3 cover the basic principles.

As you look through the example, bear in mind that the identifiers of the resources have been simplified to keep everything easy to read. In a real data set, all the identifiers would be URIs.

The example is based on a hypothetical database of references: quotations from various published works. Originally, we imagine, the data was stored in a relational database. Each reference consists of a quotation from a published work, and the database contains the author(s) of the work, its publisher, the name of the book, and other information (meta data) about the work such as its title, starting page, and a comment about the quote. Each publisher is an organization that has a name, a main URL, and other properties that aren't used here. Each author is a person who has a name and other properties.

2.5.1 *The data model*

We start with a data model of the kind that a database designer would create (see figure 2.10). We create the model in terms of a relational database—tables and their relationships. In a relational database, data is contained in the rows and columns of tables (at least, from a conceptual point of view; the internal structure, invisible to the database programmer, might be quite different). This database contains four basic tables: person, organization, publication, and reference.

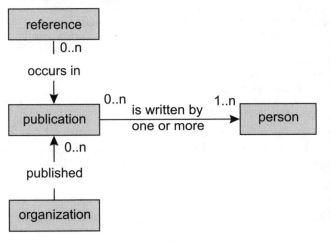

Figure 2.10
Basic data model for the RDF example. This example illustrates how data and meta data join smoothly in RDF. This figure depicts the table structure of a conventional database. The *x..n* notation means anywhere from *x* to any number of items. For example, a publication is written by one or more persons. The data is stored in the tables, and the labels, such as "reference" and "published," represent meta data about the database.

In this diagram, the notations 0..*n* and 1..*n* refer to the cardinality of the relationship. In this example, 1 or more persons (*n* indicates an unspecified number greater than 0) can be an author of a publication, and 0 or more publications can be written by any one person. However, a reference can occur in just one publication, although there can be more than one reference from the same work. Similarly, any one publication can be published by just one organization, although an organization can be the publisher of any number of publications. A more complete data model would also show the individual data items, such as the title of a book, the name of a person, and so forth.

2.5.2 *The data in table format*

Tables 2.4 and 2.5 illustrate the data stored in two of the tables, labeled with their column names. Notice that references are made to primary keys (`refid`, `sourcepub`) rather than to names. In this case, we have `sourcepub=2` instead of `sourcepub=Basic Books`. This is good relational database practice—each fundamental entity has its own identity, separate from its name.

Table 2.4   Part of the data stored in the reference table. The first column contains the identifier of each row (the primary key). The second column contains identifiers of particular rows in the publication table. This is how relationships, represented by the lines connecting the tables shown in figure 2.10, are created in a conventional database.

refid	sourcepub	reftext	startpage
1	2	Meaning has to do with the ways in which we function meaningfully in the world and make sense of it via bodily and imaginative structures.	78
2	2	As we will see, our most fundamental concerns—time, events, causation, the mind, the self, and morality—are metaphorical in multiple ways. So much of the ontology and inferential structure of these concepts is metaphorical that, if one somehow managed to eliminate metaphorical thought, the remaining skeletal concepts would be so impoverished that none of us could do any substantial everyday reasoning.	128

With a relational database, we can't embed a list of authors into the publication table directly.[4] So, we need a table to hold the list of authors for each publication. We'll call this table authorlist. Table 2.5 shows a sample of this table.

---

[4] The newest versions of SQL databases can embed lists, but this technology isn't common yet, especially in low-cost and free software.

Table 2.5 Part of the data is stored in the authorlist table. This table isn't present in the basic data model depicted in figure 2.10, but it's needed due to the restrictions of standard relational databases, which can't store a list in any one cell.

authorlistid	personid	role
2	2	author
2	3	author

Besides the tables, the relationships between them are important. A relationship tells which field in a table is related to a field in another, like the `sourceid` for a `pub`.

2.5.3 *The relationships between tables*

The diagram in figure 2.11 summarizes the tables and their relationships. In this diagram, the data element above the line is the table's primary key. The black

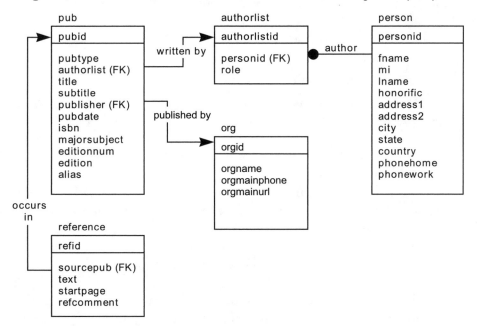

Figure 2.11 Design of the tables, showing more of the detail needed for design purposes. Each rectangular container represents a table. The label above the container is the table's name. The label in the compartment at the top of the table is its primary key—the data item that serves to distinguish one row of data from another. The black dot on the left end of the author relationship line indicates a many-to-one relationship: A list of authors may include one or more persons.

dot on the line from person to authorlist indicates a many-to-one relationship: One person may write many publications.

The FK in parentheses means *foreign key*, which is a technical database term. A foreign key is a way to reference a data item in another ("foreign") table. In a relational database, foreign keys are important for managing relationships between tables. Verb phrases like "wrote" indicate the role of the particular relationships.

2.5.4 *The RDF version of the data*

In section 2.1, we showed how a table can be pulled apart into triples, which can then be represented using RDF. When you do this, you end up with many triples representing each row of a table. For this example, we tried to stay as close as possible to the original tables. It might be better to make some design changes if we were targeting an RDF design from the beginning, but the result would be similar.

Figure 2.12 shows part of the RDF graph for one of the references—there isn't room on the page for much more. A (non-RDF) table version of the same data is shown in section 2.5.5 for comparison.

You may have noticed several things:

- The uniform, readable format of the tables has been replaced by repeating patterns in the graph.

- If you could see more of the graph, it would be hard to tell that all the references have the same structure. At a casual inspection, each one might be arranged somewhat differently from the others. This is an advantage in some situations; but normally, if a set of data is regular, it's useful to make that fact apparent.

- The RDF version is much more redundant than the relational database version. The property specifications, such as type, name, and so on, are repeated, whereas in the relational database they're contained in the column headings only once for each table. In a relational database, property specifications are contained in the table definitions, or *schema*. Why, with RDF, do we have to keep saying that a pub node has type='tt-book'? Isn't it obvious? It isn't obvious to a computer. In this database, a pub might be a book, but it might also be a magazine, an issue of a journal, or a newspaper. So, we have to say what its type is.

The tradeoffs are clear. RDF trades regularity for flexibility. This requires RDF to carry data that might otherwise be redundant. However, patterns in the data remain as patterns, whether the data is stored in tables or on RDF.

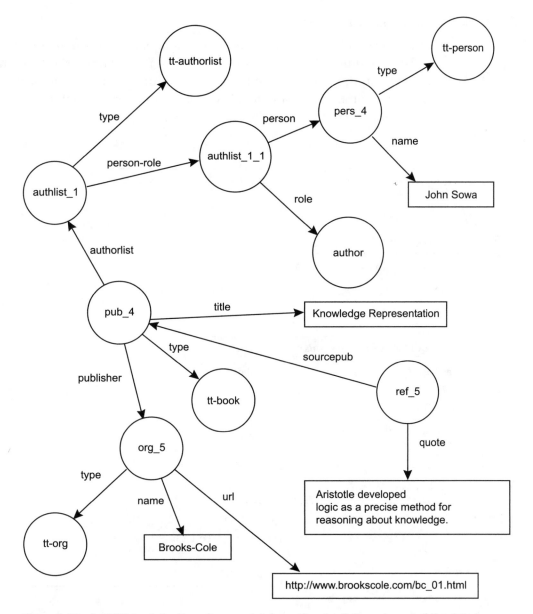

Figure 2.12   An RDF graph for the reference database (for simplicity, only part of the data is shown).

2.5.5 *Table versions of the data*

Figure 2.13 shows table versions of the same data. Note that the tables are simplified—we have omitted columns for which there is no data in the RDF graph. Also, the name in the person table has been simplified by not being broken out into first name, initial, and last name, because the RDF graph contains the name as a single string (it could have been split up, too).

publication

pubid	pubtype	title	publisher
pub_4	tt-book	Knowledge Representation	org_5

publication-Authorlist

pubid	authorlistid
pub_4	authlist_1_1

authorlist

authorlistid	personid	role
authlist_1_1	pers_4	author

person

personid	name
pers_4	John Sowa

organization

orgid	orgname	orgmainurl
org_5	Brooks-Cole	http://brookscole.com/bc_01.html

reference

refid	sourcepub	text
ref_5	pub_4	Aristotle developed logic as a precise method for reasoning about knowledge.

Figure 2.13 How the data of the example might look in a set of tables. Each table represents a kind of entity (a type of resource in the RDF version).

2.5.6 *Why bother with RDF?*

So far, the RDF version contains the same data as the relational database version. Why go to the trouble of converting to RDF? Well, if you plan to use the data exactly the same way, you shouldn't put it into RDF. A relational database will be more efficient. Here are some things you can do with the data as RDF that you can't do when it's in a conventional database:

- Combine the data with other data sets that don't follow the data model you've been using.

- Add more data that doesn't fit the table structures. You could add a book's web site to the data, give an author's nickname, or whatever you like.

- Exchange data with any other application that knows how to handle RDF. You can do this over the Web, by email, or any other way by which you can exchange a data file. There is no equivalent way to exchange the data in a relational database.

- Use an RDF processor that can do logical reasoning (more in chapter 6) to discover unstated relationships in the data.

- Use someone else's ontology to learn more about the relationships between the properties and resources in your data.

- Add statements about publications and references that have been defined somewhere else on the Web. All you have to do is to refer to the identifiers (the URIs) that they have published. You aren't limited to talking about things stored in your own database.

- Do all these things using well-defined standards, so that a wide range of software can process the data.

This isn't all, but it's enough to show that RDF can bring a lot of power to bear.

2.6 *Sharing data*

For information to be widely usable over the Web, we need a way to exchange it between computers. If RDF is to play the role of representing that information, there must be a standard format for communicating an RDF dataset over the Internet and other networks. In practice, this entails a language based on XML (Extensible Markup Language), the international framework for such languages.

RDF is defined in terms of a model (basically, statements or triples), as presented in section 2.1. The current suite of draft documents that specify RDF include a model theory, which is a formal mathematical description of how to understand and work with the model (more in chapter 6). In addition to a common model and its interpretation, there is a standard format for communicating an RDF dataset. The RDF Model and Syntax Recommendation (W3C 1999) includes an XML vocabulary for this purpose, usually called the RDF/XML serialization syntax.

This syntax has turned out to be awkward to read, understand, create by hand, and process; consequently, several more readable non-XML syntaxes have grown up. None of them is yet an official standard, but a number of tools process some of them.

2.6.1 RDF/XML syntax

We'll look at RDF/XML syntax in some detail, although not exhaustively, because it's one of the main ways in which RDF data is shared and illustrated. This section will provide you with a bit of familiarity when you encounter examples of RDF on the Web or elsewhere, and also give you a sense of how ordinary XML documents can be modified into RDF. RDF/XML syntax can be difficult to learn, partly because it allows many optional ways to construct the same statements, and partly because the long URI references used to identify resources are hard to type and read. XML namespaces also play an important role. If you aren't familiar with XML namespaces, you may want to review an introduction to XML.

RDF information is embedded into an XML document by placing it into an RDF element. The document (or file, if you prefer) may contain only RDF, or an RDF element may be just part of it. Some RDF processors may require the file to be nothing but RDF.

Start with a namespace declaration

Here's an empty RDF element, including the namespace declaration that associates the rdf prefix with the actual RDF namespace (http://www.w3.org/1999/02/22-rdf-syntax-ns#:

```
<rdf:RDF xmlns:rdf="http://www.w3.org/1999/02/22-rdf-syntax-ns#" >
    <!-- RDF statements go here -->
</rdf:RDF>
```

As with any XML element, you may declare other namespaces as well. To simplify the illustrations, we'll usually omit the rdf and rdfs namespace declarations (and use the rdf and rdfs prefixes as if they'd been declared), but you should remember to put them back if you want to create RDF of your own.

An alternative you may see uses a so-called *default namespace*, like this:

```
<RDF xmlns ="http://www.w3.org/1999/02/22-rdf-syntax-ns#" >
    <!-- RDF statements go here -->
</RDF>
```

Using a default namespace, any child element without a prefix is taken to be in the RDF namespace (but not attributes, so they may still have to be prefixed, which again requires a namespace declaration).

Identify the subject

Remember that the model for RDF contains a collection of statements (or triples), each with a subject, a predicate, and an object:

```
{subject1, predicate1, object1}
{subject1, predicate2, object2}
{subject2, predicate3, object3}
```

The simplest approach would be to have one RDF element per statement.

To be concrete, we'll use the example from section 2.5.5 about references. Let's look at just these statements, about one of the publications:

```
{pub_1; type; tt-book}
{pub_1; publisher; org_1}
{pub_1; title; Fluid Concepts and Creative Analogies}
```

In RDF, the subject is normally introduced using the Description element:

```
<rdf:RDF xmlns:rdf="http://www.w3.org/1999/02/22-rdf-syntax-ns#">
    <rdf:Description rdf:about='#pub_1'>
        <rdf:type rdf:resource='#tt-book'/>
    </rdf:Description>
</rdf:RDF>
```

The rdf:about attribute specifies the URI of the resource. Here, #pub_1 indicates that pub_1 has been declared elsewhere in the same document (although we haven't shown the declaration yet—this is done next). If pub_1 had instead been declared in a different source, we'd have to include the entire URI reference to it. That URI reference would be whatever namespace the other document assigned for pub_1. If there were none, we'd use the URI of the other document. Supposing that the right URI to use is http://example.com/references.rdf, we could refer to it like this:

```
rdf:about=' http://example.com/references.rdf#pub_1'
```

Here's how we can identify a resource if it hasn't already been referred to by means of an rdf:about assignment. We do so by assigning it an ID value:

```
<rdf:Description rdf:ID='#pub_2'>
    <rdf:type rdf:resource='#tt-book'/>
</rdf:Description>
```

Here we use the ID attribute to assign an identifier to the resource. The ID attribute lets you refer to a resource without using its full URI, in addition to giving you a way to assign an identifier. What if you forget to create an identifier? If you have a statement that refers to a resource, an RDF processor is entitled to infer that it must exist, even if you haven't declared its identifier. In other words, the RDF processor should create a node for that resource anyway.

If you had a separate Description element for each statement, the RDF file would get very long. To shorten the XML, you can put more than one property/object pair into a Description element, as long as they refer to the same subject:

```
<rdf:RDF xmlns:rdf="http://www.w3.org/1999/02/22-rdf-syntax-ns#"
    xmlns='uri:fieldguide:rdf#'>
    <rdf:Description rdf:ID='pub_1'>
        <rdf:type rdf:resource='#tt-book'/>
        <publisher rdf:resource='#org_1'/>
        <title>Fluid Concepts and Creative Analogies</title>
    </rdf:Description>
</rdf:RDF>
```

In order to specify that publisher and title are properties that we're establishing (and not properties of the same name established by, say, Dublin Core or someone else), we've added a namespace for them (uri:fieldguide:rdf#). This namespace is made up and doesn't point to any actual document that could be retrieved (although it could). The relationship between such a namespace and the document the resources are declared in turns out to involve some tricky issues (see section 2.7).

Next let's add a few statements about the organization org_1:

```
<rdf:RDF xmlns:rdf="http://www.w3.org/1999/02/22-rdf-syntax-ns#"
    xmlns='urn:fieldguide:rdf#'>
    <rdf:Description rdf:ID='pub_1'>
        <rdf:type rdf:resource='#tt-org'/>
        <publisher rdf:resource='#org_1'/>
        <title>Fluid Concepts and Creative Analogies</title>
    </rdf:Description>

    <rdf:Description rdf:ID='org_1'>
        <rdf:type rdf:resource='#tt-org'/>
        <name>Basic Books</name>
        <url>http://www.harpercollins.com</url>
    </rdf:Description>
</rdf:RDF>
```

We can also nest the description of org_1 inside the description of pub_1, under the publisher element, like this:

```
<rdf:RDF xmlns:rdf="http://www.w3.org/1999/02/22-rdf-syntax-ns#"
    xmlns='urn:fieldguide:rdf#'>
    <rdf:Description rdf:ID='pub_1'>
        <rdf:type rdf:resource='#tt-book'/>
        <publisher>
            <rdf:Description  rdf:ID='org_1' rdf:type='#tt-org'>
                <name>Basic Books</name>
                <url>http://www.harpercollins.com</url>
            </rdf:Description>
        </publisher>
        <title>Fluid Concepts and Creative Analogies</title>
    </rdf:Description>
</rdf:RDF>
```

Both of these forms cause the RDF processor to create exactly the same set of triples.

We mentioned the creation of an anonymous node—one that has no identity of its own. Here's how we could make the publisher an anonymous node. In effect, the following fragment says that pub_1 is published by something whose type is "tt-org" and whose name is "Basic Books". That "something" is the anonymous node—a resource that has no inherent identifier:

```
<rdf:RDF xmlns:rdf="http://www.w3.org/1999/02/22-rdf-syntax-ns#"
    xmlns='urn:fieldguide:rdf#'>
    <rdf:Description rdf:ID='pub_1'>
        <rdf:type rdf:resource='#tt-book'/>
        <publisher>
            <rdf:Description  rdf:type='#tt-org'>
                <name>Basic Books</name>
                <url>http://www.harpercollins.com</url>
            </rdf:Description>
        </publisher>
        <title>Fluid Concepts and Creative Analogies</title>
    </rdf:Description>
</rdf:RDF>
```

This is almost identical to the previous version except that no ID is specified for the publisher resource.

Attribute-only version

In yet another variation, element content can be converted into attributes. Doing so is useful when the RDF is to be embedded in a web page, because ordinary browsers don't display attribute values. This makes the RDF invisible to the reader while still available to processors. Here's an earlier snippet rewritten in the attribute-only format:

```
<rdf:RDF xmlns:rdf="http://www.w3.org/1999/02/22-rdf-syntax-ns#"
    xmlns:fg='urn:fieldguide:rdf#'>
    <rdf:Description rdf:ID='pub_1'
```

```
                rdf:type='#tt-book'
                fg:publisher='urn:fieldguide:rdf#org_1'
                fg:title='Fluid Concepts and Creative Analogies'/>

      <rdf:Description rdf:ID='org_1'
                rdf:type ='urn:fieldguide:rdf#tt-org'
                fg:name='Basic Books'
                fg:url='http://www.harpercollins.com'/>
    </rdf:RDF>
```

One point that isn't obvious is that we had to change the resource identifiers like
#org_1 in the fg:publisher attribute to include their entire URI, like urn:field-
guide:rdf#org_1.

The large number of ways to express the same thing, combined with tricky
parts like knowing when to use #org_1 versus the full URI reference, can make it
difficult to work with the RDF/XML syntax. Although this syntax has many more
aspects, we'll look at only one more variation, sometimes called *striped* format.
This format lets you treat ordinary XML markup as if it were RDF, if it meets certain requirements.

Striped format

Notice that an RDF graph alternates between nodes and edges. You can
treat nested XML elements as alternating nodes and edges, and so make a
correspondence between the XML and RDF statements. Figure 2.14 illustrates
this pattern.

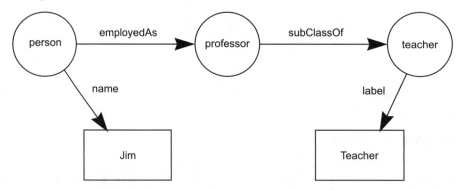

**Figure 2.14 Alternating nodes and edges. Nodes, represented by circles, are connected
by edges, represented by lines. Each node is an RDF resource, and each line is an RDF
property. Nodes and lines alternate automatically, as shown here. A piece of an XML
document that follows this alternating pattern can easily be turned into RDF statements.**

We might represent this in XML as follows:

```
<person>
    <name>Jim</name>
    <employedAs>
        <professor>
            <subClassOf>
                <teacher>
                    <label>Teacher</label>
                </teacher>
            </subClassOf>
        </professor>
    </employedAs>
</person>
```

The striping works like this:

- If an element represents a subject, then its immediate children must be properties.

- If an element represents a property, then it can only have one child, and that child must be the property value.

- If an element has character content, then that content is the literal value of the property.

- Element names represent resource types, not their identifiers.

In the previous code, the outermost element is `<person>...</person>`, which will become a resource of type `person`. `<name>` will become a property that has a literal value of "Jim" and a type of `name`. `<employedAs>` will become another property of type `employedAs`.

Notice that none of these XML elements has any RDF-type identity. This suggests that they should be represented as anonymous nodes. This is precisely what an RDF parser will do. To turn this bit of XML into RDF, all we have to do is put its elements into a namespace that we're authorized to use and wrap it inside an RDF element:[5] For purposes of illustration, we'll use the made-up namespace `urn:exlorersguide:rdf#`.

```
<rdf:RDF xmlns:rdf="http://www.w3.org/1999/02/22-rdf-syntax-ns#"
    xmlns='urn:explorersguide:rdf#'>
    <person>
        <name>Jim</name>
```

---

[5] Recently the RDF specifications have been changed so that the RDF element may be omitted if the processing application knows that the document is in RDF. Thus even the RDF wrapper used here isn't necessarily needed.

```
<employedAs>
    <professor>
        <subClassOf>
            <teacher>
                <label>Teacher</label>
            </teacher>
        </subClassOf>
    </professor>
</employedAs>
    </person>
</rdf:RDF>
```

The graph created by the RDF parser is shown in figure 2.15. It isn't precisely the same as the original in figure 2.14, but it's approximately equivalent. In other words, the graph could be read, "There is something, whose type is 'person' and whose name is 'Jim', that is employed as something of type 'professor', which is a subclass of something of type 'teacher', having a label of 'Teacher'." In this manner, an ordinary XML file that is constructed properly can be turned into a collection of RDF statements. In some cases, minor adjustments must be made to the original file.

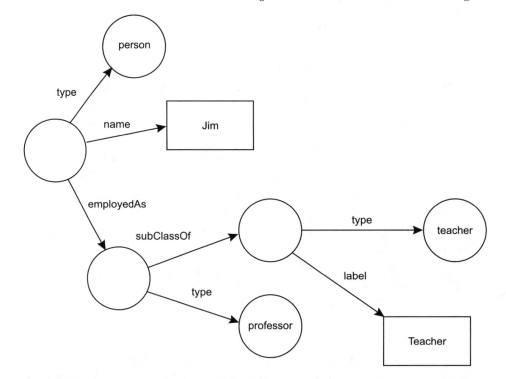

Figure 2.15 The RDF graph generated by an RDF processor for the previous code snippet.

RDF/XML example

To round out this section about RDF/XML syntax, let's look at a fragment of working RDF. Listing 2.1 is an example of RSS from O'Reilly Network.

Listing 2.1   A blog entry in an RDF version of RSS

```xml
<?xml version="1.0" encoding="utf-8"?>
<rdf:RDF
  xmlns:rdf="http://www.w3.org/1999/02/22-rdf-syntax-ns#"
  xmlns="http://my.netscape.com/rdf/simple/0.9/"
>

  <channel>
    <title>Pie-R-Squared</title>
    <description>
      Download a delicious pie from Pie-R-Squared!
    </description>
    <link>http://www.pie-r-squared.com</link>
  </channel>

  <image>
    <title>Pie-R-Squared du Jour</title>
    <url>http://www.pie-r-squared.com/images/logo88x33.gif</url>
    <link>http://www.pie-r-squared.com</link>
  </image>

  <item>
    <title>Pecan Plenty</title>
    <link>http://www.pie-r-squared.com/pies/pecan.html</link>
  </item>

  <item>
    <title>Key Lime</title>
    <link>http://www.pie-r-squared.com/pies/key_lime.html</link>
  </item>

</rdf:RDF>
```

NOTE   Because RDF syntax can be hard to get right, it's a good idea to test new RDF documents using an RDF validator. The W3C maintains one that also draws a graph of the dataset, which can be very helpful. The W3C RDF validator is online at www.w3.org/RDF/Validator.

2.6.2 *Non-XML formats*

Notation 3 (N3) and N-triples are the most common non-XML formats. N3 was developed by Tim Berners-Lee and Dan Connolly. It's unofficial, although a document describing it has been published by the W3C. A statement is written in ordinary text in the order `<subject> <predicate> <object>`. A statement is terminated by a period (.). Here's a simple example:

```
<#pat> <#knows> <#jo> .
<#pat> <#age> "24" .
```

The `"24"` represents a literal value rather than a resource. The use of the # character with the identifiers is just like its use in the RDF/XML syntax. Namespaces and prefixes can be declared in a compact way that isn't shown here.

Some N3 processors, like cwm, can perform logical inferences on the triples after ingesting them. N3 can be converted into RDF/XML format and vice versa.

N-triples is a line-oriented subset of N3. It was developed to express the desired results of test cases and to be transmittable over the Internet in a MIME format. For simple cases, there is virtually no difference between N-triples and N3, so we don't include an example.

2.7 *RDF in the real world of the Web*

You've seen that RDF can be used to make a wide range of statements or assertions about specific resources. The resources can be either concrete (that is, retrievable over the Internet) or more abstract. A set of RDF statements constitutes a kind of database and is well suited for declaring meta data. RDF can be expressed in XML form, for interchanging with other systems by Internet or some other means. RDF's flexible capabilities, its ability to use and extend statements created by several sources, and its ability to support layers of ontology and logic seem appropriate for a role in the Semantic Web.

A number of matters need to be worked out, however. Some will require little more than an agreement on a convention; others may be more fundamental. In this section we mention some of the more prominent issues.

2.7.1 *What does a URI reference indicate?*

All resources in RDF are identified by URI references, unless they're anonymous. But it isn't always clear what a particular URI reference indicates. In the case of a URL that points to a web page, when that URL is used by a browser, it identifies a particular resource—the web page. The page may change from time to time and may be sent in different formats (possibly for different browsers), but the URI always refers to a representation of the current state of that resource.

In contrast, consider this fragment of RDF, from the RDF Model and Syntax Recommendation:

```
<rdf:Description about="http://www.w3.org/staffId/85740">
    <rdf:type resource="http://description.org/schema/Person"/>
    <v:Name>Ora Lassila</v:Name>
    <v:Email>lassila@w3.org</v:Email>
</rdf:Description>
```

The chances are high that the URL http://description.org/schema/Person won't return a document. If it does, we can only hope that it returns a description of the meaning and usage of the term *Person*. Even if it does, the intended meaning is to say that the type of a resource is "Person," which is very different from being a kind of Person. Furthermore, if the URL returns a page, how can we know if the intended meaning is "Person" and not the actual document? After all, we'd suppose that a bit of RDF starting with `<rdf:Description about='http://www.whitehouse.gov'>` refers to the home page of the White House. We have no standard way to know.

There are more complications, too. Suppose we want to refer to the main idea that is the subject of a web page. There is no standard way to do this. If a resource identifier is supposed to represent something abstract that can't be retrieved over the Internet, the interpretation of its meaning can be even less clear.

Another problem with using URIs the way RDF does is knowing where to find more information about a particular URI identifier. If we encounter the identifier

```
http://description.org/schema/Person
```

it would be useful to be able to read about what the URI is intended to mean. RDF and languages built on top of it can describe to some degree how the URI should be used in an RDF document, but a person may need to know more than can be captured this way. Of course, we'll notice the string Person and guess that the URI is intended to represent the concept of "person," but it would be better to get definitive information.

If such a URI is an http: URL, it's possible to put a page at that address explaining the meaning of the identifier. However, this convention isn't universally followed. There could be a convention for making an RDF statement that states where such information could be found, but again no such convention is in widespread use.

Until these issues are dealt with successfully, the meaning of such resource identifiers will have to be established by programmers who code their understanding into their programs and their RDF.

2.7.2 *Contradictory statements*

Since anyone can create a statement that asserts practically anything about anything, there's a real possibility of encountering statements that conflict. How can they be reconciled? Doing so is likely to become complicated, involving an assessment of the reliability of the sources of the statements and the consistency of the statements with other information.

This problem and several others mentioned in the following sections arise in large part from the nature of the Web. In a closed system that you construct and control, you can purge out contradictions and mistakes. But the Web is too large for that; and in addition it's open, not closed. This means more information can be added at any time, without any central control of its contents.[6] RDF has no means of preventing contradictory statements, although a processor might be able to detect them. If it does, an RDF processor ought to put out a notification about the contradiction.

2.7.3 *Incomplete information*

If you want to draw conclusions, and facts are missing, then you can draw several different conclusions that will all be consistent with the available facts. It would be desirable for different agents to be able to draw the same conclusions. The fact that your credit history isn't available may indicate that you're a bad credit risk, but it may also indicate that your records were destroyed or that you haven't used credit before. There's no way to know without more information.

Because the Web is open, very large, and highly dynamic, it includes a great deal of incomplete information. Although RDF is only about making statements and has no means to consider incomplete information, the logic processors that will be built on top of RDF will be subject to incomplete information. How they should handle it isn't standardized.

2.7.4 *Limitations*

RDF is designed to make statements about specific resources (which can include resources that represent ideas). It has no built-in features to make general statements about, let's say, all tables or all politicians (although it can make statements about tables or politicians as generic classes). It also has no way to negate statements—that is, to say a statement isn't true.

---

[6] To be more accurate, in a closed system, data not in the system is considered not to exist. In an open system, data may exist that is not currently known by the system.

Full first-order logic (see chapter 6) requires these capabilities. Therefore, RDF by itself isn't powerful enough to support the full range of logic that might be desired. There's a question of whether RDF, even with the help of other languages built on top of it, will be powerful enough for its intended uses. With its extensions, can it support the complex logic needed by, say, autonomous software agents? This remains to be seen.

2.8 *Summary*

RDF is the W3C's candidate language to represent data and meta data in a way that lends itself to widespread use on the Web, and that has a foundation that can be built upon for building ontologies, performing logical reasoning, describing web services, and a host of other Semantic Web activities. RDF can be very useful in its own right with or without the Semantic Web; but it remains to be seen how widespread it will become.

RDF is based on a model of triples, which are three-part statements. Each statement states a single thing about its subject, by assigning it a property with a value. The property component of a triple is also called the predicate, and the property value is also called the object. The subject of any statement is called a resource, and resources are identified by URIs. Properties are also resources. Objects, the property values, may be either resources or literal values. It's also common to have resources that aren't identified by URIs but only by their connections to other resources. Such resources are called anonymous or blank nodes.

The object of one statement may be the subject of other statements. Thus, a collection of RDF data can form a kind of network of interconnected statements, forming a model of the information that represents the data. Such a model is both simple, since it's built of simple parts (the triples), and complex, because typically a great number of nodes and edges are interconnected in the graph of the data.

RDF statements can be collected from many sources, so it's possible that some will be in conflict. Given the scale of the Web, it's very likely that some statements in a collection of RDF data will conflict. Industrial-strength RDF processing will have to be designed to deal with this fact of life.

RDF is useful as a flexible way to store irregularly structured data, with or without the Semantic Web. At the time of writing, RDF is a leading candidate for representing the knowledge that Semantic Web systems will exchange and process.

3

Navigating information with topic maps

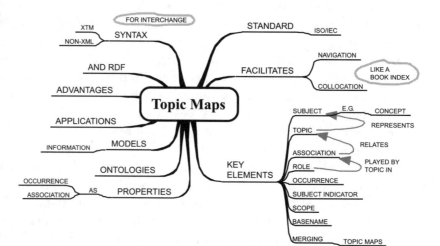

"Well! I've often seen a cat without a grin," thought Alice; "but a grin without a cat! It's the most curious thing I ever saw in my life!"

—Lewis Carroll, *Alice's Adventures in Wonderland*

So essential do I consider an Index to be to every book, that I proposed to bring a Bill into Parliament to deprive an author who publishes a book without an Index of the privilege of copyright; and, moreover, to subject him, for his offence, to a pecuniary penalty.

—Baron Campbell, *Lives of the Chief Justices*

This chapter continues our examination of modeling and representation of knowledge. *Topic Maps* is another technology for organizing information, including meta data. Whereas RDF proceeds by building up a collection of individual small facts, as you saw in chapter 2, Topic Maps evolved from efforts to develop electronic indexes. Consequently, they're especially suited for tasks that involve discovery and navigation of knowledge bases. Topic maps provide the ability to model information, but the approach is somewhat different from RDF's.

In this chapter, we look at how topic maps work, how they can model a body of information, and how they may relate to the Semantic Web.

3.1 What are topic maps?

According to Michel Biezunski, one of the key developers of Topic Maps:[1]

> Topic Maps were originally designed to handle the construction of *lists*, *glossaries*, *thesauri*, and *tables of contents*, but their applicability extends beyond that domain. (Park and Hunting 2002)

Originally developed for automated indexing systems, the Topic Maps technology has evolved to handle the wide range of information resources accessible by networks. The international standard for Topic Maps, ISO/IEC 13250, describes how a topic map is organized. It also defines XML Topic Maps (XTM), an XML-based language for exchanging topic maps between computers.[2] The Topic

---

[1] When both words are capitalized, we mean Topic Maps the concept, or Topic Maps the international standard, as opposed to a particular topic map.

[2] ISO/IEC 13250 specifies two markup languages for topic maps. The XML-based language is called XTM, and there is an older version based on the SGML HYTIME syntax. This older version has also been informally written in an XML version, but it isn't often used.

Maps technology is undergoing continual development and refinement. The descriptions and illustrations in this book follow the current version of the ISO/ IEC 13250 standard.

Book indexes are a good place to begin our examination of topic maps because they're familiar and, at least on the surface, simple. The index of a book serves the dual purposes of collocation and navigation. *Collocation* means that relevant information can be found together. If you go to the library and find a book on mountain climbing, you want to find other books about mountain climbing on the shelves nearby. *Navigation* refers to finding information by its attributes and relationships—metaphorically moving around the space of information. Topic Maps provides strong capabilities for both collocation and navigation.

A typical book index contains most of the core ideas behind the Topic Map model.

3.1.1 An example index

Let's examine an index from an actual book: *Philosophy in the Flesh* by George Lakoff [Lakoff and Johnson 1999]. Table 3.1 shows some fragments of its index (minus the page numbers).

Table 3.1   An index for the book *Philosophy in the Flesh*.

Index entry	Type of information

Vision
    folk theories of
    intellectual
    logic of
    metaphoric
	The main entry is some kind of concept or subject.
	"Intellectual vision" seems to be a subclass of "Vision".
	"Folk Theories" and "Metaphoric" seem to bring a context or perspective to "Vision."

Vision Metaphors
    Intelligence and Visual Acuity
    Seeing is Touching
	The sub-entries are specific instances of the main entry.

Understanding and common sense	Two concepts are related by occurring in the same passage.

Universals
    concepts
    experiences
    human reason
    language
	The sub-entries are subclasses or more specialized versions of the main entry

This piece of an index, small though it is, is rich in its structure and exhibits most of the key features built into Topic Maps. Each main entry is an idea or concept. Usually there are sub-entries, but these aren't always concepts in the same sense. In the first row, for instance, some entries are subclasses of the main concept (that is, they're more specialized versions). Other sub-entries give a context in which the main concept occurs. You can look up passages about vision in the context of folk theories. It's true that folk theory is a kind of concept too, but here it's used to denote a context. This indicates that a concept can provide a context for another concept.

In the third row of this index fragment, the terms *Understanding* and *common sense* are said to be related by virtue of appearing together in a particular page. Figure 3.1 depicts topic map elements that can be used to model these aspects of the index.

So far we've noticed concepts, relationships, and contexts. The information occurs not in the index but in specific pages of the book. In topic maps, concepts

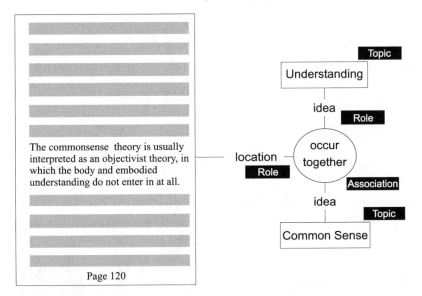

Figure 3.1 **A model of part of the index of *Philosophy in the Flesh* in the style of a topic map. Black boxes with white text label topic map elements. The two white rectangular boxes represent *topics*, which stand for concepts. The concepts *Understanding* and *Common Sense* are represented by topics. They're related by means of the fact that they're associated together on page 120. This relation is indicated by an association labeled *occur together*. Each topic of an association plays a *role*, indicated here by the labels in the lines connecting the association to its topics. There would be a topic representing the page as well, but it has been omitted for simplicity.**

are represented by *topics*. The topic is something in the computer (data stored in its memory), whereas a concept is something in the world of discourse—something that can be talked about (an idea or a physical thing). In Topic Maps, the concept a topic represents is known as its *subject*.

Relationships between concepts are usually at least as important as their properties, and topic maps use the *association* to represent relationships between concepts. Each topic that participates in an association plays a *role*, as shown in figure 3.1. The figure also shows that an association can relate more than two topics. By contrast, the basic structure in RDF is the statement, or triple, which serves to relate exactly two concepts.

Specific information about a topic, like a page number, web page, or text passage, is called an *occurrence*. An occurrence either says where the information is located (it uses a URI to do this) or contains the information in the form of a chunk of text. Figure 3.2 depicts two occurrences and also indicates that one concept is a subclass (a more specialized kind) of another.[3]

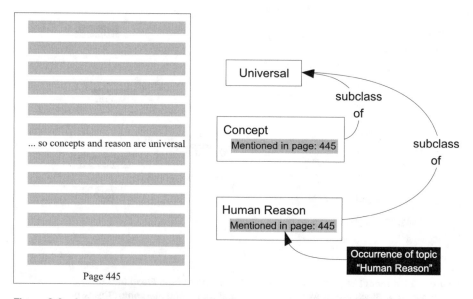

Figure 3.2   A topic represents Page 445. It's an `instanceOf` *Page*. *Page* is a topic representing the abstract ideal of a page. With the help of the *Page 445* topic, we can link concepts to the page using associations as an alternative to using occurrences.

---

[3] This would be done using associations to relate a topic to its subclass. The details have been omitted from the diagram for simplicity.

A topic can have a *name*, which isn't an identifier but rather contains a label for the topic. In fact, a topic may have more than one name. This reflects the real world, in which things often have more than one name. You probably have several, including one or more nicknames. You saw in the sample index that a subject can occur in one or another contexts, such as "folk theory." In a topic map, such a context can be indicated with a *scope*.

In the second row, both sub-entries are specific instances of a more general concept, *Vision Metaphors*. *Seeing is Touching* is one type of Vision Metaphor. So, we'd like to have a way to indicate that a concept may be of a particular type. Topic maps use a topic's instanceOf property to indicate its type. Figure 3.3 depicts the use of instanceOf.

In figure 3.2, the page numbers are modeled as occurrences. However, if we want to say anything about Page 445 itself, we need to create a topic for it. Remember, in Topic Maps, all subjects of interest are to be represented by topics. Figure 3.3 illustrates a topic for Page 445 and shows that it's a topic of type *Page*. Of course, *Page* is itself a topic that represents the abstract notion of a page. Now

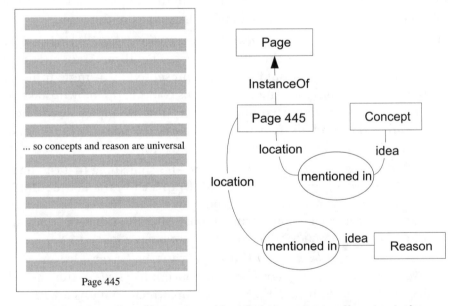

Figure 3.3   Information about a concept is called an *occurrence*. Here, two topics *Concept* and *Human Reason* are said to be subclasses—specialized versions of—the topic *Universal*. This page, page 445, contains information about the two topics. The occurrences of these topics indicate this fact. The type of these particular occurrences is *Mentioned in page*.

that there is a topic for Page 445, we can use associations to link index entries to the page, as an alternative to using occurrences.

3.1.2 *The subject of a topic*

One of the important aspects of a topic is the identity of its subject. It's possible to create perfectly good topic maps without formally indicating what the topics stand for. A person would have to guess what the topics represent based on their names. But we can do better.

How do you know what the subject of a given topic is? In general, this is a deep matter. For example, if we say that the subject is a particular URL, do we mean the subject is the URL itself, the web page, or the main concept the web page discusses (see also section 2.7.1)? In addition, a thing may have several names, and several things can have the same name. Thus a name can't, in general, uniquely identify a specific concept or individual.[4] Topic Maps has special machinery to help clarify the nature of a topic's subject.

In Topic Maps, the identity of the subject is represented by a `subjectIdentity` entity, depicted in figure 3.4. You can indicate the subject of a topic three ways, all of which use a URI reference to identify the subject of the topic:

- *The* `subjectIdentity` *entity could point to another topic*—In this case, the two topics would be about the same subject. The Topic Maps model is clear that a given subject should only be represented by a single topic. If more than one topic has the same subject (this could happen by mistake or when one topic map is imported into another), the two topics should be *merged*, meaning they and all their names, occurrences, and links to associations should be transferred to the new combined topic.

- *The subject might be an addressable resource*—It's something that can be received over a network, such as a web page. In this case, the `subjectIdentity` is stated to be a `resourceRef` that points to the address of the resource. The use of a `resourceRef` says unambiguously that the subject is that particular resource as opposed to whatever the resource is about.

- *The subject might be non-addressable*—It can't be retrieved over a network, like an automobile or a non-tangible concept like *soul*. In this case, the subject is referred to by a `subjectIndicator`, which contains a URI reference.

---

[4] Not all subjects can be accurately named. See, for example, Svenonius (2000), p. 49, which cites the concept of Moby Dick: "It makes sense to say that *Moby Dick* is about something, but this something is more than just a whale; however it's characterized, it can't be neatly packaged into a word or short phrase." Even this amorphous concept, though, can be given a label to be used as a shorthand reference.

The URI reference doesn't have to be retrievable—it need not point at an actual web page—but somewhere there must be a description that explains the meaning to be associated with the URI. At a minimum, the description should make sense to a person. If it can be made usable by a computer, so much the better.

To illustrate, the string

```
http://www.topicmaps.org/xtm/1.0/core.xtm#superclass-subclass
```

represents the superclass-subclass kind of association. A topic map application would be expected to know how to use this type of association. Even though the URI string doesn't have to be an actual network address, good practice would make it point to a web page that defines the subject indicator. The page could also contain a machine-readable ontology. Such a published identifier is called a *Published Subject Indicator (PSI)*. (The terminology can get confusing because the specifications speak of both a *subject identifier* and a *subject indicator*.)

It's possible to use subject indicators that haven't been standardized—just make them up, and put their definitions on a web site—but they're more valuable if they're widely understood. So, various efforts are in progress to specify useful collections of PSIs. More can be expected in the future.

The designation of a particular PSI might change from time to time. It might, for instance, become incorporated into a published standard as a different URI. The Topic Maps technology has a built-in way to handle such changes, by using

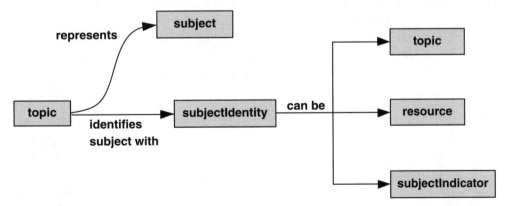

Figure 3.4 How the subject of a topic can be specified. The subject that a topic represents can be another topic, a web page, or some other addressable resource, or it can be indicated by a URI reference contained in the `subjectIndicator`. In all three possibilities, an identifier is a URI reference.

the topic merging mentioned earlier. You can prepare a small topic map that uses both the old and new URI as subject indicators for the same topic. An application that imports this map will examine the new topics to see if any of them should be merged with existing topics. During this inspection, it will discover that topics with the old PSI should be merged with topics having the new PSI. In effect, this means the new PSI can replace the old with no disruption.

The machinery of the subject identifier gives Topic Maps a way to avoid ambiguities about whether a given URI is supposed to be an abstract identifier or point to a network resource that can be retrieved. Using the exact names of the elements in the XTM specification, if the `subjectIdentity` is a `subjectIndicator-Ref`, the URI reference is an abstract identifier. If it's a `resourceRef`, it's a real address, and the subject is the retrievable resource at that address. If it's a `topicRef`, it identifies another topic.

In some cases, a topic is better known by its associations than by its formal identity (or it may lack a `subjectIdentity`). See the FOAF case study in the appendix for more on this topic.

3.1.3 *Properties*

Real things have properties. They may be colored blue, be six feet long, or be transparent. Properties are considered to be different from parts. A tree has leaves and branches, and these are thought of as parts of the tree, not properties. The tree as a whole, though, may have "size" and "health" properties. How can properties of a subject be represented in a topic map?

The notion of property isn't as simple as it seems. Is the property a {label, value} pair, or is it a separate concept in its own right? Topic maps can take either approach, as depicted in figure 3.5.[5]

These two approaches correspond to topic map constructions:

- To use the *(label, value)* method, you can use an occurrence, which might contain the text "Red" or might point to a web page that defines the color in question.

- To use the *separate concept* method, you use an association and turn the property into a topic of its own. This is a powerful method, because the property topic can participate in any number of other associations, while an occurrence can't. However, it forces the topic map to contain many more topics, one per property instance.

---

[5] I thank Steve Pepper for clarifying this subject on the XTM discussion list in response to a question of mine.

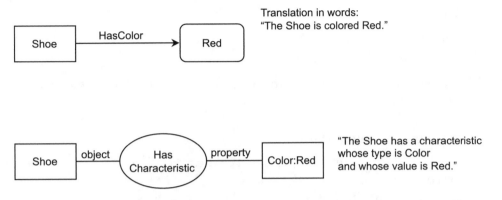

Figure 3.5 Two ways to model properties. Each approach has advantages. In this figure, the rectangles represent topics or concepts, the rounded rectangle represents a value (in this case, the string "Red"), and the circle indicates that two topics are related.

3.1.4 Scopes

Suppose you're known by a pet name. It might be embarrassing to be called Jimmikins, but as long as no one outside your family calls you that, you can live with it. So, at home you're called Jimmikins, at work you're called James or Mr. Smith, and on your passport you're called James C. Smith.

Each name has a reach, or coverage, or region of validity. Topic Maps has a way to specify such coverage: *scope*. Other candidates for a knowledge representation language for the Semantic Web don't have a similar notion. Topic map names have scope, and a scope can be said to be *applied* to a topic's name. A scope acts as a kind of context within which the use of a name is appropriate.

That which constrains a name is a concept in its own right. In Topic Map terms, that means a scope is represented by a topic. The scope of the name Jimmikins would be a topic for *family*, while the name James C. Smith might include the scopes *passport* and *formal occasions*. Because a scope might need to have more than one component, as in this last example, a Topic Maps scope is specified by a set of scoping topics rather than just one. By default, the scope is a universal scope, meaning that the name is considered valid for use in any context.

Scopes can be useful as filters, making queries more precise and reducing the amount of data returned (you only get results that are "in scope"). They can also provide additional information, a kind of annotation of the data you're looking at. With scopes, a query for your name might display results something like this:

Name

James[work]
Jimmikins[family nickname]

Scopes can also be applied to the occurrences of topics, and to associations. They're always optional.

3.1.5 *Summary of key features*

The key structural features discussed in the preceding sections are collected here for convenience:

- Topics
- Associations
- Names
- Occurrences
- Roles
- Scopes
- Subject indicators

The topic map model may seem more complicated than, say, RDF, which is based on resources and triples. But all these features (or something that simulates them) are needed in many real, complex information systems. If they don't exist natively, they must be implemented by making use of the facilities of the supposedly simpler system. The end result is often complex, and at the same time non-standard. In fact, you can look at the Topic Map approach as a *pattern* for structuring information, and that pattern is useful whether it's applied with a Topic Map system or with some other technology.

3.1.6 *Collocation, navigation, and representation of information*

We've pointed out that the index of a book serves the dual purposes of *collocation* and *navigation*. A topic map isn't limited to being an index for an individual book, of course. You've seen how topics can refer to any kind of concept that could be the subject of interest, and that the identity of the subject of a topic can point to any resource on the Web. Therefore a topic map can link any information on (or off) the Web to anything else, and also can add meta data to the description of any information it likes. In this way, a well-designed topic map can be effective at helping its users find related information and navigate through it.

The ability to have a topic play a wide variety of roles with respect to other topics gives topic maps great power and flexibility.

The metaphor of a map is frequently used. A map gives you a guide for navigating a territory. On a deeper level, a map is a model of the territory together with a user interface (the visual design of the map), just as a book index is a model of the book's information together with an interface. Topic Maps provides the model, and a topic map application provides the user interface.

Although we've presented topic maps as especially useful as a way to build computer indexes into a store of information, a topic map's ability to model the territory means that it can act as a general-purpose method of representing information.

Of course, many other systems can do some or all of these things. However, the Topic Maps technology offers many advantages compared with most alternatives:

- A standard model that's very flexible
- A standard way to interchange maps
- An extendable set of known subjects
- A way to build vocabularies
- A machine-understandable way to understand the relationships between concepts
- A way to supply appropriate contexts for concepts
- Ways to indicate the nature of the information being pointed to
- A set of related standards published by an international standards body

There would seem to be compelling advantages to using topic maps, especially if you're interested in sharing your maps with others.

3.1.7 Merging topic maps

Any one topic map is supposed to have just one topic for a given subject. To combine the information in two topic maps, the two must be merged. When that happens, it's possible that a topic in one map will have the same subject as a topic in the other. Topic Maps has rules to help determine when that's the case and other rules about how to combine the two topics into one. Naturally, if they're combined, then any related associations must be adjusted as well.

The determination takes into account the subject indicators, names, and scopes involved. As one example, two topics with the same subject indicators must be about the same subject. If the application considers names to be significant, then topics with the same name should be considered to be about the same subject unless the names have different scopes.

The merging capabilities are also useful when a new version of a vocabulary comes into use and it's necessary to say that a term (in reality, a PSI) is equivalent to an existing term. You create a topic map wherein a topic has *two* subject indicators, one with the new term and one with the old. When this topic map is merged with an existing one, the processor will detect the topics with double subject indicators and merge any topics that contain either one. In this way, newer topic map information can be seamlessly combined with the old.

3.1.8 Maturity of Topic Maps software

Until recently, software infrastructure supporting topic maps was scarce and not very mature. However, at the Extreme Markup Languages conference in August 2003 (see [Extreme]), several authors presented examples of Topic Maps systems with impressive capabilities and size. Their message was clear: Topic maps are ready for prime time.

Even though Topic Maps software is nowhere near the maturity of, say, relational database systems, it's possible to begin using topic maps on a moderately large scale. Topic maps are best seen as complementing and integrating with other systems rather than replacing them. It isn't necessary to move huge data sets into topic map storage systems. Often, a more effective strategy is to put a topic map wrapper onto another system so that it can be treated with Topic Maps techniques.

3.2 Basic models of topic maps

To work with or program for Topic Maps, we need a model. At the time of this writing, two interchange formats are specified by the ISO/IEC standard (see section 3.1.1): an XML format called XML Topic Maps (XTM) and a Standard Generalized Markup Language (SGML) format, but an interchange model isn't sufficient for processing. The set of ISO/IEC Topic Maps standards may in the future be extended with draft proposals for a Reference Model (RM) for Topic Maps and a Topic Map Data Model (TMDM).

The RM provides an abstract graph-based model showing how all the components in a topic map should be structured and connected (recall from chapter 2 how an RDF dataset can be considered a graph). An application doesn't have to use this model, but its functionality would ultimately be equivalent to that of the RM. The TMDM specifies the processing to be applied as an application performs typical operations such as creating a topic map, creating a new association, and merging topics. When they're adopted, the RM and the TMDM should help make sure everyone understands how topic maps should be put together, and applications should be able to work together more effectively than they do now.

To help explain the workings of a topic map, this section sketches an object-like static model based on the XTM specification. You can skip this section if you aren't interested in this kind of modeling detail.

3.2.1 Abstract model

An abstract model forms the best starting point for data or system modeling. Figure 3.6 depicts an abstract model of a topic map at a high level without much detail. The figure shows the basic components of a topic map as discussed in section 3.1.

Let's walk through this model in words. A topic may be an instance of another topic. A topic represents a subject and is named by a name (really, one or more names), and information about the subject occurs at (or is pointed to by) an occurrence. Finally, a topic may be related to other topics via an association.

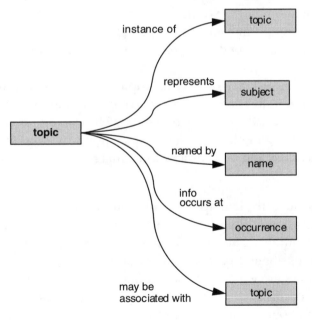

Figure 3.6
Abstract topic map model. A subject represents any concept that can be discussed or thought about. A topic represents the subject in a computer. Topics can have a type, such as *Dog* or *Color*, and these types are also topics, since they represent concepts as well.

MODELING TOPIC MAPS IN RDF   You may have noticed that the diagram in figure 3.6 looks much like an RDF graph. At a more detailed level the model looks less like RDF, but ultimately, a topic map could be modeled with an RDF graph (except for some different interpretations of what the subjects are—see section 3.1.2 for a discussion of how to identify the subject of a topic). A topic map component such as a topic or an occurrence could be represented by an entire RDF subgraph (a collection of RDF triples).

Topic maps can be considered a particular design pattern as much as a specific technology. The data in a topic map can be structured and stored in many different ways, including RDF and relational databases. If a topic map were modeled in RDF, certain kinds of recurring groupings of RDF statements would be used over and over. The RDF application would have to understand those patterns (or *idioms*) in order to process the map as intended. A topic map starts from those patterns. In a sense, any set of data whose organization bears a close resemblance to a Topic Maps pattern could be considered a topic map. However, here we're considering datasets that are designed to follow the structures specified in the ISO/IEC standard.

Names and occurrences

Figure 3.7 shows more details of names and occurrences. A name is called a `baseName` in the XTM format but in the SGML format may also include a `sortname` and a `dispname` (used for display and sorting purposes). A name has a label, the `nameString`, and it may also be scoped with one or more scoping topics, as discussed in section 3.2.

An occurrence may be an instance of another topic, allowing occurrences to be typed and to participate in taxonomies. An occurrence can represent a property, as discussed in section 3.1.3. An occurrence may either contain its value directly, in the form of a string of characters, or it may point to some network-addressable resource, such as a web page or a graphic image.

Associations

An association relates topics. Topic maps can relate more than two topics, as illustrated in figure 3.8. Although figure 3.8 depicts just two roles played by topics in the association, any number of topics may play any number of roles.

If you want to say things about a particular association, you can make a topic for it. In Topic Maps, topics are what are talked about—that is, they participate in associations and have occurrences. If there is a topic for an association, then you can make statements about it. The topic uses its `subjectIdentity` to indicate that its subject is the association.

An association may also be scoped, like a topic name or occurrence.

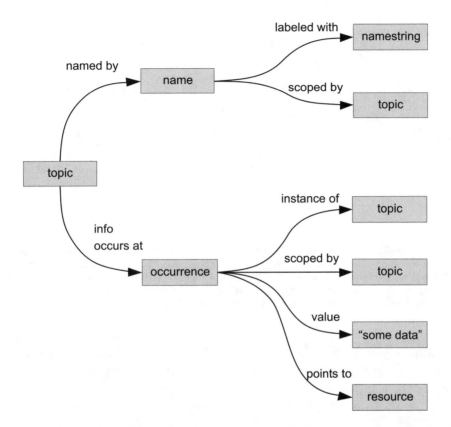

Figure 3.7   Details of topic names and occurrences. Topics can have any number of names and occurrences, each of which can have its own scopes. An occurrence can either point to a network resource—data at a URI that can be retrieved over the network—or it can contain actual data.

Association members and roles

The link between a topic and an association of which it's a member has a structure of its own, unlike an RDF predicate link. Figure 3.9 shows this structure.

Notice that the role a topic plays in an association (via its *member* entity) can itself be declared to be an instance of a topic. This is how a type is assigned to a role. In an association that represents the notion that a person owns a thing, the two roles could by given the types of "person" and "thing."

In Topic Maps, the diagram lines linking topics to associations have no arrowheads. That is because the roles supply the equivalent information. With RDF, we could have the triple (Bob → likes → Beer). The link between Bob and Beer would be directional to indicate which is the subject and which is the object. Bob plays

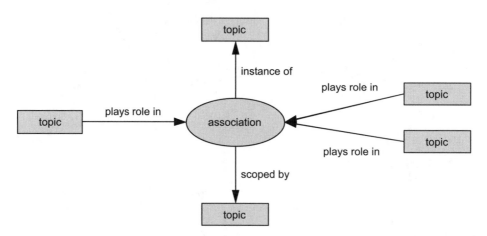

Figure 3.8   Details of an association. This particular association links three topics. Each one plays a role in the association. The association can have a type, denoted by the *instanceOf* topic. In addition, an association may have a scope (or a set of scopes) that gives it a context. (This diagram is an entity-relationship–style drawing, not a topic map–style drawing. That's why the lines have arrowheads, whereas other diagrams showing associations don't.)

the implicit role *subject*, and Beer plays the implicit role *object*. In a Topic Maps association, the roles are made explicit, so there is no need for directional indicators. Having explicit roles adds complexity, but it makes those roles available to be the subject of discussion—in other words, you can make whatever statements you like about them. This isn't possible when the roles are left implicit.

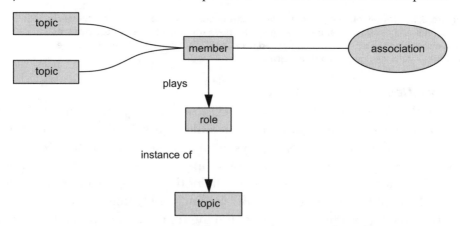

Figure 3.9   Details of association members and roles. This detail wasn't shown in figure 3.8 for simplicity. Each different role of an association is represented by a *member*. One or more topics may be part of a member, meaning that they play the member's role in the association.

3.2.2 *Implementation approaches*

This abstract model says nothing about how to implement or store a topic map in a computer. It could be modeled by a relational database, by an object database, by an object-oriented program, or in any number of other ways. Let's look at possible approaches: object-oriented, graph-oriented, and database-oriented.

Object-oriented approach

An obvious approach, especially if you have a background in object-oriented design, would be to interpret the abstract model as an object model. In the most straightforward implementation, each entity in the model would turn into a class in the program. Thus there would be a `topic` class, an `association` class, and so on. However, it may be difficult to make this approach perform well for large maps, because any program will need to look repeatedly through long lists of topics, scopes, associations, and other components, each of which can have several forms depending on how their subjects are specified. At a minimum, effective indexing would be needed. It might be well to build the system on top of an object database system, although object-oriented implementations can also be backed by a relational database.

For a large map, the program design would probably have to depart from the abstract model, just as practical databases often depart from their normalized, idealized logical data models to achieve reasonable performance.

Graph-oriented approach

A topic map resembles a graph because it has many linked components. This suggests a graph-based approach with two main types of nodes: the association node and the topic node. Merging, traversing, and searching operations could take advantage of the extensive research done on graphs over the last several decades.

Database-oriented approach

The simplified model shown in figure 3.6 appears easy enough to model with a relational database. This approach would let you take advantage of the indexing, querying, and storage abilities of relational databases. Several systems use relational databases, but doing so isn't as easy as it seems. For one thing, relational databases don't lend themselves well to representing hierarchies nor to querying lists of arbitrary length. For another, the many options available to some of the entities in the Topic Maps model can be awkward to include in a relational database, and multiple optional values are hard to extract with simple queries. So, a lot of programming must be mixed in with queries to the database, which reduces some of the presumed advantages.

3.3 *Sharing topic maps between computers*

In the current specifications, topic maps are primarily defined in terms of their *interchange syntax*. This term refers to the format of a document that can be used to send topic map data between computers. Currently, topic maps can be interchanged (between people or computers) using one of the two standard markup formats mentioned earlier. In practice, the XTM format is most widespread and has mostly replaced the older SGML format. There is also a non-XML (and nonstandard) format called Linear Topic Map (LTM), which is easier for people to read and write. A few other non-XML formats are available. Each is supported by one or a few toolsets, but none so far has become a standard in common use.

Listing 3.1 is a fragment of the XTM format to give you some flavor of how a topic map is put together. This small topic map contains information about certain weather events. It sets up topic types (which are themselves topics) like "Tornado," "Date," and "Flood." Then it defines an instance of a tornado and one of a flood. Web pages about these weather events are linked in as occurrences. For brevity, we don't show the entire topic map.

Listing 3.1   Fragment of a topic map illustrating the XTM interchange format

```
<?xml version="1.0" ?>
<topicMap xmlns="http://www.topicmaps.org/xtm/1.0/"
    xmlns:xlink = 'http://www.w3.org/1999/xlink'>      ◁─❶ Topic map
                                                             data begins
<!--========= Weather Topics ====================-->
<topic id='tt-wxtype'>          ◁─❷  Topic declared
  <baseName>                               ◁─❸ Topic's baseName specified
     <baseNameString>Weather Type</baseNameString>
  </baseName>
</topic>
<topic id='tt-tornado'>
  <instanceOf><topicRef xlink:href="#tt-wxtype"/>        ❹ Topic assigned
  </instanceOf>                                              a type
  <baseName>
    <baseNameString>Tornado</baseNameString>
  </baseName>
</topic>
<topic id='tt-flood'>
  <instanceOf><topicRef xlink:href="#tt-wxtype"/></instanceOf>
  <baseName><baseNameString>Flood</baseNameString></baseName>
</topic>
```

```
<topic id='tt-tornado1-sterling' >
  <instanceOf><topicRef xlink:href="#tt-tornado"/></instanceOf>
  <baseName>
    <baseNameString>Sterling, VA Tornado</baseNameString>
  </baseName>
  <occurrence>        ⬅➎ Occurrence assigned to topic
    <instanceOf>
      <topicRef xlink:href='#rt.referencepage'/>   ⬅➏ Type of
    </instanceOf>                                         information
    <resourceRef>http://www.nws.noaa.gov/er/lwx/
        Historic_Events/VAcnty-tornado-events.htm
    </resourceRef>   ⬅➐ Information's location
  </occurrence>
  <occurrence>
    <instanceOf><topicRef xlink:href='#rt.note'/></instanceOf>
    <resourceData>This was an F0 or F1    ⬊ Literal data contained
      Tornado</resourceData>              ➑ in occurrence
  </occurrence>
</topic>
<!--rest of map omitted-->
</topicMap>
```

➊ The topic map data begins here with standard XML namespace declarations to specify the two vocabularies used in the document (one for XTM and one for Xlink, which is used to point to various topics and web resources).

➋ A topic labeled "Weather Type" is declared starting here.

➌ The "Weather Type" topic's baseName is specified.

➍ This section shows how a topic is assigned a type. In this case, the topic "Tornado" is said to be of type "Weather Type."

➎ Next an occurrence is assigned to a topic.

➏ Information of type "Reference Page" applies to the topic called "Sterling, VA Tornado." Here, an Xlink construction is used to point to the topic that represents the type of the occurrence.

➐ This line tells where that information is located. Note that a declaration for the occurrence type representing "Reference Page" has been omitted from this fragment for brevity.

➑ Literal data is contained in an occurrence. This is in contrast to 7, which contains a web address in the form of a URI.

3.4 *Topic map examples*

Topic maps are useful when they can be navigated. Navigation is inherently dynamic, so it's difficult to portray in a book. General-purpose topic map browsers are available. Because they're general purpose, they aren't the most efficient for any particular map, but they let you examine the different parts of a map and how they're linked. A special-purpose interface would be more efficient for a particular kind of map, but with a good interface you can't tell that a topic map is involved. You simply experience well-linked screens and find it relatively easy to find information of interest, as well as to discover things you weren't necessarily looking for.

The rest of this section depicts two topic map examples. Although these printed illustrations can't respond interactively, they may give you a sense of the rich navigation possibilities that topic maps can provide.

3.4.1 *Weather events*

Figure 3.10 depicts a view of the weather event topic map from listing 3.1, as seen in a general-purpose topic map browser.[6] The Xenia tornado has been

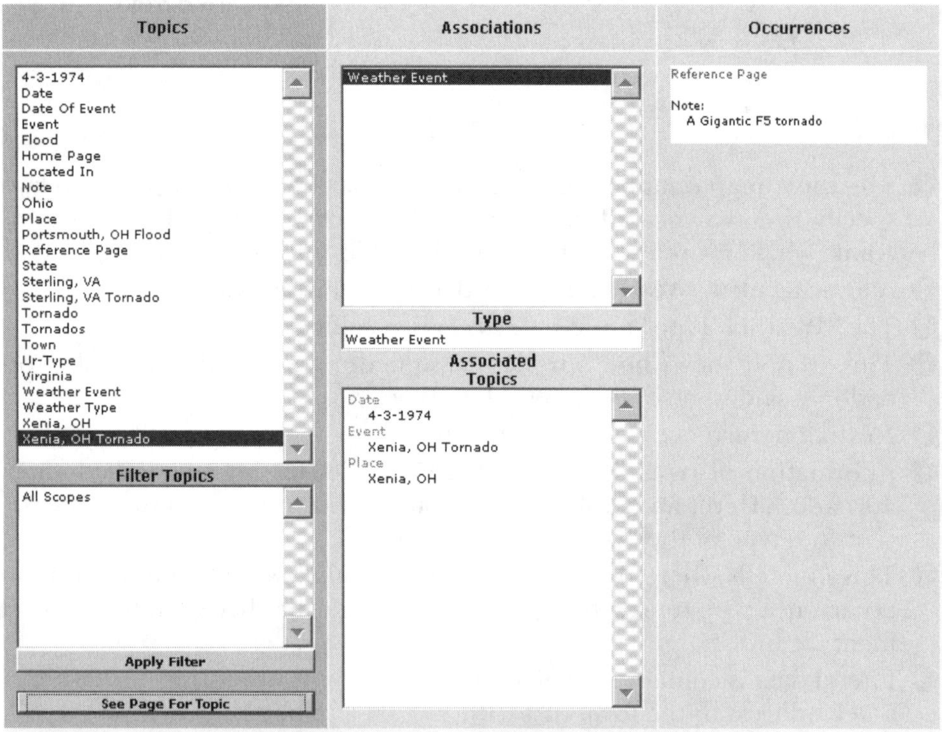

Figure 3.10   View of the weather topic map in a general-purpose browser.

---

[6] This topic map browser runs in an ordinary web browser, because it's written in JavaScript. The code, written by the author, is available from an open source project on SourceForge (TM4Jscript). The package is very useful for hand-authoring topic maps.

selected, and you can see that it has two occurrences: a hyperlink to a web page and a note. This topic plays the *Event* role in a *Weather Event* association. From the association, you see that the event took place in Xenia, OH on April 3, 1974. All the facts (occurrences) and related topics have been pulled together in one place—this is *collocation*, discussed earlier.

In another view, shown (with a few annotations) in figure 3.11, you can click any topic in the display to see all of its information. Between these two views, you have extensive *navigation* capability. Of course, the full impact is hard to portray in a static printed page.

3.4.2 Conference proceedings

The conference papers of the XML Europe 2002 conference are available online at www.idealliance.org/papers/xmle02/. The site provides a topic map for the papers, as well as a conventional HTML index. It's interesting to compare the two. They're quite similar, in that they make comparable use of keywords, and so on, and display similar groupings of information. I was able to find a collection of papers that contained the keyword *topic map* with about the same ease using both indexes. The topic map version had some extra features, such as the graphical hyperbolic display (also called a star display), but that's a user interface enhancement rather than a fundamental benefit of using a topic map.

Figure 3.11
Another view of the weather topic map in a general-purpose browser.

Despite this superficial similarity, the two indexes are distinguished because the topic map is downloadable in the ISO/IEC standard XTM format. It will work in virtually all topic map applications. Figure 3.12 shows a view of the conference map in the same browser used to make figures 3.10 and 3.11. In the actual display depicted in figure 3.12, every one of the related topics is also a hyperlink; this is not obvious in the figure.

This is remarkable. The topic map browser used to make the previous figures was designed independently of the application that displays the conference map at the conference web site, and independently of the applications that created the map. In addition, this topic map browser has no notion about the detailed design of this particular topic map. But because the map is organized according to the topic map pattern, it can be navigated conveniently using a general-purpose topic map viewing application. This wouldn't be possible for most other knowledge representation systems such as RDF, because a general-purpose browser wouldn't be aware of the patterns in the map that allow such navigation.

3.5 *Topic maps and the Web*

The examples in section 3.4 contain topics that aren't defined except insofar as their names suggest their meaning. These examples are convenient for explaining the basic model, but the Semantic Web is about making information available to software as well as to people, and about gaining access to resources everywhere. To tie such topics into the Semantic Web, many of them would be given URIs that reference published definitions or descriptions that would serve to establish the nature of their subjects.

Once a topic map has been tied in, there are many ways it can participate in the Semantic Web. This section discusses some roles that topic maps can play:

- *Integrated information across the Web*—A topic map can refer to information distributed across the Web. There are well-defined procedures for merging information about the same subject. Thus topic maps can integrate a wide variety of information.

- *Shared vocabularies*—Shared vocabularies (or ontologies, to be more precise) can be created using a topic map to specify relationships and constraints between published subject indicators. For this purpose, a suitable language will be necessary. Work on such a standardized Topic Maps Constraint Language is under way, although it will probably be several years before it's ready for widespread use.

Unravelling Complexity With 'Forensic' XML

Type: Presentation

Subject Identity Reference: 03-04-06

Resources

- **Time of Presentation:** 14.45
- **Abstract:** Developing an XML-based transaction model has required creating some basic transformations which manipulate dissimilar (but XML marked-up) data structures to discover, first of all, what common ground there is on which transactions might be executed. It is now clear that these same techniques can expose the net transactional effects of complex multiple-step, multi-party dealings, even where that complexity may have been intended to conceal precisely that simple reality. The need to pierce such intentional obfuscation has become newsworthy through coverage of the investigation of the Enron collapse. This presentation will examine three complex transactions as described in the New York Times coverage of Enron, in order to demonstrate how 1) applying a certain style of markup to the apparently unrelated components of such complex deals, and then 2) subjecting those marked-up documents to some straightforward, simple transformations quickly reveals the underlying simple transactional reality.
- **Presentation Level:** In-The-Middle
- **Date of Presentation:** Wednesday, 22 May
- Paper

Relationships

- **(unnamed association):**
  - **Presentation:** (This topic)
  - **Presenter:** Perry, W. E.
- **(unnamed association):**
  - **Track:** Late Breaking News
  - **Presentation:** (This topic)
- **(unnamed association):**
  - **Keyword:** TRANSACTIONAL COMPLEXITY
  - **Presentation:** (This topic)
- **(unnamed association):**
  - **Keyword:** HIERARCHICAL STRUCTURE
  - **Presentation:** (This topic)
- **(unnamed association):**
  - **Keyword:** OBFUSCATE
  - **Presentation:** (This topic)
- **(unnamed association):**
  - **Keyword:** FORENSIC ACCOUNTING
  - **Presentation:** (This topic)

Figure 3.12   A view of the topic map for the XML Europe 2002 conference.

- *Integrated vocabularies*—Once standardized ontologies become available, Topic Maps can piece several together from distributed sources and apply them to the integration of Semantic Web information.
- *Support for navigation of distributed collections of information*—Topic maps support effective navigation of integrated information.
- *Distributed meta data*—Topic maps can capture meta data about web resources that is comparable to RDF's.

3.6 *Topic maps and RDF*

Topic maps and RDF both model information. RDF is an initiative of the W3C, whereas Topic Maps is a collaborative development between a number of individuals and companies whose efforts have been adopted by the international standards organizations known jointly as ISO/IEC. Since Topic Maps and RDF have overlapping domains, it's interesting to compare them. There have been some suggestions that they could be made more compatible, perhaps to the degree that the same processor could process both of them. This is unlikely to happen in practice. It's more likely that certain RDF datasets (perhaps most) will be transformed into topic maps and vice versa. Ontologies developed for RDF-based systems could be also adapted for Topic Maps applications.

3.6.1 *RDF: information by the atom*

RDF has a simpler basic model than Topic Maps. To reprise from chapter 2, RDF uses *resources*, represented by URI references. Resources are related by *statements*. A statement has a *subject* and assigns a value called an *object*. The relation between subject and object is called a property, or a *predicate*. (The object of a statement can also be a literal value, like a string). A resource is more or less comparable to a concept or topic map subject. Metaphorically, a statement is like a molecule in which the predicate is the chemical bond between two atoms. The only structures in RDF are statements, and each statement associates exactly one subject with exactly one object.

More complex structures, like topic map associations, must be built up one statement at a time. To make a statement about another statement, for instance, you have to create a statement-type resource that collects three other statements: one saying that the target statement has a certain resource as its subject, one that the target statement has a certain other resource as its predicate, and so on. Only then can you make assertions about this new statement-type resource. This process is like building complex materials atom by atom.

3.6.2 *Topic maps: proteins of knowledge*

Topic maps also have resources, as well as pre-defined structures. They can fit together in specific ways, like complex molecules. They aren't as complex as genes, but you can think of them as proteins, building blocks for the assembly of complex systems. The tradeoff between RDF and Topic Maps is flexibility: a great deal of processing on the one hand versus less flexibility but more specialized capabilities on the other. RDF can represent anything in a topic map, and a topic map could represent anything in an RDF database, but this is a rather theoretical *could*. It doesn't mean that the two models could be processed by the same processing methods in a practical way.

Topic maps are better suited to the kinds of tasks they were first developed for—collocation, navigation, and integration of concepts and addressable resources. Of course, these objectives cover many of the needs for using information on the Semantic Web. RDF may be better for representing other kinds of tasks, such supporting logical reasoning over large datasets. There is a large area of overlap. Thus, RDF and Topic Maps have both been used to define the structure and detail of entire web sites.

3.6.3 *The subject, revisited*

The objects of interest to Topic Maps are called *subjects*, and to RDF are called *resources*. In Topic Maps, there is a clear distinction between the subject and the topic, its proxy in the computer. RDF doesn't have that distinction. An RDF resource is identified by its URI (unless it's a blank node). In theory, that URI doesn't need to point to an actual resource, as long as it isn't used to identify more than one resource (recall that RDF resources can be abstract as well as network-retrievable). However, if the URI is retrievable, then there can be confusion about whether the resource is or isn't the thing the URI points to. And even if it's agreed that it *is* the thing pointed to by the URI, we can't know whether what's intended is that *actual resource* or the apparent *subject of the resource*. In other words, are we talking about a web page itself, or about the content of the web page?

Either one is a possible subject of discussion, but it's important to know which is intended. With RDF, there's currently no way to be certain which possibility is intended. With Topic Maps, it's easy to be certain.

3.6.4 *Theoretical basis*

RDF has a more advanced theoretical base than Topic Maps (which has virtually no formal mathematical analysis to date).[7] Thus RDF is currently more amenable to analysis and therefore more suited to the application of formal logical reasoning (see chapter 6 for more on logic). RDF's simpler design may also make theoretical analysis more practical in the long run, although this remains to be seen. To the extent that advanced logical reasoning will become important to the Semantic Web (and many people think that it will be highly important), RDF will likely have an advantage over Topic Maps for some time to come.

3.6.5 *Data structures as first-class citizens*

In Topic Maps, you can make any data structure in the map the object of discussion by either giving it a unique identifier or creating a topic that points to it. This includes associations, occurrences, names, and so on. An association is approximately the equivalent of an RDF statement (although a Topic Maps association can have many more participating topics). However, in RDF there is no way to refer to any statement directly. Statements aren't resources, and only resources can be the subject of statements. That is to say, with RDF, you can't talk directly about assertions.

Consequently, it's difficult (or impossible) to adequately qualify any RDF statement. Chapter 10 points out that it will be essential in the Semantic Web to be able to assign reliability assessments to statements and their sources, because all data won't be equally reliable. With Topic Maps this assignment would be straightforward, but with RDF it would only be possible using awkward workarounds or a significant language extension.

3.6.6 *Strengths and weaknesses*

Clearly, RDF and Topic Maps have their own strong points and weaknesses. RDF's primary strengths are its simple, uniform data structures and its theoretical base. Topic Maps' strengths are its predefined patterns of information, such as topics and associations, its ability to make statements about the components of data within a topic map data store, and its ability to distinguish the subject of a topic in a way that RDF doesn't. Otherwise, both technologies are roughly equivalent in their potential usefulness for the Semantic Web.

---

[7] Recently, Neill Kipp presented an initial draft of a set-theoretic description of Topic Maps; see http://www.kippsoftware.com/rm20031014.pdf.

3.7 *How topic maps are used in practice*

Today, as this chapter is written, most topic maps are relatively local in scope. Topic maps have been created with the order of a million topics, but by and large they're used more like local databases than as semantically integrated, distributed systems. An increasing number of smallish topic map systems are coming into use. These are being used to organize a person's own information, to create and manage web sites, and other tasks of a similar scope. Here are some examples:

- Mondeca (www.mondeca.com) has developed systems holding the equivalent of several hundred thousand records.

- A Topic Maps system is used at Oak Ridge National Laboratory; it's part of a system to assist officers in applying security classification rules to documents, which can be extremely complicated. The topic map holds the rules and documents, and an inference engine applies the rules to the data in the topic map.

- The U.S. Internal Revenue Service released a CD containing all of the year's tax regulations and forms. It was indexed with a topic map.

- Starbase Corporation, now part of Borland International, created a system that integrates several separate databases by adding a software layer that makes them look like topic maps (Seidl 2001). The virtual topic map is available over the company's network. This application of Topic Maps starts to approach the vision of linking and navigating a range of different resources distributed over a network.

- LexisNexis, which maintains an enormous online reference collection for subscribers, has developed a prototype topic map system that makes it easier for a person to locate information of interest (Freese 2003). Note that this system doesn't store the main data in the topic map. Instead, the topic map contains meta data that can be used to identify and find information in the main data stores.

- The U.S. Social Security Administration has developed a content-management system for policy-related documents that's accessed using an enterprise-wide topic map (Degler and Battle 2003), using earlier work that collected references to a vast amount of Medicare information for legal users. The original impetus was a need to handle complex medical appeals cases more quickly. The system allows document owners to index documents using common topics related to agency processes and terminology. Policy subject experts add and maintain all the keywords in the topic map without having to rely on specialist technical staff. This helps to keep the topics familiar to people seeking content, and improves end users' ability to find complex, interrelated content.

The software systems used for these topic maps vary widely. Some use commercially available topic map software, some are built using existing database systems, and some have been developed specially for particular projects. At the time of this writing, several open source topic map projects are available and are suitable at the least for smaller scale projects.

3.8 Summary

Topic maps are fundamentally about linking concepts to information about those concepts, with the goals of promoting collocation and navigation of the information—finding the right information and finding all related information nearby. Topic maps are based on the idea of concepts—anything that can be discussed or thought about. A topic is a computer representation of a concept. Concepts are significant because of their relationships to other concepts. To model this, topics can be related to other topics by means of associations. They can also contain or point to other relevant information, using the occurrence structure for this purpose.

Subject identity is one of the key ideas of topic maps. The subject of a topic map means the concept it refers to. The identity can be established in several ways. One is by specifying a publicly published identifier (a PSI), which contains a human-readable description of the subject, and possibly machine-readable meta data as well. Another way is to point to a resource, such as a web page, and say that the resource "indicates" the subject. A third way is to state that a given resource *is* the subject in question. In all cases, human judgment may be needed to determine exactly what the subject of a given topic is. These capabilities make topic maps unique in their ability to specify the nature of their subjects.

Although they were originally designed to act as indexes into bodies of information, topic maps can store and organize data of all kinds. Their origin as indexing systems is reflected in a tendency for topic map developers to use topic maps as overlays to existing information rather than as primary databases.

This chapter presented examples of topic maps and sketched some of the ways topic maps are being used. We briefly compared topic maps and RDF, since they can do similar things. Topic maps can be seen as a particular pattern for organizing information. As such, they can be implemented in many ways, including the use of RDF.

Topic maps are potentially well suited to be part of the Semantic Web because they can refer to any subject anywhere on the Web (as well as to concepts that aren't network retrievable), they can combine information in well-specified ways, they can integrate disparate information sources and ontologies, and they're specified by an international standard.

4 *Annotation*

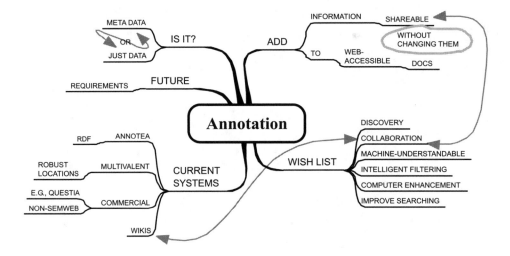

META DATA

OR
JUST DATA

IS IT?

INFORMATION — SHAREABLE

ADD
TO — WEB-ACCESSIBLE — DOCS

WITHOUT CHANGING THEM

REQUIREMENTS — FUTURE

Annotation

RDF — ANNOTEA

ROBUST LOCATIONS — MULTIVALENT

E.G., QUESTIA
NON-SEMWEB — COMMERCIAL

CURRENT SYSTEMS

WIKIS

WISH LIST

DISCOVERY
COLLABORATION
MACHINE-UNDERSTANDABLE
INTELLIGENT FILTERING
COMPUTER ENHANCEMENT
IMPROVE SEARCHING

"UNimportant, of course, I meant," the King hastily said, and went on to himself in an undertone, "important—unimportant—unimportant—important—" as if he were trying which word sounded best.

Some of the jury wrote it down "important," and some "unimportant." Alice could see this, as she was near enough to look over their slates; "but it doesn't matter a bit," she thought to herself.

—Lewis Carroll, *Alice's Adventures in Wonderland*

Some of my books have little tags stuck to pages so I can find items I thought were important. Some pages have notes or highlighting. I want to be able to mark up documents that I read in my browser, too. The trouble is, they live on someone else's server, and I can't change them. I want to share my notes and comments with other people, and I want to see theirs. Can this be done?

Annotation of documents, especially ones that you don't control, may seem far removed from a web of smart services and accessible data, but the two overlap. As will become clear, effective and distributed annotation will require many Semantic Web threads to work together, including advanced searches, ontologies, agents, and annotations. This chapter discusses annotation as it may relate to the Semantic Web.

4.1 What is annotation?

What do we mean by the word *annotation*? Dictionaries define it like this:

1. The act or process of furnishing critical commentary or explanatory notes (American Heritage).
2. A critical or explanatory note; a commentary (American Heritage).
3. A comment (usually added to a text).
4. The act of adding notes (WordNet).
5. <hypertext> A new commentary node linked to an existing node. If readers, as well as authors, can annotate nodes, then they can immediately provide feedback if the information is misleading, out of date or plain wrong (FOLDOC).

These definitions cover quite a range. The first two are scholarly activities, sometimes complex, and often produce separate works rather than notations marked in the original document. This kind of annotation isn't quite what we want here. On the other hand, this usage suggests that we could look upon annotations as a kind of meta data, a notion that we'll examine further in the next section.

The third and fourth definitions are right on target. Think of writing notes in the margin or highlighting a passage, or perhaps writing between the lines. How often have you wanted to add notes to a web page or an email without printing it out?

The last definition is more oriented towards the Web, since it refers to hypertext, nodes, and links. It also brings in interactivity.

In this chapter, *annotation* means adding information (such as notes, commentary, links to source material, and so on) to existing web-accessible documents without changing the originals. These annotations are meant to be shareable, also over the network, although notes would be useful even if they couldn't be shared. In the main, then, we'll consider a merger of the last three definitions, with some extensions.

In a sense, annotations are just more data. However, an annotation is tied to the work that it annotates in a very immediate and fine-grained way. It doesn't merely represent information about the work, but arises from the interaction between the work and its reader. Also, the knowledge captured by a collection of annotations represents a larger body of knowledge of which the work itself is only a part. These characteristics serve to distinguish annotations from the general category of "just more data," such as news feeds.

4.2 Annotations at full power

Adding notes to existing documents might be useful, but can it be considered a Semantic Web activity? Remember, most people think that the job of the Semantic Web is to make information on the web machine-processable as well as human-readable. How could annotation fit into this notion?

Let's say you're reading an article online. You find a passage you think is especially cogent, and you want to highlight it and also add a remark that supplies some context. So far this is a personal act, useful but only involving you.

Next, suppose it were possible to make that highlighted passage and your remark available on the Web, so that each time you went back to the article, the passage would be highlighted and marked. A number of commercial and non-commercial systems can do some version of this today; section 4.3 has some examples. Going further, suppose other people could see your notations for that passage when they went to the page. This too is possible today to a limited extent (again, section 4.3 has examples). Unfortunately, most of the current systems are too limited and clumsy, or too proprietary, to be widely usable.

Capabilities like these would be valuable for sharing thoughts and knowledge over the Web, and they're starting to get into the realm of the Semantic

Web. The Semantic Web could support other functionality that would enhance annotation:

- *Annotation discovery*—Your computer should be able to discover annotations for you. Possibly a document could contain embedded meta data
  pointing toward annotation servers it uses, or there might be well-known
  repositories that a software agent would check for you. If you were referred
  to the document from someone else's page, the link might include meta
  data about annotation sources. However it might be done, your computer
  or software agent would be able to locate annotations and display them
  for you.

- *Machine-understandable annotations*—You should be able to create machine-
  readable annotations, as well as human-readable highlighting, notes, and
  so on. You could annotate a book review to indicate the publisher, and
  include a web service pointer so that someone else's software agent would
  be able to go to the service and order the book.

- *Intelligent filtering*—It should be possible to filter annotations intelligently.
  Without filtering, a page could collect so many notes that it couldn't be
  read, and many of those notes might be of low quality, or even unpleasant.
  If you were reading a historical work, you might want to see only commentary by historians who were experts in related fields. This suggests that it
  would be useful to include meta data about the annotations within the
  annotations themselves. It might be possible to filter based on the author
  of the annotation, the type of remark, or a quality rating.

- *Improved searching*—Adequate meta data about annotations to a resource
  might help search engines locate the right information.

- *Enhancement by computer*—It's possible that a smart software agent could
  improve the quality of annotations or even generate useful new ones.
  Among other ideas, it might be possible to apply anti-spam techniques to
  weed out low-quality notes. Indeed, if anyone can annotate a web resource,
  those notes may end up including spam, slanderous or pornographic
  material, or other unwanted material. The right software could correct bad
  URLs in notes, add links to other relevant resources, update a price if
  someone included a price in a note, and enhance the body of annotated
  information in many other ways.

- *Collaboration*—When several people collaborate, they usually have points to
  make, positions, and decisions to support. A kind of inverse annotation
  can be useful, in which sources of supporting data and rationales annotate

the arguments, statements, and published decisions. I call this *inverse annotation*, because normally annotations are small additions to an existing work. In contrast, inverse annotations may be voluminous—they may be one of the most important parts of the body of work. In this kind of collaboration, it should be possible to mark portions of all kinds of resources—such as sentence fragments or parts of photographs—and to attach them to the body of work together with information on their source and why they're considered relevant. These complex annotations should use standard ontologies so that they can be searched and analyzed by computer. The results should be accessible to the collaborators, and often a wide distribution will be desirable.

It's clear that there are many opportunities for improving the state of annotations, and it's clear that Semantic Web technologies can and should play a role. We'll look at current annotation systems to highlight some of their weaknesses. Next we'll examine newly evolving systems for annotation (and collaboration), to see how early Semantic Web technology is starting to work its way into this area. Then we'll briefly sketch some possibilities for the future.

NOTE   Can annotations be considered a kind of meta data? Personally, I don't look at them that way. Meta data is data about something else, like the name of the author of a book, and as such is intrinsically associated with the subject. Annotations, however, are generally about a third party's thoughts, data, information, or experience. These things aren't intrinsically associated with the thing being annotated. Instead, they arise from the association between object and annotator. Annotations can capture a person's experiences, thoughts, and feelings about the item being annotated so that they can be shared. From a personal point of view, these kinds of annotations are much more than meta data. Some researchers, on the other hand, consider annotations to be meta data that's created after a work has been published.[1]

4.3 Current web annotation systems

The simplest way to annotate a web page is to download it to your own computer and then use an editor to add highlighting, insert notes, and so on. This approach

---

[1] For example, see Shabajee, Miller, and Dingley (2002), who used annotations to provide new indexes into a multimedia database, making it useful for new purposes.

only works for pages that can be edited, like HTML pages. Typically, the annotation tool changes the document by adding new elements and hyperlinks. Often an icon is inserted where a note exists, or a passage is highlighted. The Amaya browser, which is a testbed browser that the W3C uses to experiment with and advance new technology, makes it especially easy to highlight passages. This approach usually puts a copy of the document on your hard drive, because few web sites will let you save a changed page back to the site.

The next step up in sophistication is for the annotations to be saved separately from the document. When the browser loads the document, it also loads the annotation data, which it merges with the document on the fly. The annotations may be saved on your own computer or on a remote server. Of course, it's faster for the browser to load the annotations from your system; but if they're stored remotely, they can be viewed when you aren't at your computer, and the server can also make other annotations available to you.

Another approach is for the annotated view to be created by the remote server. Usually the server keeps the documents in a database, along with each user's annotations. This approach can be fast and convenient, since the server has control over the appearance of the document and the annotations. Performance can be good, and the site can offer many services (such as searches) because it has complete control over the collection, but a great deal of control is yielded to the server. Proprietary systems tend to use this approach. The Questia (www.questia.com) online library is an excellent example of this kind of system.

Some of these systems work reasonably well, especially for your personal notes, but you're out of luck if they go out of business. Either you can't get your annotations, or you can't do much with them when you do, or the software doesn't work on newer computers. There is also the question of how to make annotation server systems that can scale up to the large capabilities needed for widespread operation on the Web.

In the next several sections, we describe some simple systems that are easy to experiment with and don't require a subscription to a commercial site.

4.3.1 *Wiki collaboratives*

A *Wiki* (short for *WikiWiki*) is a site that lets its members (and, often, any reader) edit its articles and add comments. Typically, each paragraph or page ends with a link that takes you to an editor. Often there are conventions so you can apply formatting as you type. With a typical convention, typing "this is ***bold***" might cause the word **bold** to be displayed in boldface. Other conventions let you include hyperlinks. Other web site frameworks exist that provide similar capabilities, although few are willing to allow readers to change the original text—usually, only a series of comments is allowed.

The original Wiki was created by Ward Cunningham and is at http://c2.com/ cgi-bin/wiki?WikiWikiWeb. To give you a flavor of the core concept, here are some quotes from its home and tutorial pages:

> This is a web site written by its users, people like you and me. Anyone can change any page or create new pages! Read the TextFormattingRules to find out how, and then go to the WikiWikiSandbox to try it yourself. If you make a page you don't want to keep, just replace its text with the word "delete".

> **Read:** You can use this website just like any other. NewUserPages may help you start.

> **Navigate:** This website has many extra features not found on most other sites. For example, all internal links are bi-directional. Click the title above to see all pages which link to this page. Also check out RecentChanges, VisualTour, LikePages, etc.

> **Write:** Click the **EditText** link at the bottom of the page, edit the text (using the TextFormattingRules), and then click the Save button that appears at the top of the page when editing.

Clearly, collaborative sites like these are about sharing information over the Web, and they provide some sharable annotation capabilities. However, they provide only coarse-grain control over the annotations—they apply to a paragraph or to the whole page, and they can only be textual.

Some Wiki sites also provide blogging and news summaries. A range of free and commercial software is available.

4.3.2 Annotea

The W3C has been working on an experimental annotation system that uses RDF to describe annotations. The content of each note is a small XHTML document. The W3C's experimental browser, Amaya, can read and write Annotea annotations. Annotations can be stored either on the browser's computer, in which case they're private and local to that computer, or on an Annotea server. The Mozilla browser can also create and load annotations from an Annotea server.

The W3C maintains a public server on which anyone can get an account. The server software is also available to others. When Amaya loads a page from the Web, it checks the note repository (on the server or the local computer) to see whether

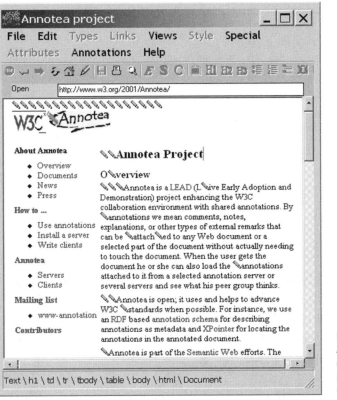

Figure 4.1
An annotated page displayed in Amaya. Each pencil icon represents a separate annotation.

there are any annotations for the page. If there are, the annotations are loaded, and clickable icons are displayed at the appropriate places in the document. When you click one of the icons, a window opens, showing the note. Figure 4.1 illustrates the Annotea home page after the annotations have been loaded.

This system is currently limited to attaching notes to selected portions of an HTML document. The user interface needs a great deal of development, as is natural at this stage. See section 4.4 for a discussion of the pros and cons of using a central repository for annotations.

Example of an Annotea note

Annotea notes are simple XHTML files, but the index to the notes is in RDF. For illustration, here's an example of the RDF for an index containing just one of the notes shown in figure 4.1. It isn't essential for understanding the general operations of the system; if such details don't interest you, skip to the next section:

```
<?xml version="1.0" ?>
<r:RDF xmlns:r="http://www.w3.org/1999/02/22-rdf-syntax-ns#"
xmlns:a="http://www.w3.org/2000/10/annotation-ns#"
xmlns:http="http://www.w3.org/1999/xx/http#"
xmlns:d="http://purl.org/dc/elements/1.0/">
<r:Description>
<r:type resource=
    "http://www.w3.org/2000/10/annotation-ns#Annotation" />
<r:type resource=
    "http://www.w3.org/2000/10/annotationType#Comment" />
<a:annotates r:resource="file:///D:/test/html/select.html" />
<a:context>file:///D:/test/html/select.html#xpointer/html]
</a:context>
<d:creator>Guest</d:creator>
<a:created>2002-06-09T20:18:59</a:created>
<d:date>2002-06-09T20:19:17</d:date>
<a:body r:resource="file:///D:/PROGRAM FILES/AMAYA/users/Guest/annotations/
    annots3vsua57.23.html" />
</r:Description>
</r:RDF>
```

The r:Description element represents the annotation. In RDF terms, it creates an anonymous node. We know it represents an annotation because the two r:type elements say that this node is of "Annotation" and also of "Comment" types. To be more specific, these two types are

```
http://www.w3.org/2000/10/annotation-ns#Annotation
http://www.w3.org/2000/10/annotationType#Comment
```

As you saw in chapter 2, these URI references uniquely designate the type of the resource (the annotation node). The creators of these types were kind enough to make them readable, to give hints as to their purpose—annotation, in this case.

The next element, a:annotates, says that the anonymous node annotates the file D:\test\html\select.html. Notice that this is a location on my computer, although it could have been a document on the Web instead.

Next we see a:context. This tells what part of the document the note applies to. It uses Xpointer methods to represent the context:

```
file:///D:/test/html/select.html#xpointer(/html[1]
```

The Xpointer expression starts with an ordinary URL to indicate the document. The part after the # sign (also called the *fragment identifier*) says that the note applies to the first html element in the document, which is always the top-level element in an HTML document. Therefore, this note applies to the document as a whole.

XPointer is the standard W3C method to point to sections of documents. Currently it can only point to XML documents and can't be used for other document types. (See section 4.3.3 for an approach that can.)

The `a:body` element contains the name and location of the file that displays the note. The rest of the elements are obvious.

How notes get misplaced when their document is changed

This is a straightforward application of RDF. One problem shows up when the target document is changed. Sometimes the links for the notes then point to the wrong place. If a note is supposed to be located at the fourth paragraph of the second division (represented as `/html[1]/body[1]/div[2]/p[4]`), and the fourth paragraph is deleted, then what? The note is now linked to the wrong paragraph, or it's linked to a non-existent location. Or, if the third paragraph was deleted, the note would now link to the previous fifth paragraph.

Any of these outcomes is undesirable. Amaya notifies you about links that point to non-existent targets, but it can't recognize any of the other changes. This problem isn't unique to the Annotea system. Any annotation system that wants to be robust against changes needs to deal with it effectively. The next program has more effective ways to deal with problems arising from editorial changes, and it can also annotate a wider range of document types.

4.3.3 Multivalent browser

The Annotea system is one of the few annotation systems so far that uses RDF. The Multivalent browser (http://www.cs.berkeley.edu/~phelps/Multivalent) uses creative technology to solve several of the problems brought out in the previous section. Even though it's still buggy and a bit difficult to use, and even though there are no assurances that it will continue to be developed, the Multivalent browser is worth looking at.

Annotating any kind of document

The Multivalent browser aims to let you annotate many different kinds of documents, not just HTML and XML. To do that, it uses its own model of a document, and it uses document adapters that build Multivalent document models so the browser can work with all kinds of documents in the same way. You can annotate any kind of document the browser can display, even bitmapped graphic images, the same way. You can even annotate some kinds of annotations.

The browser can also maintain several layers for one document and register them onscreen. For example, a scanned document that contains both the scanned image and text extracted from it by an optical character reader turns into two layers, one for the scanned image and one for the text. Either layer can be shown, and any part of the document can be highlighted and annotated.

Local storage

Annotations are kept in a separate layer and saved in separate files. They're in an XML format, although not RDF. It would be simple to convert them to an RDF format. An annotation file can be emailed to someone else so they can view the annotations. Obviously the annotations could be made available over a server, although this isn't possible at the time of this writing.

You can change words in text, display styles, and insert anchor points and hyperlinks in any document type for which there is an adapter. However, if you can't save the document back to the server it came from, most of these kinds of changes won't be permanent (since they affect the document itself). Only the annotations in a separate layer can be saved separately from the document.

Figure 4.2 shows the browser's introductory page with some annotations, which are circled for clarity. A word has been highlighted, and two notations

Figure 4.2
Multivalent browser showing three separate annotations (circled for clarity).

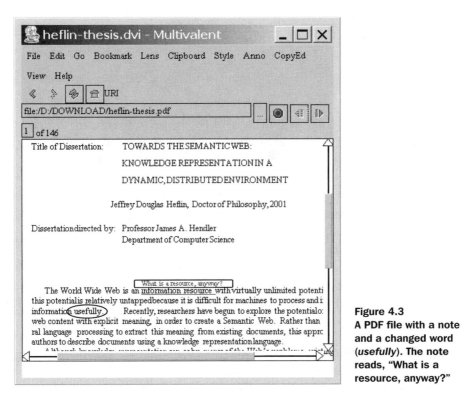

Figure 4.3
A PDF file with a note and a changed word (*usefully*). The note reads, "What is a resource, anyway?"

have been inserted. You can also add a note in a colored box that will scroll with the window.

Figure 4.3 shows an annotated PDF document. Once again, the annotations are circled to point them out.

Example of a Multivalent annotation

Here is an example of the format the Multivalent browser uses. You can compare it with the format used by Annotea in the previous section. The annotation describes the inserted note visible in figure 4.3 (you can skip the details if they don't interest you):

```
<saved Behavior='Layer'
   URI='file:/D:/download/heflin-thesis.pdf'>
   <page  page='1'>
     <copied  Behavior='multivalent.std.span.AwkSpan'
        CreatedAt='1070045234730'
        comment='What is a resource, anyway?'>
      <start  Behavior='Location'
        tree='0  6/information 7/line 0/text 0/mediabox 0/pdf'
```

```
            context='information an resource' />
        <end  Behavior='Location'
            tree='8  7/resource 7/line 0/text 0/mediabox 0/pdf'
            context='resource information with' />
        </copyed>
    </page>
</saved>
```

Each kind of annotation or effect has a `Behavior` property, like `Layer`, `multivalent.std.span.AwkSpan`, or `Highlight`, as well as start and end locations. The `Behavior` property describes the kind of annotation to be made.

Each location has a `tree` and a `context`. The `tree` expression describes the location down to the paragraph and word or character in the document model. The `context` expression gives a bit of adjacent text. The use of both a `tree` expression and a `context` to identify the location of the annotation provides redundancy that protects against changes to the document, as discussed next. The Multivalent `tree` corresponds to the Annotea `context`.

Note that these expressions don't use the W3C formats used by Annotea (RDF and XPointer), but they capture much the same information. Actually, the Multivalent annotation captures more and is more flexible, as you'll see.

Protecting against editing changes

Annotations have an ongoing problem, as mentioned in the previous section about the Annotea system: If the document changes, the annotation may end up being attached to the wrong point, or its attachment point may disappear. An Annotea note uses an XPointer expression to point to a place in the document tree, much like the `tree` expression that Multivalent uses (for example, the 5 characters located 40 characters after the start of the fourth paragraph of the first body of the first HTML node).

The Multivalent approach is to use a nearby text fragment together with the text of the target location to make sure the right place is found. The text of the `context` is compared with the text near the tree location. If the adjacent text doesn't match, the browser follows a systematic search, looking first for matches nearby, then in adjacent paragraphs, and then farther away in the document tree. According to the Multivalent designer, this method is extremely likely to find the intended target even after significant editing. This approach is called *Robust Locations*.

It would be possible to use RDF and XPointer with the Multivalent approach. Doing so would make the Annotea system more robust. However, it wouldn't allow Annotea to annotate non-HTML or non-XML documents, because there is no standard document model for general documents, and because XPointer doesn't apply for other document types.

4.4 *Improving annotation*

You've seen the current state of the annotation art. Some commercial systems provide easier interfaces and create more effects, but they aren't fundamentally different. Either a system uses standards like XML and RDF, or it uses proprietary formats. The annotations are stored either on the local computer or on a remote server. Notations are entered by hand and read by people. There are also specialized commercial systems for scholarly work, like ATLAS.ti (www.atlasti.de), but they do a different kind of annotation than we're dealing with here.

A number of research projects are developing more advanced systems. These are at an early stage (at the time of this writing). Many of them attempt to use a predefined ontology to provide categories for annotation data and also for classifying the material being annotated. This kind of approach tends to be hard for a user to work with as well as inflexible. More ambitious projects try to analyze the material the user reads and annotates, with the aim of providing intelligent assistance by classifying the material and learning progressively more about the user's interests and needs.

There is an intermediate ground. Some news sites, such as Slashdot, and many web logs, allow readers to comment on their stories. Often these comments are indexed by search engines so that they can be found by the right search. You can picture the stories and their comments indexed, categorized, and otherwise semantically enriched with little change to the way they work today.

Future annotation systems will have to deal with the following:

- Storage, retrieval, and discovery of annotations must be made more convenient and less dependent on a few servers that are proprietary and may not persist. Services (see chapter 8) share this problem.

- The annotation locator mechanisms need to become more robust so that normal editorial changes won't orphan annotations.

- It should be possible to apply annotations to a wide range of documents, as with the Multivalent browser.

- It should be possible to link machine-readable annotations to documents. Thus an RDF block describing a service for purchasing an item could be associated with a review of the item.

- Convenient ways are needed to filter associations so that the reader won't be overwhelmed by large numbers of unwanted annotations from a range of annotators. This is possible today to a limited extent, but more capability is needed.

- More and better display methods are needed so that a reader can tell what and how many annotations exist.

- Much better user interfaces are needed.

- It should be convenient to attach hyperlinks to other resources for use as annotations. These should be both machine- and human-readable.

- Browsers and similar annotation readers should allow programmatic access to the annotations, just as they currently do for the parts of a document (that is, by means of a Document Object Model [DOM]).

- Collaborative access to networks of annotations should be possible, and communities should be able to create shared annotations in their area of interest.

- Annotation systems should be able to use whatever ontology may be relevant to the subject being annotated. Those ontologies may be pieced together from various parts, possibly on the fly.

With capabilities like these in place, annotations will play a useful, even exciting role in the future Web. Imagine that after you create an annotation, your computer creates an agent (see chapter 9) for it. The agent works in the background over the next few minutes, hours, or even days. It uses the context of the document and the wording of the annotation to perform semantically focused searches on the Web (see chapter 5). It monitors any URLs in the annotation for validity and changes, and communicates with other annotation agents, exchanging information that helps it to assess the quality of the information it's receiving.

After some time, when the agent has collected and integrated all this information, it offers you a selection of information related to your note and to the part of the work you were annotating, possibly along with related information you may not have been aware of. The agent might even offer an opinion that your note is misguided, based on a review of authoritative research!

Is a scenario like this possible? No one knows for sure, but parts certainly are.

4.5 *Summary*

In this chapter, we've looked at the current capabilities for the annotation of web resources. The potential number of annotation types is large, ranging—to name just a few—from personal notes, to formal meta data about the provenance of a work, to creating new indexes for databases. More kinds of meta data are being created all the time, and existing meta data constantly gets reused in new ways.

Several systems are available that help you annotate web pages right in the browser; they're mostly experimental, but we have a long way to go before annotation capabilities get to a useful level. A great deal of work is needed in the areas of user interface, automated assistance in categorizing and marking documents, and merging retrieved annotations with the original work. Search and discovery methods that let people locate annotations of interest while not being overwhelmed by irrelevant ones are just as important for finding annotations as for any other kind of search.

Once the basic machinery is in place, it should be possible for computers in general (and especially software agents) to use annotations in many creative ways. The chapter ended with a fairly futuristic list of desirable capabilities that may or may not be realizable, but that are intriguing. This list requires several threads in the book to work together, including advanced searches, ontologies, agents, and annotations.

5

Searching

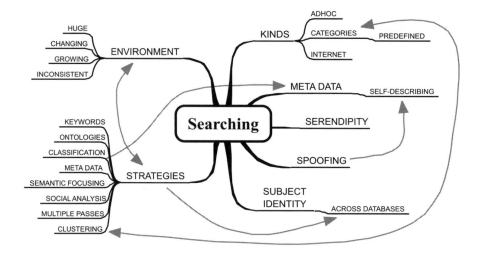

...which gave the Pigeon the opportunity of adding, "You're looking for eggs, I know THAT well enough; and what does it matter to me whether you're a little girl or a serpent?"

—Lewis Carroll, *Alice's Adventures in Wonderland*

Anyone who searches for specific information on the Web learns to put up with frustration. Sometimes things go well, but other times irrelevant information buries those bits we seek. Here are two typical examples from my experience.

First, I want to find the home page for the Python XML project. I type "python xml" into the Google search page. In less than a second I get back 10 pages of hits, but soon I find that the third item is the one I want. If I remember that the project is also called pyxml, I still get 10 pages of hits, but now the first hit is the page I want.

Next, I need to get a replacement cooktop heating coil for my old stove, and I want to find a store in my area. Because I'm working on this chapter, I decide to try an online search. I enter the following search phrases in order, based on words I saw in otherwise useless hits:

- burner jennair
- burner jennair replace
- burner jennair new
- burner jennair distributor
- jennair distributor va
- jennair distributor virginia

The last phrase gives a few hits—only six—but they're useless too. They include a site that offers agricultural businesses for sale.

I know that I've saved a bookmark in my browser for a real store that carries the replacement parts I need. I find the bookmark and enter its URL into the search engine. I get back a page that contains the search engine's category for the URL and also a description. The category seems to make sense:

```
Shopping > Home and Garden > ... > Appliances > Parts
```

It's also a clickable hyperlink that gives me a page of 14 online appliance dealers. Adding the stove brand to the search finally gives me a list of seven dealers that apparently handle the brand. However, none of them are actual stores, let alone stores in Virginia, and the list doesn't even include the original store whose URL I tried. Later, I discover that, had I typed "jennair" in the first place, the return page would have displayed the category for the query. This would have helped, except that it's wrong—the site changed its categories and failed to update that part of the database.

These two experiences epitomize the strengths and weaknesses of searching the Web today. Search engines have indexed a staggering number of web pages, but a user has no good way to know which search terms have good chances of success. And each user has a different and often imprecise mental hierarchy of categories and terms, none of which may match what the search engines offer.

5.1 Searching the Web

Surely every reader of this book has performed searches. On the Internet, there are search engines like Google and Altavista. Libraries have their card catalogs and electronic search terminals, and books have their indexes. These are also varieties of search aids. This section looks at current Internet searches, to suggest potential areas where the Semantic Web could bring substantial improvement.

5.1.1 Kinds of searches

The act of searching for information can be classified in many ways. One way is by the location—you can search your own computer, or your company's intranet, or the Internet. Another classification concerns the type of query. The distinction here is between an ad hoc search (which is what you do when, for example, you type "black Labrador kennel" into a search engine) and a more structured search in which you use predefined categories set up by the search site. Figure 5.1 depicts some of Yahoo's (www.yahoo.com) predefined categories.

A different kind of distinction can be made between a closed system, like a stable collection of reference documents that are similarly structured, and an open system containing a large number of different kinds of information. Library science knows many specialized distinctions between kinds of information to search for: inventory control, establishing the provenance of documents (their source or origin), locating similar items, finding similar sets (such as different editions of the same work), and many more.

In this book, we're most interested in information that can be found using the Internet and that can preferably be used by both people and computers. This covers quite a range.

Business and Economy
Directory > **Business and Economy**

Search [   ] ⦿ the Web ○ just this category   [Search]

CATEGORIES

Commercial Categories
- **Business to Business (288092)** NEW!
- **Shopping and Services (442351)** NEW!

Additional Categories
- **Booksellers@**
- **Business Libraries@**
- **Business Schools@**
- **Business Weblogs@**
- **Chats and Forums (3)**
- **Classifieds (2700)**
- **Cooperatives (22)**
- **Directories (308)** NEW!
- **Economics@**
- **Education@**
- **Employment and Work (678)**
- **Ethics and Responsibility@**
- **Finance and Investment (1361)** NEW!
- **Global Economy@**
- **History@**
- **Intellectual Property@**
- **Labor@**
- **Law@**
- **Marketing and Advertising (246)**
- **News and Media@**
- **Organizations (12094)**
- **Taxes@**
- **Trade (306)**
- **Transportation@**

Figure 5.1 An example of predefined categories, as presented by the Yahoo search site. Selecting any one category brings up a page presenting a more specialized list of categories. Categories like these work well when they match the words a person thinks of. When the categories don't match well, it can be hard to decide which ones to choose.

5.1.2 *So near and yet so far*

Today, Internet searches are usually done by people who type words into the input box of a search engine's web page. Some people also run search engine programs that index their hard drives and find files by name or text phrases. Either way, the results come back as text listings that a person can read, perhaps with hyperlinks to other web pages.

Search engines are also starting to provide interfaces so that programs can request and receive information; Google has such a service, for example. However, no standards exist yet for either the form of the request or the form of the response.

Web users everywhere have shared the experience of trying to guess the right words that will return a useful result, as the second vignette at the start of the chapter exemplifies. Some sites give no guidance; some, like Yahoo and Open

Directory (www.dmoz.org), have a hierarchy of terms you can navigate like an index; and some provide active help in focusing your search by showing additional terms to add to your search, like the wonderfully creative graphic interface at KartOO (www.kartoo.com/).[1]

Whatever search site you use, it can be difficult to get useful results. Either you get too many hits, or none of the results gives the information you want, or you get general information when you wanted specifics. The best search engines are much better at discovering useful results than lower grade sites, but the quality of results is erratic even at the best sites.

It can also be difficult to use search results in a program. A program that wants to look for a book in many different bookstores may receive data from each bookstore; this data can be read by a person, but it's difficult to combine and process automatically. The sites use different and incompatible data formats that don't lend themselves to machine processing. Fortunately, as search engines begin to return data in XML formats, this situation is improving.

Search engines today are sometimes so effective that it can be faster and easier to do a search than to find a site in your list of saved bookmarks. When I planned a vacation in Alaska, I found that I could type "alaska railroad schedule" into Google to get railroad schedules more easily than I could navigate to the bookmark saved in my browser.[2] To my way of thinking, for a large and distant search engine to find a reference faster that I can in my list of bookmarks is a stunning accomplishment, notwithstanding the limitations of current web searches.

5.1.3 *Behind the scenes*

The Internet must be the most difficult environment conceivable for search engines. It's huge, growing, always changing, and inconsistent, and it contains documents of all kinds and structures. Those documents may contradict each other, and no central registry lists them all. Of course, these facts are also precisely the strength and richness of the Internet, the reason it's so interesting and vital.

---

[1] Trying my search for the stove part on KartOO resulted in a small number of hits, essentially the top hits from the regular search engine. But the ingenious graphical display made it easy to see which hits might be useful. In fact, one of the hits led through an intermediate link to the manufacturer's page, where I got a listing of dealers near my home.

[2] Since I began to use the bookmark application discussed in the appendix, I can usually find my own bookmarks faster than using Google.

What Internet search sites do behind the scenes is amazing. They deal with so many information sources—millions or hundreds of millions of documents—and they usually give results within seconds:

1   A search engine must find web sites and documents for indexing (and there's a huge number of candidates).

2   The engine must analyze each page and each web site in many ways to be ready for the unknown queries that users will submit. The relationships between linked pages must be analyzed and a strategy developed to deal with those linked pages. Many sites *cache* (that is, save copies of) the pages they index in case the original page becomes unavailable. The search engine must analyze the contents of a wide range of document types, from the highly structured to the almost unstructured, from the informal to the highly technical.

3   Once the information has been stored and indexed for later retrieval, the search engine has to analyze queries, locate candidate results in its huge databases, select the best results from those candidates, possibly group them into sensible divisions, order them by their relevance, and present them to the user in a very short time.

Later in this chapter, we'll look at how Semantic Web technologies can help to improve this process, and how the results from a search could be made more useful for computer consumption.

SERENDIPITY: SURPRISE AS A GOAL Search sites and users place a lot of emphasis on returning results that satisfy the original request as closely as possible, even when that request may have been vague. But it can be valuable for people to discover things they weren't looking for and didn't expect. In pre-Internet days, when we spent time in libraries (some of us still do), it was common to stumble across something tremendously interesting but previously unknown. (I myself acquired two new hobbies that way, thanks to the excellent library system of Shaker Heights, Ohio.)

We don't want to lose those opportunities in the name of efficiency and focused results. This is a subject I haven't seen discussed, and it shouldn't get lost. As I prepared to write this chapter, I accidentally stumbled across an unexpected and amusing site, using the AltaVista search engine (www.altavista.com): the Political Impersonator Speakers Bureau site (www.counterfeitbill.com/), which has links to comedians who impersonate presidents and other politicians. I was glad to have found it.

5.2 Search strategies

In this section, we look at some issues involved in searching. It isn't a comprehensive and detailed discussion, but it tries to frame the potential contributions of a future Semantic Web. At the time of this writing, no standards exist for indexing, cataloging, analyzing, or specifying the quality and performance of search engines, nor for specifying request and response message formats. Therefore we can't give specific technical examples of Semantic Web–oriented standard technologies—although many research papers delineate experimental approaches.[3] Of course, we expect the usual suspects—RDF, Topic Maps, and OWL (see chapters 2, 3, and 7)—to play a prominent role. Topic Maps could be used to organize and structure data, and OWL could define categories and relationships between them.

5.2.1 Keywords

The most straightforward approach to indexing the Web is to search web resources for a list of keywords and store their locations. When the user types in one or more search terms, the engine attempts to find them in its index; if it can't, it tries to find equivalent terms that it does contain. Pages known to contain the keywords are returned.

Aside from the fact that pages not containing any of the keywords may not be returned, there is the *natural language* issue. In language, as people use it every day, words can have many different *senses*, or classes of meaning. For example, according to the WordNet lexical dictionary (WordNet), the word *tool* has four senses when used as a noun and four more when used as a verb (for example, to "work with a tool" and to "joyride"). Some of these senses are closely related, and some aren't. To make effective use of keywords, the search engine must figure out the right sense when it analyzes a page and also when it analyzes a query. This gets into the difficult area of natural language processing (NLP). In addition, the search engine normally receives no context for analyzing the query; but in natural languages words often have different meanings according to the context (polysemy), which can lead to ambiguity.

---

[3] Many research papers discuss searching—far more than could be reported in this book. This chapter mentions only a few efforts that seem likely to be useful now or in the relatively near future, and that clearly involve Semantic Web technologies.

Another problem is that users often don't think of the same keywords that the search system uses. Keywords, although they can be useful, don't provide enough utility to support the kinds of search activity that goes on over the Web.

5.2.2 *Ontologies*

The classic AI-oriented (Artificial Intelligence) view would be that by classifying the words and concepts in web resources into categories defined by a suitable ontology, the essential contents of the resources could be captured and matched to the concepts behind the categories. Failing that, the terms used in a query could at least be automatically related to known terms from the ontology. Alternatively, terms from the ontology could be presented to the user, who would pick one or more for the query. This approach would be made more feasible if web pages were marked up with the right information.

There are two issues here: the analysis of documents on the Web and the creation of queries. For the creation of queries, the use of terms from ontologies hasn't been demonstrated to be nearly as effective as you might think. It can be useful in relatively small, closed systems where the vocabulary is small and well controlled, but a query for information on the Internet is very different.

A person who wants to find information is unlikely to have the same working ontology as the system uses for its classification. In other words, people have different associations to different words and concepts, and one person's hierarchy of concepts may not suit another's. In addition, the use of words is dependent on the context of the query and the expectations of the searcher. A real, useful ontology will probably be too large for a user to easily look through to find the right terms to use. Finding the proper terms can become a search exercise in itself, as I found when I tried to locate a heating coil for my stove. I started with *hob* because that's the term used in the restaurant industry, switched to *burner,* and ended up with *appliance* and *jennair distributor.* It's also hard to devise a good user interface that allows a user to choose terms from an ontology without disrupting their thoughts.

Whatever the reason, to date, the use of ontologies hasn't been particularly effective for helping users construct queries that produce good results. Note that this isn't the same as saying that that classification of terms is useless during analysis of either documents or queries, nor that classification systems can't help a person to craft a query. Still, ontology-based queries don't seem to be the largest part of the answer. This amounts to observing that a good index in a book can be invaluable for finding specific material; but for a large book written about many different subjects by many different authors, it's much harder to find what you want, index or no.

On the other hand, an approach in which the computer silently augments a query by using an ontology to relate the query terms to a knowledge base will probably be much more successful (see section 5.2.7).

5.2.3 *Meta data*

There are several kinds of meta data about any document or resource. There is meta data that is explicitly contained in a work, such as its author, keywords about its content, and its publisher. Other metadata is published separately from the work, perhaps in reviews or in annotations (see chapter 4 for more on annotations). In some cases, it may be possible to infer meta data that isn't explicitly stated.

Today, most documents and web pages contain little meta data. It has often been assumed that one of the most important consequences of the Semantic Web will be that most resources will be marked up with meta data in a few standard formats. It's undoubtedly true that more pages will be marked up with meta data, but it seems certain that most resources on the Web will continue to lack labeled meta data. Most web pages won't contain markup that says, "This is an important concept," or "This page uses terms drawn from the XYZ ontology."

Therefore, search engines need to analyze resources to deduce or extract the implicit and explicit meta data they may contain, and to do so even without marked-up sections in the documents. Some of this already takes place, and quite a lot of research focuses on such analysis. Two approaches, which may also be combined, appear frequently in the research: analysis of the language of the document (more in the next section) and analysis of common structural patterns to identify parts of particular cogency. Typically, such parts are consecutive sentences, or paragraphs with links, or runs of sequential paragraphs with certain kinds of links and terms. Even the visual layout of web pages has been shown to provide helpful information for identifying important concepts and links.

Identification of sections that have strategic hyperlinks is sometimes combined with what the discussion in section 5.2.6 calls *social analysis*. Social analysis is a key feature of Google's approach.

5.2.4 *Semantic analysis*

All web resources are about one or more themes and contain some number of concepts. Most of the time, the themes and concepts are expressed in natural language. If these concepts can be discovered and matched with the concepts contained in a query, it ought to make for better retrieval of the desired information. The discovery process will probably entail classification according to an ontology (as covered in section 5.2.2).

In the future, some resources' major concepts will be marked up with a standard language like Resource Description Framework (RDF). When this happens, it will make the analysis much easier. But a vast number of pages and documents aren't so tagged now and probably never will be. A great deal of research has gone into the subject of automatic analysis of natural language; it's a large and difficult subject. To be practical for search engines, the analysis must not only be reasonably accurate but also very fast. As another benefit, natural language analysis can also help a search engine to understand queries and to let a user type queries that are more like everyday questions.

However, there's more to it than just inferring concepts. Suppose you type in the name of a well-known person. Some research papers use Bill Clinton, the former American president, as an example. What kind of information should a system return for the query "Bill Clinton"? A biography? His current health? A history of the Clinton presidency? His email address? Let's try it: Table 5.1 lists the top hits for several major search engines.[4]

Table 5.1   Top search engine results for the query "Bill Clinton"

Search engine	Top results
AltaVista	Counterfeit Bill Productions—George W. Bush, Laura Bush, Bill Clinton, Hillary Clinton, Jesse Ventura, and Al Gore The "Unofficial" Bill Clinton New Book of Knowledge: Bill Clinton
Google	Welcome to the White House Clinton Presidential Center The "Unofficial" Bill Clinton
Netscape Search	Welcome to the White House Clinton Presidential Center www.whitehouse.gov/WH/Mail/html/Mail_President.html
Teoma	Clinton Presidential Materials White House Search Engine Clinton Library Book—satirizing the Clinton Library aka Clinton Presidential Center LindaTripp.com The Journal of Linda Tripp's fight for justice against the Bill Clinton Whi...
Ask Jeeves	Clinton Presidential Materials White House Search Engine Clinton Library Book—satirizing the Clinton Library aka Clinton Presidential Center Town Hall: Conservative News and Information—The Conservative Movement Starts Here

---

[4] Of course, these results will probably be different by the time this book is published.

The top response of both Google and Netscape is completely inappropriate, since at the time of writing Clinton hasn't been president for some time. All five search sites have satirical or comic sites in the top three, which probably isn't what most people expect (although it's a good example of the serendipitous response mentioned earlier). Ask Jeeves also produced a sidebar of suggested topics, each a hyperlink of its own, to narrow the search:

- Bill Clinton, Biography
- President Clinton
- Impeachment of Bill Clinton
- Monica Lewinsky
- Bill Clinton Jokes
- Bill Clinton Photos
- Bill Clinton Schedule
- Clinton Lewinsky
- Bill Hillary Clinton
- Bill Clinton Picture

Although helpful, the first return under "Bill Clinton, Biography" was for a biography of Hillary Clinton, not Bill.

All in all, the hits have some cogency but aren't particularly responsive. But what should the response have been, with such a plain question? That isn't easy to know, and the better search engines try to come up with something that makes sense, such as biographic material or primary employment.

The methods that commercial search engines use at any particular time are generally not known in detail. The principles behind Google were published while it was still an academic project, but no doubt it has extended its methods since then. The results of our test search do indicate two things. First, a number of sites evidently use some kind of semantic analysis, because the results tend to be about Clinton rather than, say, collections of his speeches or lists of old addresses. Second, the elevated position of satirical pages seems to reflect a measure of their popularity. How else would such pages rate so highly? (Section 5.2.6 goes further into this question.)

Clearly, the use of semantic analysis to discover concepts and word senses in resources can help find the right information during a search. Just as clearly, an understanding of the intended meaning of the search request is needed for searches to become substantially more effective. The next section discusses how a system could improve its understanding of a query.

5.2.5 *Semantic focusing*

What can be done at the query end to improve a search engine's understanding of a query? In some way, the query needs to be put into a context that will help a search engine do a productive search.

Context from the user

When a user makes a query because they're reading part of a document, the system could analyze that part of the document. Suppose you're reading a news story. You highlight a phrase and ask for more information. The system would try to analyze that part of the story, including any hyperlinks. The analysis would yield concepts and relationships between them, and the system would use them to augment the query.

This process would be useful even if the story contained no semantic markup. If it did, the system would be able to do its job with more precision. If the user's system could enhance the query using terms and concepts known to the search engine, the whole process of query-search-results could be much more effective.

Context from databases

Another strategy is to try to classify the user's query and then search a knowledge base using that classification. Information from the knowledge base would then be used to enhance the query sent to the search engine. Even better would be to combine information about the subject from several knowledge bases. For this to work, the system must be able to identify the subject of a query, even if it was called different things in different places. The project known as *TAP* (http://tap.stanford.edu/), being developed at Stanford University, has evolved a scheme for doing this that dovetails well with the design of RDF.

TAP has developed a way to ask a server to supply a graph containing information about a subject. A server that receives a request for information on "a person whose name is 'Tom Passin', who is writing a book about the Semantic Web, who has an email address of tpassin@example.com, who lives in such-and-such a town, and who is interested in flying" might find that it has data on a person named Thomas Passin, who lives in the same state as the town, who has a silver car, who has an email address of tpassin@example.com, and who likes flying and music. Putting the two together, the system can discover that there is a person who has the two names Tom Passin and Thomas Passin, who has an email address of tpassin@example.com, who lives in such-and-such a town in such-and-such a state, and who likes both flying and music.

TAP has built a knowledge base that can identify many well-known people and concepts. One example from TAP documents is a query for information about Yo Yo Ma, the famous cellist. The query is likely to be about music the cellist is involved with, and TAP can discover this from its knowledge base. So, TAP tries to get information about recordings, concerts, musical venues, and so on that relate to Yo Yo, as well as his current concert schedule. All this information is assembled and presented to the user. The result seems like an ordinary search result, except that it's much more focused on music-related information than usual. Most of the typical scattered, irrelevant results are gone. (The TAP site doesn't explain how to get non-music-related information about Yo Yo. Presumably this can be done as well.)

Subject identity—again

Recall from chapter 2 that RDF saves its information as a series of simple statements called triples, because they have three parts—for example, (Mycar, has-Color, Silver). Also recall from chapters 2 and 3 that a name may or may not identify a resource. RDF uses unique URIs as identifiers. But it's also possible to describe something without using its identifier: "my car is the small silver convertible parked near the end of the block."

Some statements are good for identifying their subject, and some aren't. "The person who has Social Security number xxx-yy-zzzz" is good for identifying a person in the U.S., because only one person is supposed to have a given Social Security number. By contrast, "The person who has brown hair" isn't good for identification, because many people have brown hair. Now, suppose we have some statements about a person in one database and some different statements in another database. If they're about the same person, and they're sufficiently good for identification, then certain parts of the two graphs—the two graphs that represent the data in the two databases—will match. The match can indicate that the two are really the same, as illustrated is figure 5.2.

In this way, the information in one database can sometimes be related to that in another, even though neither one knows the other's identifiers. (TAP) has more on this subject.

5.2.6 Social analysis

The apparent influence of popularity on the results found in section 5.2.4 is no accident. In the study of the influence of scientific research, one of the most effective measures turned out to be how often a given work is cited in other research papers. In a like manner, some search engines (notably Google) analyze

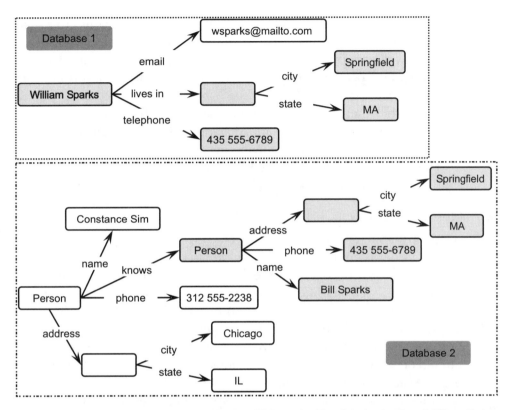

Figure 5.2 Data in two databases, depicted as RDF graphs. The data is structured differently in the two databases, but there are some similarities. A suitable processor could match "lives in" from database 1 with "address" from database 2. It could then discover that parts of the two graphs have essentially the same shape and type of connections. From this, it could infer that database 2 may contain the same person, William Sparks, as database 1, because the address has the same city and state, and the telephone numbers match. The fact that "Bill" is a common alternative for "William" strengthens the conclusion. The matching parts of the two graphs are shaded.

the pattern and number of links to a page, and the results play an important role in ranking a page's importance.[5] The analysis can become complicated, with certain pages being weighted more heavily depending on the patterns of links coming to them. The more a page or web site is judged to be of high quality, the more influence it has on the ranking of a page.

---

[5] Google calls its system PageRank. You can read more about PageRank on the Google web site at www.google.com/technology/ (they also have a delightful spoof of this at www.google.com/technology/ pigeonrank.html) and in the research paper "The Anatomy of a Large-Scale Hypertextual Web Search Engine" by Sergey Brin and Lawrence Page at www-db.stanford.edu/pub/papers/google.pdf.

What could be more web-like than using the very hyperlinks that characterize the Web to guide the discovery of information? Of course, popularity alone doesn't make something accurate (think of urban legends that are repeated over and over), but social ranking has a long history. Polls are a form of social ranking. Amazon.com, the bookselling site (which has branched out and now sells all kinds of other merchandise), makes it easy to see the opinions of other people who have bought the same item. Amazon includes the entire text of people's reviews, so these ratings affect buying decisions.

The ability of technologies like RDF to annotate resources (see chapter 4) could contribute powerfully to social analysis and thereby play a role in search strategies.

5.2.7 *Multiple passes*

It's clear that no one approach (or even two) to indexing Web resources and analyzing queries is enough. An approach that is frequently used in research papers and is now starting to show up on some search sites is to make a preliminary query using a web site like Google (or more than one site) and then to perform additional analysis. In (Amitay 2000), the work starts by searching for "Albert Einstein" on Google and other search sites. Each hit is analyzed by computer to find the best description of its contents, which are then presented to the user or filtered out. The hits are analyzed by looking for certain structural features in the pages; other research uses different strategies.

Some of these experiments have apparently delivered much better results than the methods normally used at present, with many fewer irrelevant hits and fewer cases of omitted pages that should have been returned.

5.2.8 *Peer to peer*

Another search strategy is to use peer-to-peer networks to allow a query to be answered by other computers that are likely to know useful information. The Neuro-Grid project (www.neurogrid.net) takes this approach. A person who participates stores bookmark references into a database, which can be shared with other participants. A query is directed by the system to those peers most likely to answer it, based on past experience. The NeuroGrid software on a person's computer is also supposed to improve its performance over time by noticing the user's behavior in making queries and deciding which proposed sources to select.

NeuroGrid doesn't use RDF or any other standard language, but it does store its data in the form of triples. Thus it seems reasonable that it could be modified to use RDF if desired. Then the system could be adapted to use some of the other strategies mentioned earlier. For example, it could participate in a TAP-like system.

NeuroGrid is interesting, although it's still in an early stage of development. With all peer-to-peer systems, there is a question about how well they can scale up to large sizes. Still, NeuroGrid's use of peer information and its attempts to adapt its performance according to the actions of its users may prove useful for other systems.

5.2.9 *Clustering*

Many search engines return their results in a plain list, usually with the (presumably) most relevant results near the top. But an undifferentiated list can be cumbersome to deal with, especially when the search term has many possible meanings. It's desirable to group the search results into sensible categories. The term *swing* could bring results for the Java Swing user interface code library, swing music of the big band era, improving one's golf swing, a child's swing, and so on. Grouping the results is often called *clustering*.

Table 5.2 compares Google's results for a search on "child's swing" with those of today's apparent leader in result clustering, Vivisimo (www.vivisimo.com).[6] For brevity, the Vivisimo results show only the clusters and not the actual hits; the numbers after the cluster headings indicate the number of results for each head-

Table 5.2   Results for a search on the term "child's swing" from Google and Vivisimo

Google	Vivisimo
CHILD'S SWING JACKET	child's swing (185)
Playland Adventures Inc. is a child's swing world of fun	Garden, Verses (27)
Little Tikes Toys, Beds and Playhouses at Just Little Tykes	Sets (24)
	Plans (12)
Child's Glider Swing	Seat (11)
Colerain Township Classified Ads: Wanted, Child's Swing Set	Furniture (11)
	Slide, Residential (9)
National Safety Council Fact Sheet Library … Install the swing set legs in concrete below ground level to avoid a tripping hazard. … more than five inches but less than 10 inches, since a child's head may …	Safety, Dangerous (10)
	Toys, Little Tykes (8)
	Tree (9)
	Child's Play (9)
Seller's Past Listings … has ended. 71187, Antique Wooden Child's Swing, $88.00, 0, 2/15/2001	Parent (2)
	Art (6)
4:37:14 PM, Auction has ended. 71189, Antique Wooden Child's Swing, …	Swing Jacket (3)
	[… other minor headings omitted …]

---

[6] Some other sites that use a form of on-the-fly clustering are iBoogie (http://iboogie.tv/), Kartoo (www.kartoo.com), and Mooter (www.mooter.com).

ing. Many of the headings in the Vivisimo results also have their own subheadings, but they aren't shown for simplicity.

Which set of results would you rather work with? Most people would probably say "the clustered results on the right"—at least, provided the results were good hits. This isn't intended to take anything away from the accomplishments of the mainstream search sites, but to indicate one fruitful area for them to move into next.

Until recently, automatic clustering has generally been less than satisfactory, so the capabilities illustrated here are especially striking. The increase of computer capability has combined with progress in academic research (for example, Zamir and Etzioni [1998]) with surprisingly good results. But more is involved than first meets the eye.

Where should the clustering of results take place? The obvious thing to do would be to devise a set of categories—an ontology—based on the entire collection of indexed documents, and to tag each one with its appropriate classification. This approach has some drawbacks, but two stand out: Documents are rarely about one thing, and they should frequently be put into more than one category.

What's more, a set of categories that represents the entire collection known to the search engine may not suit the particular set of results for your current query. It can be more useful to cluster results on the fly as they come back from the search. That's what Vivisimo does—it performs its clustering using the short quotes that a search engine returns with each document. It's also possible to combine this ad hoc, on-the-fly clustering with predefined categories, although the Vivisimo site doesn't do so. Vivisimo is happy to put a given document into many categories if that's how the results turn out. The bookmark case study in the appendix also discusses the usefulness of ad hoc categories and multiple classifications.

The effectiveness of ad hoc clustering leads to a second point, a conundrum of sorts. For clustering like this to be usable on the Semantic Web, it should be possible to make the clustering available in a way that can be readily acted on by other computers. That's easy enough. But how can other computers know what these ad hoc categories mean? They wouldn't by definition be standard terms, since they would be created on the fly.

Chapter 7 discusses the design, construction, and interchange of ontologies. Usually it's taken for granted that this means the definition of a predefined set of categories, which again is at odds with the ad hoc nature of these clustered results. The OWL ontology language can state that one category or term is equivalent to another. Perhaps in the future a clustering engine will be able to link its ad hoc clusters to other vocabularies using such methods. Since clustering can also be done against terms from an ontology, it should be possible to relate those clusters to the ad hoc clusters.

Clearly, some basic work needs to be done in this area. Clustering results is an important way to present a large number of results so that people can work with them effectively, so it's important that the work be done.

5.3 *Distorting results and spoofing search engines*

HTML pages can include simple meta data by using the META element. A page designer can include keywords describing that page, and a search engine can use them for cataloging the page. It sounds ideal and well suited for extension with Semantic Web capabilities. The trouble is, people began packing their pages with multiple copies of the same keywords, and they added keywords that seemed to be popular with search engines even though they didn't suit the page. This (mal)practice can cause bad results and damage the utility of a search engine. As a result, the better search engines no longer make much use of self-describing META tags in a page.

There are other ways to fool search engines or users. A site can be *hijacked*—its home page can be hacked so that visitors are sent to a different web site that may look like the original one but belongs to someone else. Or, a URL can mislead a user into going to the wrong site. Here's an example. The Open Directory Project is found at www.dmoz.org. Open Directory aims to produce a directory in a noncommercial way, using the services of many volunteer editors. It uses a home-grown, changeable taxonomy—for example, Science/Biology/Agriculture/ Forestry/Urban Forestry. But if you (by a perfectly natural mistake) visit www. opendirectory.org, you'll see a site that superficially looks like the www.dmoz.org site but is actually an advertising directory. Links to www.opendirectory.org might be misanalyzed by a page-ranking system.

Another source of bias is paid ranking. Some sites allow advertisers to buy the top places in the returned hits. Nowadays the better sites that do this keep the paid returns, sometimes called *sponsored links*, in a separate and well-labeled area, which is an improvement. Still, advertisers can be favored by having the site fail to return certain pages (possibly those of competitors).

The upshot is that there are many ways to distort or bias search results, and searches on the Semantic Web will have to take these into account (more in the next section). The issue of ensuring the reliability of Semantic Web data and operations is a difficult subject that is discussed further in chapter 10, "Distributed Trust and Belief."

5.4 *Searching and the Semantic Web*

There has been a tendency for the potential contribution of the Semantic Web to be presented largely in terms of adding classification and standard ontologies to resources on the Web. Search engines would add software that could extract that data, and thereby searching would become far more reliable. This seems logical, but we've seen that it will fall short in several areas.

5.4.1 *Self-describing meta data: no panacea*

As we've discussed in this chapter, the use of self-describing meta data for web searches has some limitations:

- Much of the material on the Web is likely to remain untouched by semantic markup.

- The value of classification beyond simple keywords hasn't been demonstrated, and there is some evidence suggesting that it doesn't bring materially better results.

- Nonstandard meta data may be ineffective (see [Utah]).

- Incorrect meta data inevitably provides worse results than no meta data (see [Sokvitne 2000]).

- Meta data can be expensive to create (see [St. Laurent 2003] and [Bray 2003]).

- The potential for spoofing and distortion is inherent in any self-describing markup.

The second and third points suggest that semantic markup and classification contained in each page could be useful within a company's intranet; where access is controlled, self-promotion would (presumably) be minimized, and the domains of interest would be relatively restricted. But for the fully connected Web, the situation is very different. Semantic markup should still be useful, but less for pure search purposes than for processing once a resource has been found.

5.4.2 *Semantic Web possibilities for improving searching*

Since self-describing meta data can be unreliable for general Web searches and social analysis is turning out to be increasingly valuable, it would seem that Semantic Web technologies could be the most useful in several general ways:

- *Make self-description more reliable*—This involves issues of trustworthiness, the subject of chapter 10. Meta data within a page could be digitally signed to attest to its source, and search engines would be able to take into account the source and its potential motives in using that information to rate the page. Social analysis might be applied to the trustworthiness of different sites or authors that added semantic data to their own documents, so that appropriate weights could be applied in deriving page rankings. So far, I haven't seen this approach discussed in literature or online technical discussion groups, but it seems logical and potentially powerful.

- *Make more information available for social analysis*—This could involve third-party annotations. That is, people would publish comments on particular web pages in a knowledge-representation language like RDF. Of course, people comment on web pages all the time now, but they do so in natural language terms. One way this approach could evolve would be for advanced natural and link analysis results to be transformed into RDF and published on the Web. Any pages that contained semantic markup would be that much easier to analyze and add to the data store. Such a movement—grass-roots social analysis—is starting to take place in the web logging (or *blogging*) communities. Bloggers link to each others' blogs, and rankings showing the blogs with the most links pointing to them are becoming available. Some people are experimenting with tools to do further analysis. The results aren't yet created in something like RDF, but the point is that there is a low-key spread of social analysis.

- *Use data integration techniques, such as those used by TAP*—This approach would require servers to present the data stored in their databases in a standard way, such as with RDF. A server would have to be able to retrieve data by matching graph fragments as well as by its identifier.

There are obviously other ways in which technologies developed for the Semantic Web could potentially improve search capabilities; many of them have been mentioned previously. Other search improvements are being developed that seem, at least on the surface, to not really involve the Semantic Web per se, and so they haven't been covered here. But the line is not always easy to draw.

5.4.3 *Searching and web services*

Chapter 8 discusses services. The search for services has a lot in common with the search for other kinds of information on the Internet. There is a difference in motivation for the information provider, especially for business and commercial services, because the service provider has a financial stake in having the service found and chosen.

If businesses are to cooperate in making services findable and usable on the Internet, they will have to adopt a means that will minimize any advantage one company has over the others. Is it better for a travel service to be able to find flights on any airline or just on those airlines that pay enough money to be privileged members of the service? Increasingly, businesses are coming to see that common access is good for everyone in the long run. If this trend prevails, the Semantic Web will have much to offer in the way of discovery and description of services.

5.5 *Summary*

This chapter has ended up in a surprising place. At first glance, it would seem that the future of searching, from a Semantic Web point of view, would be the large-scale introduction of marked-up semantic information into web resources, augmented by carefully developed ontologies. Classical logical reasoning techniques would be applied to the classification of the pages, and consequently searches would be far more effective than they are now.

Instead, you've seen that self-description in pages is unreliable and that social analysis of links and opinions together with the semantic analysis of the natural language of pages will probably continue to be of the greatest importance. You've also seen that intelligent analysis of the context of the queries themselves is likely to add significant effectiveness to searches. These realizations lead to questions about the trustworthiness of self-supplied information even if it's impeccably marked up with the latest technologies, and to the possibility that the stores of annotations and opinions the Semantic Web will make available may be an important contribution to searching.

The role of logic

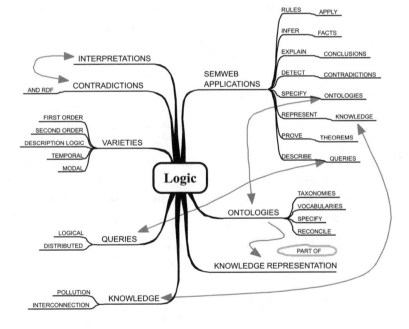

…Other truths are immutable, such as "I am not elsewhere." I mean, wherever I go I cannot get away from me! It is sort of frightening. That would be called "TRUTH."

—Severn Darden, *Lecture on Metaphysics*

In daily life, we encounter this sort of thing all the time: "OK, you say you're Mr. Robert Smith, your driver's license says you're Mr. Robert Smith, the picture looks like you, the age seems right, and a Mr. Robert Smith of the same address has an account at this bank, so according to our bank rules I can cash your check."

This is one form—a familiar, everyday form—of *reasoning*: the art or science of drawing conclusions. Logic as a branch of philosophy is the study of correct reasoning, used as a means to arrive at correct conclusions. As a closely related branch of mathematics, Logic is the study of systems of reasoning. You're probably familiar with the use of logical reasoning to prove mathematical theorems—if you studied geometry in school, you'll remember wrestling with proofs. Logical reasoning, however, is commonly applied to all kinds of statements—not just statements pertaining to branches of mathematics, but also statements in natural language. For the Semantic Web, computers will need to apply logical reasoning to all kinds of "statements" (which may be data in various forms), and those statements will be distributed across the Web.

6.1 *What logic is good for*

Logic is likely to play many different roles for the Semantic Web. The term *logic*, as used here, is intended to indicate formal logic, the result of technical study. Where and how would logic be useful in the design of software for the Semantic Web? Putting together the many visions and scenarios that are sketched in chapter 1, we can expect to see logic at work in at least the following ways:

- Applying and evaluating rules, as in Mr. Smith's check-cashing adventure.
- Inferring facts that haven't been explicitly stated. If Mr. Smith is found to have a mother named Susan, then it may be inferred that there is a female person called by that name.
- Explaining why a particular conclusion has been reached. A system could explain why Mr. Smith should be granted the privilege of having his check cashed. This capability may turn out be quite important.
- Detecting contradictory statements and claims.
- Specifying ontologies and vocabularies of all kinds. This subject is discussed in chapter 7.

- Representing knowledge. Logic plays an important role here. In part, logic describes the kinds of things that may be said about a subject, and how those statements are to be understood.

- Playing a key role in the statement and execution of queries to obtain information from stores of data on the Semantic Web.

- Combining information from distributed sources in a coherent way.

Many of these capabilities have been implemented in one or another piece of software for years. We'll briefly look at how the Semantic Web may relate to them.

6.1.1 *Rules*

The use of rules to prescribe the behavior of software may be the oldest practice in the field of computing. Indeed, most programs can be considered to consist of a series of rules. However, here we mean a more specialized kind of rule, the kind often used by so-called expert systems:

```
IF <logical conditions are met>
THEN <perform specified actions>
```

Obviously, evaluating the truth of the logical conditions involves logic, but there is more to it. Rules are often *chained* together. Here's an example in which part of a recipe for making bread has been rewritten in the form of a collection of rules:

```
1   IF the first rising is finished
         THEN form loaf AND place it into loaf pan.
2   IF loaf has been rising for 1.5 hours
         THEN begin preheating oven.
3   IF dough is in loaf pan AND dough volume has doubled
         THEN set condition "dough has risen".
4   IF oven is hot AND dough has risen
         THEN insert bread in oven.
```

A processor can work backward from one condition to work out what had to happen to get there. For example, if the condition "dough is risen" is true, then steps 1 and 2 must have happened already. Conversely, a processor can work forward to figure out the consequences that must ensue if a certain condition has been met. Thus you can ask, say, whether a certain outcome is possible. If the processor can trace its way through the rule set and arrive at the result, it can report that the outcome is possible and how to get to it. In this way, a rules-based system can go beyond simply controlling a system according to the rules and simulate a reasoner that has practical knowledge of a particular field.

Of course, a real set of rules is likely to be much more complicated. There will probably be many alternatives that could be taken according to the conditions, so the rules can be diagrammed as a kind of branching tree. The Semantic Web will have several additional needs:

- *A Web-compatible language for expressing rules*—Currently, no such standard exists. There are developing proposals for using rules with RDF (Resource Description Framework; see chapter 2), and some work is in progress. Topic Map systems (see chapter 3) have been used to define sets of rules.

- *The ability to specify the kinds of rules and their relationships and constraints*— This by rights should be part of ontology (see chapter 7), but rules capability hasn't yet been integrated with the likely standard ontology languages. There have been proposals, and work is in progress.

- *Ways to handle incompatible rules*—If rules are collected from several sources distributed across the Web, some of them might be incompatible. There need to be practical ways to deal with this possibility.

6.1.2 *Inferring facts*

In the example, Mr. Smith is said to have a mother named Susan, but the system has no record of a person with that name. Provided that the system's knowledge base contains the right information, a system could find that

- Mr. Smith is a person.

- A mother is a female of the same species as its child. Therefore, Mr. Smith's mother is a female person named Susan.

- A person known to the system must have a record.

Thereupon, the system might create such a record, linked by a *child* relationship to Mr. Smith. Notice that the system had to infer that the record to be added concerned a person, and that the person was female. These facts weren't stored previously but were implied by others that were known. For the Semantic Web, the known collection of facts may be very large and possibly not fully consistent.

There is an important distinction between an *open world* and a *closed world*. In a closed world, all relevant facts are known, so the absence of a data record is just as definitive as the existence of one. When information is missing, a negative conclusion is justified. In a closed world, Mr. Smith does *not* work here if he isn't in the database. An open world doesn't contain all relevant information— more might become available at any time. In an open world, Mr. Smith *might* work here even if there is no such record. Clearly, an open-world system works differently from a closed-world one. The Semantic Web will be a very large, open system.

In a large, open, and relatively uncontrolled world, there is a considerable risk that a system will absorb contradictory or incorrect information. This has some potential to lead to serious problems, a concern that surfaces in several places in this and other chapters.

6.1.3 *Explanations*

In a scenario in chapter 1, a digital personal assistant explains itself:

> I checked his affiliation with university of Montana, he is cited several times in their web pages: reasonably trusted; I checked his publication records from publishers' DAML sources and asked bill assistant a rating of the journals: highly trusted.

The ability to explain a train of reasoning may emerge as one of the most important capabilities a Semantic Web reasoning system can have. If Mr. Smith is allowed access to a bank account, it may become important *why* the conclusion was reached. Some reasoning systems can capture explanations, but so far those that can emit the results do so in specialized, hardly readable ways.

6.1.4 *Contradictions and interpretations*

You've seen that the Semantic Web will be a large, open system that may contain contradictory information. What will happen if a Semantic Web system encounters a contradiction? This isn't a trivial matter, because in pure logic, a contradiction would allow *anything* to be proven. This would probably lead to many unpleasant consequences.

The obvious thing to do would be to regard each statement known to the system—let's suppose we're dealing with RDF statements—as a kind of claim that may or may not be strongly supported. This would be hard to do with RDF, because there's no simple and direct way in RDF to talk about a statement itself. A program could do so using its own specially developed techniques, but there would be no ready way to exchange the information with other systems.

To provide an alternative, the current version of the RDF specifications (which have recently replaced the W3C's original RDF Recommendation) define a way to understand the meaning of a collection of RDF statements that can deal with the possibility of contradictory information, albeit at the cost of more computing power. In this approach, you consider a hypothetical world that might be compatible with the statements in question. If two statements are contradictory, there would be no such worlds—no state of affairs—in which both statements are true. This situation might be unfortunate, but it wouldn't be a disaster.

A hypothetical state of affairs of this nature is called an *interpretation*. To make this abstract notion more concrete, let's look at an example.

Bob and his house

Suppose we're given this statement:

Bob is standing in front of his house.

This brings to mind a man and a house. We may suppose that it's a man because Bob is usually the name of a man rather than of a woman. Let's add the statement:

Bob is a dog.

Suddenly we realize that Bob might have been a dog all along. Either interpretation would have been consistent with the known facts.

The two statements together are consistent with Bob being in front of either a human house—the house of his owner, where he (Bob) lives—or in front of his dog house in the back yard. Each possibility corresponds to a different interpretation. Of course, there are many other possible interpretations. Bob may be a female dog and could be any variety of dog. Interpretations in which Bob is male or female, and in which Bob is one or another breed of dog, are all consistent with the two statements. Interpretations in which Bob is a horse or a Martian aren't.

If we add to our knowledge base a taxonomy of types of creatures, we could infer that Bob is a mammal. In terms of interpretation and entailment, we can say that our knowledge base entails that Bob is a mammal, because in any interpretation in which our two statements are true and our taxonomy holds, Bob must be a mammal. We don't have to know that everything in our knowledge base is true, just that it's all consistent for any feasible interpretation. Under the right conditions, a computer can make such a determination.

In any practical situation, it's unlikely that we could have enough information to eliminate all but one interpretation. It's more productive to seek those things that can be true for any feasible interpretation.

This approach, making use of interpretations, helps to prevent disasters in the face of contradictions, but contradictions must still be dealt with. A practical reasoner for the Semantic Web will have to be able to detect and report apparent contradictions, giving the user a chance to decide how they should be handled.

6.1.5 *Ontologies*

Another area of great importance for the Semantic Web involves ontologies. An ontology establishes the things that a system can talk and reason about. This means the vocabulary, but as chapter 7 discusses, there's more to it than just a collection of words and names—the terms have logical relationships to each other that need to be specified, and this in turn means that any ontology system must adopt some variety of logic, either formally or informally.

On an abstract level, logic is used to represent knowledge, at least the kind of knowledge that is well defined enough to be clearly stated and discussed. Ontology supplies the concepts and terms; logic provides ways to make statements that define and use them, and to reason about collections of statements that use the concepts and terms. Where will those "collections of statements" come from? From web pages, from databases, and from other knowledge bases. They may be expressed in RDF, stored as a topic map, or contained in a SOAP message[1]—there are many possibilities, but some degree of standardization in the description of the underlying ontologies is needed to piece everything together.

In the Semantic Web, the role of logic will be very different from the role of most other components of the Semantic Web layer cake. In areas from meta data to knowledge representation to web services to searching, information will be exchanged, normally with standardized formats like RDF, and then processed by a program that may in turn obtain further data from sources spread across the Web. Ontologies will be shared and merged. But logic comes into play differently, because it isn't information to be exchanged.

In mathematics classes, we usually don't receive instructions about the logic of arithmetic with each problem we're given to solve. The necessary logic to use is normally assumed. Only in exceptional cases would it be necessary to say, "Solve this problem using logic of type *X*." Similarly, no languages are yet being standardized for the Web to define the specific kind of logic to be used as part of an exchange of information. It's assumed that a suitable form of logic will be applied to information by the users of that information, and that valid conclusions can be formed, even if the provider of that information has made different assumptions about the form of logic or its interpretation. In some cases, such as the latest work on RDF, constraints have been placed on the rules of logic to be applied, but this practice is still uncommon. The closest thing to a transmission

---

[1] SOAP is a standard for packaging a message, usually in XML. It's most often used with web services (see chapter 8).

of logic will probably be an exchange of the results of a logical calculation, namely the results of a proof or the steps of reasoning that led to it. Otherwise, the variety of logic may be indicated only by the ontology in use.

6.1.6 *The representation of knowledge*

Logic as a formal discipline deals mostly with formal languages that can express a subset of everything that can be articulated using natural languages. The formal description of data and information thus naturally involves logic. Many systems of notation have been developed to express logical descriptions. RDF, for one, has a basis in formal logic. Not all languages have the same ability to express information, and RDF's ability is fairly weak, although it's adequate for capturing simple data and meta data about specific subjects.

Ontology languages can increase RDF's power, but other, more expressive languages exist. At the time of this writing, though, these older, more expressive languages aren't well suited for use on the Web. It's unclear whether one or another of these older languages will be redesigned, whether current languages like RDF will be extended, or whether an entirely new language may be developed to provide more expressive power. What is certain is that RDF as it exists now can't express many things that will need to be communicated. Some of these are discussed elsewhere in the chapter, including *negation* of a statement, *quantification* ("for all..."), and *modal logic*. However, it's also clear that RDF and Topic Maps can contain the kinds of data that are normally captured in databases, and that capability will go a long way as the Semantic Web evolves.

6.1.7 *Queries*

A *query* can be thought of as a logical description of information to be retrieved from a database. For an effective Semantic Web, queries will need to operate across distributed sources of data. In turn, this means they will have to be able to reconcile the different ontologies in use and to deal effectively with the problems of contradictory information discussed in section 6.1.4. In addition, a thorough response to a query may require the queried system to perform a lot of inference to satisfy the request.

To illustrate, a query about birds would be expected to return information about eagles and flamingos. A flamingo, however, might have been recorded as an aquatic bird, and the system would have to discover that an aquatic bird is a kind of bird before it could know that it should return information about flamingos as well as about eagles. In many cases, this process could be very resource intensive.

Queries that wish to take full advantage of the expected capabilities of the Semantic Web systems are likely to be more complex and require more computing power than ordinary database queries we're familiar with. They will have to exploit a number of these systems' logical capabilities.

6.1.8 *Combining information*

In previous parts of section 6.1, you've seen that problems can arise from trying to combine information from multiple sources on the Semantic Web. Here are some of the most prominent:

- *Different sources may use different ontologies (different vocabularies for the same things)*—Considerable work has gone into the development of an ontology language for the Semantic Web to make it suitable for piecing together different ontologies; but even so, there will be no easy, universal solutions.

- *Different sources may have different semantics for the (apparently) same things*—As an example, a Person in one database might mean a human who works for the company, whereas a Person in another database might mean any human being. The more precisely these things are defined (which again involves ontologies), the less of a problem such discrepancies will be, but here too there will be no easy solutions.

- *Different sources may contain contradictory information*—This topic is covered in section 6.1.4 and also in chapter 10.

- *Different sources may have different degrees of reliability*—This is a complex problem, also discussed in chapter 10. Whatever solutions may be developed, they will involve logical descriptions and reasoning to capture reliability information and apply it effectively. This area is likely to be important in the future, and it's currently not well developed.

6.2 *All logics aren't created equal*

Philosophers and mathematicians, have thought and argued about logic and reasoning for thousands of years. Over this long stretch of time, many systems of logic have been developed, many fine distinctions have been drawn, and new interpretations have been applied to older ideas. The variety of "logics" can seem overwhelming: first-order logic, second-order logic, temporal logic, modal logic, fuzzy logic, description logic, and many more.

By and large, only specialists need to be concerned about the types of logic, except that the terminology shows up from time to time in discussions about

Semantic Web technologies. This section discusses some of the more common terms and notions you may encounter in articles and discussion lists. You can skip the section if this sort of detail doesn't interest you.

6.2.1 *First-order logic: the logic of individual things*

First-order logic (FOL) lets you make statements about things and collections of things, their types and properties, and to qualify them, describe them, or relate them to other things. Statements like "This ball is red" and "Robert Smith is married to Jane Smith" are simple examples. FOL doesn't (in its usual flavors) say much about properties or relationships—usually called *predicates*—themselves (predicates like "red" and "is married to," for example), beyond specifying their types and where they may be used.

FOL is generally considered the most significant and most complete logic, because the higher-order logics can be considered extensions of it.[2] FOL is also considered fundamental because (with a bit of extension) it can define all of mathematics. This represents a great deal of *expressive power*.

6.2.2 *Second-order logic: the logic of types and relationships*

In addition to specific individual things, we're often interested in properties and also in the kinds of things there are. *Second-order logic* adds extensions that allow general statements to be made about whole classes of properties and relationships. This provides a capability to describe them in great detail, at the expense of more demanding computation.

To be able to classify things, we need FOL; but to define the classification categories themselves and to talk about their relationships, we also need higher-order logic. That would be undesirable because solving even full FOL problems, let alone second-order logic problems, can be intractable. In many cases, the computations are resource intensive; in some cases, no answer can be computed, even in principle. In one well-known case, it isn't possible to prove whether an arbitrary computer program will ever stop or whether it will continue to execute indefinitely (some programs can be proven to stop eventually, like a program that plays tic-tac-toe, but not all). This wouldn't be good for widespread deployment on the Semantic Web. The trick is to find subsets of logic that are useful but, in the kinds of situations usually encountered, will be practical to compute.

---

[2] Any short statement like this about logic, especially by a non-specialist, is bound to be an oversimplification. Our intent here is to be informative, not rigorous.

6.2.3 *Finessing complexity*

To make it possible to control the complexity of reasoning tasks, it's necessary to impose restrictions on the forms of logic that are allowed. With a judicious design, it turns out to be possible to talk about types and properties and still be sure (or just reasonably sure, in some cases) that the computations can be accomplished.

Logicians have been developing FOL subsets specialized for classifying things for many years. A certain group of these forms of logic has come to be called *Description Logics*.[3] (Nardi and Brachman 2003, *Description Logics*, Horrocks 2002) Since they're designed for classification tasks, they're good for creating ontologies. There are multiple families of Description Logics, representing slightly different subsets of FOL. Description Logics are carefully designed so that they're amenable to mathematical analysis and so that results can be mathematically proven to be computable. This is a strength. On the other hand, the price of this mathematical tractability comes in the form of limitations on their expressive power—that is, in the kinds of things that can be said using them.

Description Logics have been used in the design of certain ontology languages for the Semantic Web (more in chapter 7).

6.2.4 *Life beyond first-order logic*

Many variants of logic might be useful but aren't yet provided for in the standards under development for the Semantic Web. With *temporal logic*, a statement may be true at one time but not at another ("Today I turned 60 years old"). There are various *modal logics*, in which statements may be contingent in various ways instead of just being true (or false)—that is, they might be true but aren't necessarily true. One such contingency or mode is possibility ("It's *possible* that I own a Jaguar automobile"). There are many others ("I *intend* to go to work this morning;" "I *know* that 2 + 2 = 4"), each of which potentially has its own variety of modal logic.

Much of the information that is likely to be available on the Web will probably be modal to some degree, so we can expect the knowledge representation languages to be extended over time to provide support for modal expressions.

---

[3] "In a Description Logic–based Knowledge Representation System such as NeoClassic, a model of a domain consists of a description of the *concepts* (kinds of individuals) that exist in the domain plus a description of each of the *individuals* in terms of these concepts and relationships between individuals." (Patel-Schneider et al 1998a)

6.3 Two pitfalls

The open nature of the Semantic Web will bring with it many difficulties along with the hoped-for benefits. This section talks about two of them. They are chosen because they are both, in a way, unusual and non-intuitive, and both, of course, involve the application of logic for representing and manipulating information.

6.3.1 Don't swallow the whole Web

Suppose we're collecting information to put into a knowledge base. We find a statement that refers to information in another knowledge base—or ontology—on a remote web site. To understand more about the thing referred to, we might seek to import more of the remote data—that is, to combine it with our own knowledge base. Now, the bit we're looking at is probably tied into a network of interconnected information (perhaps a whole collection of RDF statements). A big question is, how much should we import from the remote site?

The obvious answer would be to import the whole data set from the remote site. That way, we could understand everything the remote site understands, and we might need to do so to understand the item we started with. There are two problems, however, one of which is moderate and the other of which could be catastrophic:

■ *Size of the remote knowledge base*—The remote knowledge base might be very large, so large that it would overwhelm our resources. This would be akin to starting to download a huge video file without knowing how big it is.

■ *How much is interconnected?*—The potentially more serious issue is this: Once we imported the remote knowledge base, we presumably would examine it and probably discover statements that referred to yet another remote knowledge base. Presumably we should import that one as well. If there is a web of interconnected knowledge bases, we could end up trying to ingest the entire Web, one site after another. We have to stop somewhere, or we'll be in big trouble.

Dealing with an import that is too large isn't difficult. But a world-wide trail of interconnected facts and sites is another. How can we prevent such an unbridled and indigestible meal? There is no standard answer so far. Obviously, we don't want to automatically trigger an import just because we've acquired a new statement or new information. Fortunately, an RDF engine doesn't have to import one graph of statements after another. It's allowed to stop. A topic map can refer to a topic located in a remote topic map, but the behavior of a topic map engine that encounters such a reference isn't defined. It will probably be defined in the next round of specifications, which are in draft form at the time of this writing.

6.3.2 *Knowledge pollution*

If a system imports unreliable information, it could conceivably contaminate much of the good data it already has. From what we said earlier in this chapter, certain lessons are clear. Obviously, all statements (information or knowledge) should be regarded as claims rather than simply taken as true. Reasoning software must be designed to handle the real possibility that it might encounter conflicting information—we don't want an automatic proving mechanism to prove that Bob should get access to sensitive information just because we have conflicting data. Think how easily a malicious person could arrange to poison whole systems otherwise. The notion of interpretations (section 6.1.4) has some ability to resist this kind of knowledge pollution. Well, poisoning would still be possible, but it would have a milder consequence—instead of allowing unauthorized access (in this example of Bob's access), we wouldn't allow any access (which is safer), but we would also get a warning about the problem.

On the other hand, the calculations required to perform some of these reasoning tasks can take a long time. It's even possible that certain calculations might not ever finish. What's more, we can't always prove whether some calculations will finish, depending on the complexity of the problem. As mentioned in section 6.2.3, by restricting the kind of logical descriptions that are allowed, calculations can at least be guaranteed to complete and possibly to complete within known times. Once again a tradeoff exists between computational complexity and the ability to decide on the one hand, versus expressiveness on the other. It's the old tradeoff of risk versus opportunity; only experience will let us learn the proper mix.

6.4 *Patchwork quilt or seamless whole?*

Because computer systems can't communicate without sharing a language, it's sometimes argued that universal, world-wide vocabularies will be necessary for the Semantic Web. Otherwise, how could my computer understand yours? Historically, such universality has happened only a few times, most notably with the World Wide Web and its Universal Resource Locators, Hypertext Transfer Protocol, and Hypertext Markup Language. As you know, these things allow computers to interchange information without necessarily understanding anything about it. They're also fairly simple, as computer technologies go.

In other words, there's the possibility of a common infrastructure (if it doesn't get too complicated)—for example, RDF + OWL + HTTP + URIs—but there's little hope for widespread agreement on complex ontologies. And without universal ontologies, pessimists see practically no likelihood of there ever being a Semantic Web. But there is a different view.

A Semantic Web system need not be able to understand everything on the Web at any one time. Rather, depending on its task, it must be able to access information anywhere, but only if it's of an appropriate variety. Such information can be built up in a piecemeal fashion. Vocabularies can be patched together as they're needed. In some cases, the knowledge base and ontology would be pieced together from sources distributed across the Web, whereas in other cases they might be supplied by the system developers. What will be important is the ability to apply such knowledge across the Web and to augment local knowledge as necessary to do so. The foundational Semantic Web technologies, like RDF and OWL, are designed to make this kind of piecework approach feasible.

6.5 *Summary*

This chapter has given you something of an overview of the relation between the Semantic Web and the field of logic. To learn more about this ancient and complex discipline, you might start with (Enderton 2001) and (Joseph 2002).[4] Logic as a discipline is extremely technical and doesn't lend itself to brief descriptions, but some aspects should be clear.

Perhaps the most important point is that the Semantic Web will be an open world. Everything must be designed with this in mind. It will be not only open but unreliable, since any given resource on the Web may be unavailable at any time, and also because any resource may contain errors (maybe even intentional lies). Any logic system will have to deal with these facts and do so on a very large scale.

You saw that the Semantic Web will, at best, give us conclusions that are entailed by interpretations of our knowledge bases. We'd rather have absolute truth, but that, as always, will be elusive.

---

[4] These two works could hardly be more different. Enderton (2001) is a modern textbook on logic, filled with current-day notations and concepts. Joseph (2002) is an exposition of classical logic and grammar as taught in generations of Catholic schools. Yet this second work is connected to the foundations of the study of logic as it was developed by, for example, Aristotle.

7

Ontology

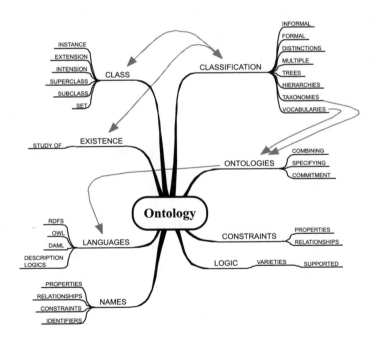

Metaphysics is "What is everything, anyhow?" and what's more is more than what's less—generally.

—Severn Darden, *Lecture on Metaphysics*

"What's the use of their having names" the Gnat said, "if they won't answer to them?"
"No use to THEM," said Alice; "but it's useful to the people who name them, I suppose. If not, why do things have names at all?"

—Lewis Carroll, *Through the Looking Glass*

People classify things easily, invisibly, and constantly. At this moment, you yourself may be silently classifying this chapter as "vital" or "peripheral." There is some scholarly dispute as to whether most of us use the same simple, perhaps built-in, underlying hierarchical classification system; but if we do that system is nearly invisible in daily life. People use complex rules in their classifications, and they bend or change those rules all the time; but so far machines need more formality and stability.

Ontology is the study of "being" or existence. In knowledge management and computer science, it has come to mean the kinds of things that can be talked about in a system or context. Ontology provides the means to classify these things, to give these classifications names and labels, and to define the kind of properties and relationships they can be assigned. In this way, Ontology and Logic (the subject of the previous chapter) are closely connected.

The arrangement of kinds of things into types and categories with a well-defined structure is also called an ontology. There is *Ontology*, the discipline, and there are specific *ontologies*. The kinds of things described by an ontology are, of course, normally given names so people can read and speak them. An ontology thus provides a vocabulary of terms for use in a specific domain. The arrangement of these terms and their organization is sometimes called a *taxonomy*, meaning both "the study of the general principles of scientific classification" and "orderly classification of plants and animals according to their presumed natural relationships."[1] However, ontologies usually contain more information than just an arrangement of terms into a hierarchy, as you'll see.

For the purposes of the Semantic Web, we want to have standard languages to define ontologies, we want them to be well adapted to the forms of logic to be used, we want to access them over the Web so ontologies can be shared and put

---

[1] *Merriam-Webster Collegiate Dictionary* online, www.merriam-webstercollegiate.com.

into widespread use, and we want to be able to combine parts of different ontologies. We also want to be able to classify all kinds of concepts and resources, both network-accessible and not.

7.1 Basic classification

The classification that people do so easily every day might be called *informal*. More formality is in order when precision is needed, as it is for scientific work and for computer systems that want to understand each other's information. Formal classification systems need a plan for their organization. The simplest kind of organization is the hierarchical list.

7.1.1 Lists, hierarchies, and trees

People naturally understand lists and hierarchies. If you're asked to write down a menu, chances are, you'll create a hierarchical list. Here's a dinner menu that has just two levels in its hierarchy:

```
Dinner
     Chicken
     Potatoes
     Asparagus
Dessert
     Ice Cream
     Flan
Beverages
     Water
     White Wine
```

This example isn't a truly a classification scheme—for example, Chicken isn't some kind of Dinner, but rather a part of a dinner. But it's natural to try to classify things with a hierarchy.

In a more strict classification hierarchy, which is sometimes called a *tree*, each term is a *kind* of its parent term, as opposed to being a *part*. Figure 7.1 shows an example.

In such a classification tree, the branching is based on judgments about distinctions that can be drawn between the categories, such as Animal *versus* Plant. Naturally, this won't work well if the distinctions aren't clear. Tree diagrams, like lists, are often drawn so that a more general classification is higher in the diagram than a more specific classification. The classification term immediately above another is sometimes called its *parent*.

The example shown in figure 7.1 is a typical kind of classification scheme; similar ones have been proposed for thousands of years. However, the world is

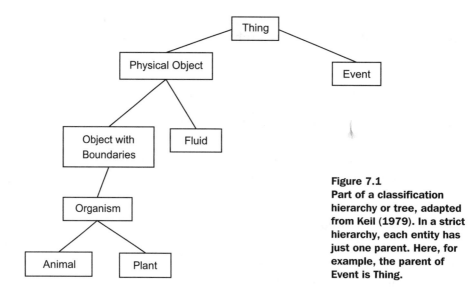

Figure 7.1
Part of a classification hierarchy or tree, adapted from Keil (1979). In a strict hierarchy, each entity has just one parent. Here, for example, the parent of Event is Thing.

complex, and a hierarchy is often too simple to capture the essence of the relationship between things. For instance, entities may partake of some qualities from more than one parent. Figure 7.2, which depicts a small part of the Cyc ontology,

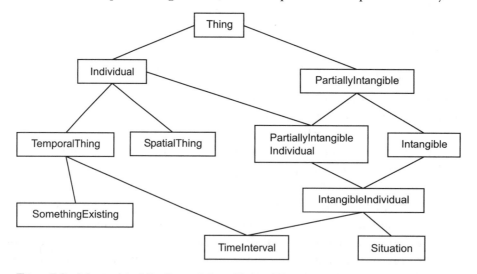

Figure 7.2 A fragment of the Cyc ontology. Many of the categories have more than one ancestor—higher-level categories—and many categories have more than one descendant. Many real-world situations require such an interconnected design since they're too complex for a single hierarchy. An automobile might be classified as Internal Combustion—Petroleum Fueled—Gasoline and also as Passenger Car-Two Seater at the same time.

is an example. Cyc is an extremely complicated semantic system that aims to capture enough knowledge so that a computer can perform everyday-style reasoning. Doing so takes an enormous amount of knowledge with a complex and subtle structure, part of which is depicted in the diagram.

7.1.2 Classification groups

Things are grouped into categories variously called *types*, *kinds*, *sorts*, or *classes*. Which word people use depends on their background. In this chapter, we'll use the word *class* to denote classification categories. We'll sometimes also use the word *type*, as in "a car is a type of vehicle."

Classification by enumeration: the extension

You can group things into classes in two basic ways: by their properties or by listing all the members. Take, for instance, the members of a club. What distinguishes the club members from everyone else? Obviously, the fact that they belong to the club. You can list the members, and if you're on the list, then you're a member. The list of members of a class is sometimes called the *extension* of the class. When you query a database, you get back the extension of the class of data objects that match the query.

Classification by definition: the intension

Alternatively, the club might say that a person is a member if they have paid their dues this year. This method specifies a criterion rather than an enumeration. A definition that defines the criteria for inclusion in a class is sometimes called its *intension* (*not* its *intention*).

An amusement park may have a sign that says, "You must be at least 4½ feet tall for these rides." This is the intension of the class of allowed riders. In a way, the duality of intension-extension parallels the duality in which a specific thing may be known by an identifier or by its collection of properties and relationships.

Classes, subclasses, and instances

Suppose we have invented a class, Cat. This class may have actual instances—that is to say, cats. Of those cats, some may be calico cats: female cats that have patches of orange, white, and black coloring their bodies. We're free to invent a new class, called CalicoCat. All our calico cats belong to this new class (by definition). But they still belong to the class Cat, too. CalicoCat is called a *subclass* of Cat, and Cat is the *superclass* of CalicoCat. Figure 7.3 illustrates these relationships.

Other terminology may also be used for the relationship of such related categories, depending on your viewpoint and the system of organization: You may

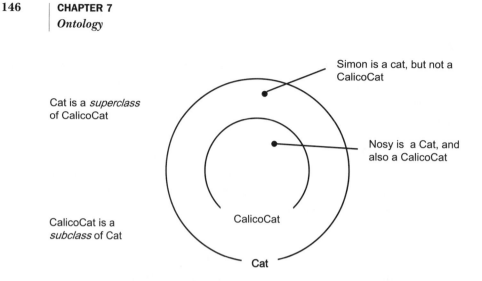

Cat is a *superclass* of CalicoCat

Simon is a cat, but not a CalicoCat

Nosy is a Cat, and also a CalicoCat

CalicoCat is a *subclass* of Cat

CalicoCat

Cat

Figure 7.3   Illustrating the relationship between classes and subclasses. All instances of the subclass, like Nosy the calico cat, are also instances of the superclass Cat. Instances of a superclass aren't necessarily instances of subclasses, just as Simon isn't an instance of CalicoCat (because Simon isn't calico colored).

speak of a *class-subclass, superclass-subclass, type-subtype,* or *supertype-subtype* relationship between connected classes or between two adjacent levels in a classification hierarchy.

A specific, individual thing such as a particular cat is called an *instance* of its class. This isn't a unique relationship, though, because the thing is also an instance of its class's superclass, and so on up the classification scheme. In figure 7.3, Nosy, a calico-colored cat, is an instance of CalicoCat, and she is also an instance of Cat (and she would also be an instance of Mammal, if we defined such a class).

Multiple classes

A thing can be an instance of more than one classification system. Our cat Nosy could also be placed in the class CityResidents, defined as beings that live in a city. The different classification systems don't need to have anything to do with each other. Figures 7.4 and 7.5 illustrate multiple classification systems applying to a brown dog.

Classes as sets

There are many ways to define classes, but most current ontology languages for the Web base them on *sets*. A class is considered to be a set of individuals that are collected together for the purpose of classification. A set is a mathematical structure

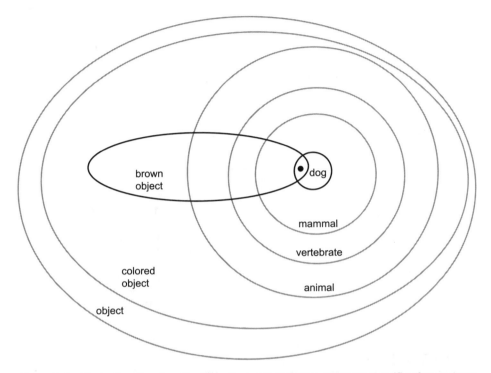

Figure 7.4 Illustrating the classification of an object by two different classification systems at the same time. In one, the object is a dog. In the other, it's a brown object. *Dog* and *brown object* have a small area of overlap, because a few brown objects are also dogs (and some dogs are brown objects). Figure 7.5 depicts the same classification schemes in a different view.

representing a collection of individuals, one that has no duplicates and in which the members of the collection aren't ordered. Sets are well understood mathematically, which helps ontology language designers devise systems that have certain desired characteristics. Ontology languages that use sets can be fairly easily aligned with theoretical results about logic.

Using sets, a class is the set whose members are exactly those instances that meet the criteria for the class. A subclass is a subset. This makes it clear that the subclass's members have all the same characteristics of their parent class, because the members of the subclass are (by definition) also members of the parent class.

The Web Ontology Language (OWL) family of languages, which you'll meet in section 7.4, has a subtly different definition of a class. Instead of having the class *contain* the instances, it's considered to be *associated* with them. This slight shift allows various mathematical theorems to be proven that would otherwise be difficult to prove.

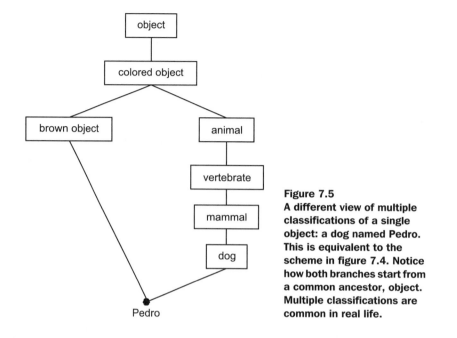

Figure 7.5
A different view of multiple classifications of a single object: a dog named Pedro. This is equivalent to the scheme in figure 7.4. Notice how both branches start from a common ancestor, object. Multiple classifications are common in real life.

7.2 *Arranging names*

In a very real sense, an ontology is about names and how they're related to each other. The names stand for concepts, categories, classes—call them what you will. The things named have various relationships with each other. A cat is a kind—a subclass—of animal. A rock isn't. The things named also have properties, and those properties have names as well. An ontology specifies the names in play, the properties of interest, and the relationships between them along with constraints on their proper use. An automobile, for instance, may have four wheels (or possibly three, depending on your definition of an automobile), but no more and no fewer. The names are used to specify the named concepts, so it's probably better to call them *identifiers*.

7.2.1 *Names and identifiers*

To build ontologies, we need a system of identifiers to refer to the types, classes, and properties we plan to create. People use names, but names aren't unique identifiers. As you saw in chapter 2, RDF has adopted the plan of identifying things by unique URI references, whether or not the identified things are addressable over the Web. Ambiguity is possible when the URI used for a concept also works to retrieve data from a web site. Does the URI indicate the specific web page or a concept defined on the page? You saw in chapter 3 that topic maps are able to avoid this kind of ambiguity; still, topic maps often use publicly published URIs to identify the subjects of topics. These two cases illustrate the use of URIs as identifiers, the current as standard practice for the Web, even when they don't point to any actual resource that could be received over the network.

The ontology frameworks currently being standardized for the Web (and they're specifically intended to be used for Semantic Web applications as well) are built on top of RDF, and so they also use URIs as identifiers. An ontology framework for Topic Maps won't be standardized for some time to come.

Unique identifiers are all very well, but people need to be able to read familiar names. Almost always, a thing or concept is assigned a readable name (or more than one) for this purpose. To make it clear that these names aren't the actual identifiers, we'll usually use the word *label* instead of *name*, because the term *name* is often used for identification purposes. A name or label can be considered to be a property of a thing or concept, and that's how they're frequently modeled.

7.2.2 *Properties*

In addition to classification categories, an ontology has to provide for properties. Properties, as you saw in earlier chapters, are often described as {name,value} pairs or some equivalent form. An example is {color,red}. In the graph model that underlies RDF, a property value is represented as a node connected to the property owner by an arc or *edge* that names the property. As you saw in chapter 2, the property type (such as `color`) is often called a *predicate*, implying a more general relationship than just *property*. A predicate refers to any binary relationship between two things; properties such as `color` and `weight` are particular types of binary relationships.

There are other different approaches to representing properties (such as the frame/slot method), but they're usually more or less equivalent from a logical point of view.

In object-oriented programming languages, objects have attributes or properties as part of their definitions. Their values are assigned when the program executes. This agrees with common usage, whereby an object owns its properties. If a ball is red, the color red "belongs" to the ball in a sense. When knowledge is represented on a computer system, the object representing the ball would be assigned a `color` property whose value would be "red" (chapter 3 discusses other ways to represent properties).

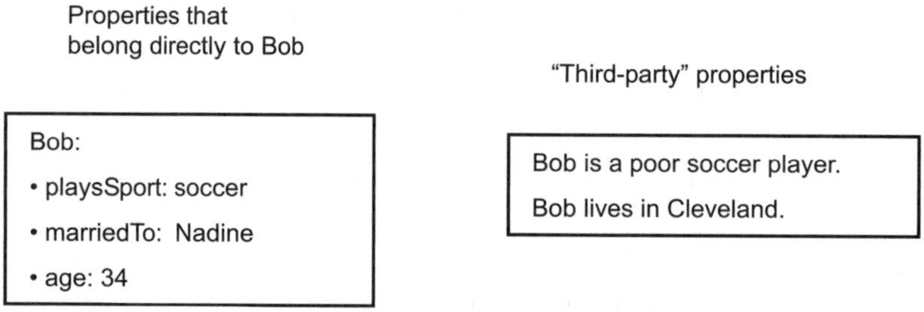

Properties that
belong directly to Bob

"Third-party" properties

Bob:

• playsSport: soccer

• marriedTo: Nadine

• age: 34

Bob is a poor soccer player.

Bob lives in Cleveland.

Figure 7.6 Contrasting owned properties with third-party properties. In programming, most properties *belong*—are directly associated with—the programming object they apply to. In the Semantic Web, most properties will be asserted by a third party rather than being an intrinsic part of their subject.

But in real life, objects can also have properties that they don't own. Consider a story in a magazine that says, "Robert Smith is a poor soccer player." We can write this claim as follows: {"Robert Smith", has-soccer-ability, "poor"}. This claim has been levied against Smith by a third party and may have nothing to do with Smith's intrinsic nature. On the Semantic Web, where the goal is to say anything about anything, most properties will be asserted in such a third-party way. The properties need not belong to the subject, unlike the case of programming objects. RDF, for one, provides this third-party capability. Figure 7.6 illustrates this distinction.

When a property isn't an inherent part of the definition of a thing, but instead is asserted separately, it's possible for the property to be applied in an inappropriate way. For example, let's say the property shows-time has a value "5:00 PM" and that it applies to a clock. It can't have a value "green", and shows-time would make no sense as a property of an ocean wave. The study of which natural-language predicates can have which kinds of values, and to which subjects they can apply—or better, which combinations are thought to be absurd versus which ones are seen as conceivable—is a fascinating piece of psychology. Ontologies establish which properties and types of values are appropriate by means of various constraints.

7.3 *Building ontologies*

One of the major functions of a specific ontology is to define a set of classes that together cover a domain of interest. For example, an ontology for sales would need to cover customers, purchase orders, sales receipts, catalog or inventory items, and so on. Many ontologies already in existence cover a variety of areas, and many more will exist in the future. Specific ontologies must be constructed with known vocabularies and rules of construction.

7.3.1 *Frameworks*

Section 7.4 discusses some of the more prominent ontology languages—which might better be called ontology construction languages—that are likely to play a role in the Semantic Web. They aren't specific ontologies but rather provide frameworks for constructing ontologies. Typically, the framework will provide a syntax, a vocabulary, and some predefined terms. You could almost say that an ontology framework is an ontology for constructing ontologies.

An ontology will generally define classes or categories, terms, and relationships. It will define what classes can be used with the relationships. It may also define datatypes, and it will define constraints on the uses of the classes and properties.

Ontologies aren't systems of logic—they provide the objects that are the subject of logical reasoning—but they may specify rules to support certain logical inferences. For example, an ontology system or framework may provide a standard way to specify that two classes are equivalent. A logical reasoner that encounters an instance of one of the classes would know that all the characteristics of the equivalent class apply as well.

7.3.2 *On designing ontologies*

Creating a good-quality ontology that is well-structured, is free from contradictions, and expresses the intent of the designers isn't easy. Of course, anyone can whip up a vocabulary of sorts in a minute. Here's one:

```
Living Thing
Plant
Animal
    Wild
    Pet
        Dog
        Cat
    Healthy
    Sick
```

We'd better stop here, because we already have big problems. For one thing, there can be wild cats and dogs as well as pet ones, but we probably don't want to repeat cats and dogs under Wild. For another, Wild, Pet, Healthy, and Sick aren't organisms. They describe certain qualities or states of organisms, and they don't belong in a hierarchy of living organisms. They may belong somewhere else in the ontology, but probably as values of as-yet-unnamed properties.

We might see a structure like this in a collection of browser bookmarks, but it isn't a proper ontology—it just looks something like one. The concepts aren't thought out or well structured.

The designer of a good ontology requires the ability to conceptualize and articulate the underlying ideas, a skill for modeling abstractions—it's much like creating a data model—and a good knowledge of the syntax of the ontology language so that the model is expressed correctly. Any one of these skills is hard to acquire, let alone all of them together. Besides that, an ontology is usually a compromise between different sets of needs, and often several groups are involved in the design. Like any other good design, a really good ontology will have artistic qualities too.

Although people will always create small ontologies for special purposes, you can see that it's a good idea to use a well-developed and accepted ontology whenever possible.

7.3.3 Other considerations

A variety of other practical considerations come up when you're using ontologies on a larger scale (larger, that is, than a personal or single-purpose application). You'll often want to use parts of more than one ontology; and since ontologies, like anything that is engineered, change over time through a process of evolution, you need to be able to adapt to version changes.

Merging ontologies

Sometimes you may want to use terms or classes from one ontology along with some from another. Suppose, for example, you have a software agent to make travel arrangements for you. The agent needs to understand the concepts and terms of airline companies, and also of, say, hotels. There are areas of possible overlap, because airlines and hotels might use different terms and formats for times and dates, and they probably use different concepts for the size and makeup of the traveling party. The agent doesn't need to know everything about the hotel business, but just enough to make a reservation at the right time for the right people. Figure 7.7 depicts a possible pair of ontologies your agent might need to work with.

Bringing one ontology into another is sometimes called *merging*. Another term is *import*—one ontology may import another. This process sounds simple but can be tricky. The obvious question is whether the merger can even be accomplished. If the two were built using the same system (like OWL, for example), a merger will usually be technically feasible. If the two were built with different

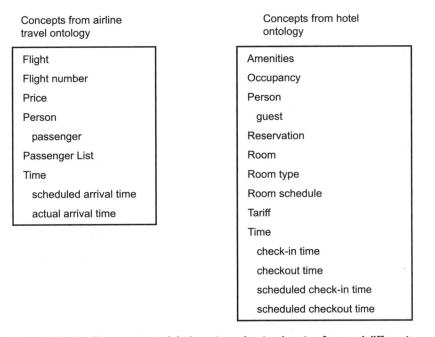

Concepts from airline travel ontology

Flight
Flight number
Price
Person
  passenger
Passenger List
Time
  scheduled arrival time
  actual arrival time

Concepts from hotel ontology

Amenities
Occupancy
Person
  guest
Reservation
Room
Room type
Room schedule
Tariff
Time
  check-in time
  checkout time
  scheduled check-in time
  scheduled checkout time

Figure 7.7 A software agent might have to understand parts of several different ontologies to make travel arrangements. Some terms might appear to be the same, yet they have differences in meaning. *Time* **might be one of these cases. Other terms might appear different but be essentially equivalent.** *Passenger* **and** *guest* **might fall into this category. And what is the relationship between** *actual arrival time* **and** *check-in time***?**

systems, it isn't clear whether they could be merged, even in principle. One must be mapped to the form of the other; but if they use incompatible design principles this may not be possible, or it may require that some information be ignored or added.

Even if two ontologies can be merged, the two may not be consistent. When there are inconsistencies, one of several outcomes will probably happen: Different conclusions could be reached by a reasoning engine, depending on the other statements known to the system and the design of the reasoner; or the conflicting classes will never have any instances (since no instances can satisfy the conflicting conditions); or the reasoner will discover the conflict and stop working on the task. An example would be a class representing a car, which in one ontology is restricted to having four wheels but in another is allowed to have three as well as four. What should happen when the system encounters a three-wheeled vehicle that is a car according to one ontology but not in the other?

In practice, the system would probably be able to distinguish two such classes, since coming from different ontologies, they would no doubt have different identifiers. But it's also likely that the system would know the two classes were supposed to represent the same kind of thing. This could happen because someone constructed a map between the two ontologies, or because the system itself was able to discover it. The safest way to prevent this kind of conflict would be to avoid including classes that apply to the same things. But this could be assured only if the merged ontologies covered completely separate domains.

More often, you don't want to bring in an entire ontology, possibly because it's very large and you only need a few bits. English uses some French words, but it hasn't imported the whole French language. The trick is to know how little of the second ontology you can import. Do you need to import all the parents of the classes you're interested in? All the relationships they participate in? All the rules?

The degree of support for merging ontologies varies from one ontology language to another.

Commitment

When you decide to use a particular ontology, you're said to *commit* to it. This indicates that you accept or assert all assertions and implications entailed by that ontology. In the example illustrated in figure 7.7, the agent trying to make travel arrangements would commit to the airline travel ontology. What if you want to use parts of an ontology, but you don't want to commit to everything in it, such as the hotel ontology in the example? Perhaps it's too big, perhaps you can't determine if you agree with everything, or perhaps you disagree but find some parts useful anyway. Imagine, if you will, that the Hotel ontology from figure 7.7 contains 2,000 terms, and that you only want to use Person, Room Type, and Reservation. Not only do you want to avoid cramming 1,997 unused terms into your system, but you also use the term *Amenities* differently than the Hotel ontology does. So, you don't want to commit to the entire ontology but only to those three bits.

There are no standard ways to handle such a case. In the future, this issue is likely to become increasingly important, so reliable methods will have to be developed.

Changes

In the real world of natural language, the meanings and usage of words change over time and often depend on context. Ontologies also change. Terms may be added or removed, and the definitions of existing ones may be changed or extended. Therefore, it's desirable for an ontology to be able to declare its version. But even if it can, there are still complex issues to consider.

Suppose an ontology you've been using changes to a new version. That could change inferences and conclusions you previously made. It could change significant parts of your knowledge base, or affect communications with agents or business partners. Of course, the ontology designer will try to make changes in such a way as to avoid these problems, but the designer may not fully succeed. There are no standard solutions at the time of this writing.

7.4 *Languages for ontologies*

After reading the preceding section, you may wonder whether ontologies will be more trouble than they're worth. Some people do feel repulsed; but in one form or another, communication requires a shared vocabulary at least. Even a simple list of terms is an ontology of sorts, as is a collection of definitions making the terms precise, so there is no getting away from them.

In this section, we'll look briefly at some of the ontology frameworks that seem likely to play an important part as the Semantic Web develops. They don't all occupy the same niche, and any of them may be superceded or extended. There are plenty of ontology languages and frameworks besides these, but most weren't designed with web-like uses in mind. Either they aren't yet expressed in a typical web language (meaning in practice an XML-based language) or they don't use identifiers that are suitable for large-scale Semantic Web deployment, or they don't look like they will become widely deployed. Of course, all these considerations may change over time.

The rest of this section includes a certain amount of detail. You may skip over it if the detail isn't for you. It's provided to illustrate how certain key frameworks operate, for those who find that sort of thing interesting.

7.4.1 *RDFS*

RDFS is the base RDF language for describing ontologies. In the 1999 version, which was a called a Proposed Recommendation, RDFS was short for Resource Description Framework Schema Specification. That version of RDFS was never issued as a final Recommendation by the W3C, but it came to be used anyway.

As part of the rework of RDF, RDFS has received attention too. Now it's called the RDF Vocabulary Description Language, but it's still known as RDFS. At the time of this writing, the revised version has developed past the Proposed Recommendation status to full Recommendation status.

Despite this rework, the form of RDFS hasn't changed much. Most of the changes have been in the documentation and formal interpretation. RDFS has been fairly stable in its form, and it's used by a number of other ontology language projects.

The language of RDFS

RDFS is built on top of RDF. Recall the bare bones of RDF from chapter 2. RDF is designed to make *statements* about *resources*. A resource represents a concept and is given a unique URI to identify it. A statement consists of three parts: a *subject*, a *predicate* (or *property),* and an *object*, which is to say, the value of a property. Because of the three parts, an RDF statement is often called a *triple*. A statement makes an assertion about its subject, like this:

```
{Bob, livesIn, Cleveland}
```

This statement, presumably about a person named "Bob", says Bob has a property called "livesIn" whose value is "Cleveland". These labels are put in quotes to indicate that the RDF processor may or may not know anything else about them. In a real bit of RDF, each of these three items would be a URI. "Bob", for example, might really be this URI: http://www.example.com/people#bob.

A collection of statements or triples can be called a *triples store* for convenience. A collection of triples is also called a *graph*, because it can be represented as a collection of nodes (the resources and literal values) connected by lines (the properties). Any given resource may be the subject of more than one statement, depending on the amount of information available about it. To say that RDFS is built on top of RDF is to say that everything that can be said in RDFS is stated in the language of RDF—which is to say, by RDF statements.

Every RDFS statement is therefore a legal RDF statement. The difference between RDF and RDFS is that the RDFS terms have no special meaning in RDF per se. The meaning of RDFS terms is defined by the W3C RDFS documents. That means a plain RDF processor, one that isn't programmed with knowledge of RDFS, will create the right triple in its triples store when it processes an RDFS statement, but it won't know what to do with it after that.

RDF classes and properties

The RDFS and RDF documents[2] define 13 classes between them. Here are those standard classes:

---

[2] That is, the current versions of these documents, as opposed to the 1999 RDF Recommendation.

`rdfs:Resource`—The Resource class

`rdfs:Class`—The class of classes

`rdf:Property`—The class of RDF properties

`rdfs:Literal`—The class of literal values (strings and integers)

`rdfs:XMLLiteral`—The class of XML literal values

`rdf:Statement`—The class of RDF statements

`rdfs:Container`—The class of Containers

`rdf:Bag`—The class of unordered containers

`rdf:Seq`—The class of ordered containers

`rdf:Alt`—The class of containers of alternatives

`rdfs:Container`—The class of RDF containers

`rdfs:ContainerMembershipProperty`—The class of container membership properties (`rdf:_1`, `rdf:_2`, and so on)

`rdf:list`—The class of RDF lists

These classes, along with the standard properties listed below, have enough expressive power to delineate ontologies but not enough to express many constraints or logical properties for them. RDFS also defines certain standard properties and uses certain RDF properties, shown here:

`rdf:type`—Gives the class of a resource

`rdfs:subClassOf`—States that a class is a subclass of another

`rdfs:subPropertyOf`—States that a property is a sub-property of another

`rdfs:domain`—The domain of a property

`rdfs:range`—The range of a property

`rdfs:label`—A readable name for the subject

`rdfs:comment`—A description of the subject

`rdf:member`—A member of a container

`rdf:first`—The first item in an RDF list

`rdf:rest`—The list of all items in an RDF list after the first one

`rdfs:seeAlso`—A resource that may have more information about the subject

`rdfs:isDefinedBy`—A resource that defines the subject

`rdf:value`—Assigns structured values to a subject

`rdf:subject`—The subject of an RDF statement

`rdf:predicate`—The predicate of an RDF statement

`rdf:object`—The object of an RDF statement

Together with the standard classes, it's possible to give basic characteristics of classes for an ontology. More advanced ontology languages, like OWL, discussed in section 7.4.2, bring considerably more power to the design of ontologies.

Of these standard classes and properties, the most used are probably `Resource`, `Class`, `Property`, `type`, `label`, `subClassOf`, `subPropertyOf`, `domain`, and `range`. Recall that everything in RDF is a `Resource` (except for literal property values), and all `Resources` are identified by URIs.

You've already met all of these except the last three: `SubPropertyOf` is like a subclass, except it's applied to properties; `domain` and `range` describe how a property may be used. The *range* defines the values a property is allowed to take. The *domain* defines the kinds of things the property may apply to. If we have a property called `numberOfChildren`, meaning how many children a person has, then its range is the set of integers zero or larger and its domain is `person`, because only a person is allowed to have the property `numberOfChildren` according to the ground rules for this example.

To express an ontology in RDFS, you usually start by "defining" classes that represent the concepts you want to make statements about. "Defining" is in quotes because a statement that appears to define a class really just asserts that there is such a class. We say "usually" because the order of statements doesn't matter in RDF—what matters is the whole collection, regardless of order. But it's usually best to start with the outline and then fill in the details. After that, you can add properties and any restrictions on them.

An RDFS example

As an example, let's use parts of a schema from a presentation on the W3C web site (www.w3.org/2001/Talks/0710-ep-grid/slide21-0.html). To make it more readable, we use a simplified syntax and omit some technical details. The syntax goes like this:

```
{subject,predicate,object}
```

When more than one property is assigned to the same subject, we write

```
{subject,
    {predicate1,object1}
    {predicate2,object2}
}
```

When an anonymous node (or *b-node*) is used (see section 2.3), we write

```
{subject,predicate,
    {predicate-of-bnode,object-of-bnode}
```

Also, we'll use prefixes like rdf without declaring the URI that they represent. Strings in quotes represent literal values. A resource beginning with #, such as #ResourceAccessRule, denotes a resource declared in the same document, the one we're constructing.

Now let's look at the example, which describes a vocabulary for access rights to web resources (see listing 7.1).

Listing 7.1 Example of a schema for RDF data describing access rights

```
{rdf:Description,
   {about, http://www.w3.org/2001/02/acls/ns#}      ◁┐ Resource described
   {rdfs:comment,"A namespace for describing Access │ by RDF fragment
      Control Lists"}
   {rdfs:seeAlso, http://www.w3.org/2001/02/acls/acls-for-ns}
}

{rdfs:Class,      ◁─┘ Defines new class │ In this document, refer to class
   {ID,"ResourceAccessRule"}       ◁─┘ as "#ResourceAccessRule"
   {rdfs:label,"Access Rule"}
   {rdfs:comment,"An assertion of access privileges to
      a resource."}
   {rdfs:isDefinedBy, http://www.w3.org/2001/02/acls/ns#}
}

{rdf:Class,
   {ID,"Identity"}
   {rdfs:label,"Identity"}
   {rdfs:comment,"Any entity to which access may be granted
      to a resource. "}
   {rdfs:subClassOf,      ◁─┘ Subclass of rdfs:Resource
               http://www.w3.org/2000/01/rdf-schema#Resource}
}

{rdf:Class,
   {ID,"Principle"}
   {rdfs:label,Principle}
   {rdfs:comment,"An Identity to which credentials or
      other uniquely distinguishing characteristics
      may be assigned."}
   {rdfs:subClassOf,   #Identity}      ◁┐ Subclass of "Identity",
}                                        │ defined earlier

{rdf:Property,   ◁─❶ Property with range and
   {ID,"access"}        domain specified
   {rdfs:label,"access"}
   {rdfs:comment,"The access privileges extended
```

```
        to an accessor."}
    {rdfs:range, http://www.w3.org/2000/01/rdf-schema#Literal}
    {rdfs:domain, #ResourceAccessRule}
    {rdfs:isDefinedBy, http://www.w3.org/2001/02/acls/ns#}
}
```

Notice how the new `Identity` class is defined as a subclass of the standard RDFS class `Resource`, whereas `Principle` is defined as a subclass of `Identity`. We can infer that `Principle` is also a subclass of `Resource`. This gives us the following hierarchy:

```
Resource
    Identity
        Principle
```

This schema constructs a hierarchy across ontologies, since `Resource` is in the RDFS Working Draft, but `Identity` and `Principle` are in the example schema.

Notice how at ❶, the domain and range are defined for `access`. The `domain` property specifies that the `access` property can only be applied to an instance of the class `ResourceAccessRule` (or of any its subclasses). More than one domain can be specified, in which case the complete domain is the union of the individual domains, meaning that any of them are permissible. Similarly, the `range` property says that only literal values can be the value of an `access` property.

How can these restrictions be enforced? Doing so requires a logical processor that can find all the relevant constraints in the set of RDF triples and then check each triple against the constraints recorded for its type of property. The processor will also have to take into account any constraints that apply to the super-properties and superclasses of each class and property, so this isn't a trivial task.

These new classes and properties, each identified by its own URI, are available for use by the rest of the RDF document. Since they have unique URIs, they can be referenced by other documents, too.

This more or less covers the abilities of RDFS, minus some details like using datatypes and containers. You can create hierarchies of classes and properties,[3] and you can declare the domain and range of a property. You can make such statements about any resource identified by a URI, not just the ones you create. Most, if not all, other ontology languages that are built on RDF also incorporate at least parts of RDFS.

---

[3] A class can be stated to be a subclass of more than one class, so you aren't limited to strict hierarchies.

7.4.2 OWL

Sometimes it's enough to sketch out several classes and properties. More often, that's only the beginning. You find that you need to restrict the cardinality ("a Car may have no more than 4 Wheels"), to express optionality ("a Car may have a CD player"), to combine classes ("participants are members of both the High School and of the town's marching band"), or in myriad other ways be more precise about the design of your ontology.

OWL (which stands for Web Ontology Language—the acronym is out of order, but nevertheless, OWL it is) is a W3C project to standardize a more capable ontology framework language than RDFS. OWL evolved from DAML + OIL, a relatively successful ontology project of DARPA, the United States Defense Advanced Research Projects Agency. In fact, many of the same people who helped to develop DAML (as it's known for short) have been working on OWL.

OWL has just been released as a final Recommendation; much DAML work is being migrated to OWL. DAML is discussed later in this chapter, despite this migration, because it's still the foundation for certain projects of interest, such as DAML-S (see chapter 8).

Flavors of OWL

OWL comes in three sublanguages or flavors, called OWL Lite, OWL DL, and OWL Full. OWL Full is the complete language; the other two are subsets or restrictions of OWL Full. There are three flavors because OWL Full allows an RDF *datastore*—a collection of RDF statements—to be complex enough to give a logical reasoner serious trouble. The two subsets of OWL have less power but reduce the computing demands on a processor.

OWL DL supports a form of what is called *description logic*. Description logics apply certain carefully chosen restrictions to the kind of things that can be said in order to gain computing advantages. This allows you to be sure that description logic processors can successfully compute results—in the jargon, it's "complete and decidable." To quote from the OWL Language Reference document, "In particular, the OWL DL restrictions allow the maximal subset of OWL Full against which current research can assure that a decidable reasoning procedure can exist for an OWL reasoner."

OWL Lite is OWL DL with more restrictions. The idea is to make it easy to start with and easy to implement processors, so that people can begin using OWL Lite easily and later graduate to more complicated uses.

OWL uses RDFS classes and properties and defines additional ones. OWL modifies the definition of a class. An `owl:Class` is basically the same as in RDFS—

that is, a class is a classification scheme associated with a set of individuals—but in OWL DL and OWL Lite, the instances of a class must be individuals, not other classes. In OWL Full and RDFS, the instances of a class may also be classes.

OWL classes and properties

To give you a sense for how much richer OWL is than RDFS, below is a list of the classes and properties that OWL defines. Their names give a good sense of their purpose. Names in boldface are defined only for OWL DL and OWL Full, not for OWL Lite. Names in italics are used in OWL Lite, but with some restrictions.

Classes	Properties
owl:AllDifferent	owl:allValuesFrom
owl:Class	owl:backwardCompatibleWith
owl:DataRange	*owl:cardinality*
owl:DatatypeProperty	**owl:complementOf**
owl:DeprecatedClass	owl:differentFrom
owl:DeprecatedProperty	**owl:disjointWith**
owl:FunctionalProperty	**owl:distinctMembers**
owl:InverseFunctionalProperty	owl:equivalentClass
owl:Nothing	owl:equivalentProperty
owl:ObjectProperty	**owl:hasValue**
owl:Ontology	owl:imports
owl:Restriction	owl:incompatibleWith
owl:SymmetricProperty	*owl:intersectionOf*
	owl:inverseOf
	owl:maxCardinality
	owl:minCardinality
	owl:oneOf
	owl:onProperty
	owl:priorVersion
	owl:sameAs
	owl:sameIndividualAs
	owl:someValuesFrom
	owl:subClassOf
	owl:TransitiveProperty
	owl:unionOf
	owl:versionInfo

In OWL, everything that can be talked about is a subclass of `owl:Thing`. `owl:Nothing` comes at the other end of the scale, being a class with no members. With all these language features, an OWL-aware processor could deduce quite a bit that a plain RDF processor couldn't. For example, suppose we say that the property `contains` is transitive. We do so by assigning to `contains` the type `owl:transitiveProperty`. Now a processor would know (by the definition of `transitiveProperty`) that if A contains B and B contains C, then A must contain C as well. Things nest inside each other. If Boston is in Massachusetts, and Massachusetts is in the USA, Boston must be in the USA. Figure 7.8 illustrates this.

Ontology versions

Notice in table 7.1 that OWL has a vocabulary for talking about ontologies and their versions, with properties like `owl:priorVersion` and `owl:versionInfo`. This capability makes it possible to distinguish between different versions of an ontology and to trace their heritage to some degree.

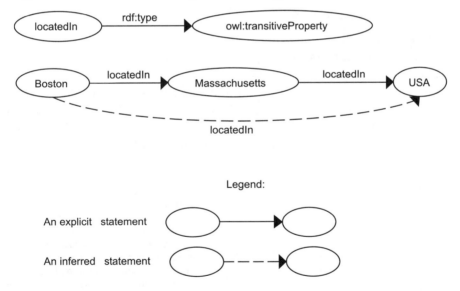

Figure 7.8 An OWL processor figures out that Boston is in the USA. In this scenario, the collection of RDF statements (that is, the knowledge base) doesn't actually say that Boston is in the USA. By knowing that the `locatedIn` property is a `transitiveProperty`, the processor can understand that the resources nest inside each other.

OWL is RDF

Like RDFS, OWL uses RDF to express everything it has to say. This works in reverse as well. Any RDF graph is also legal OWL Full, although OWL may not assign special meaning to all the resources. OWL Full doesn't impose any restrictions on the RDF statements you might like to make, regardless of whether they use OWL constructs.

We mention this because it's possible to make statements in RDF that aren't allowed under OWL DL and OWL Lite. OWL DL uses all the constructs of OWL Full, but with some restrictions on their use. Similarly, a set of RDF statements that is compatible with OWL Lite is also compatible with OWL DL, but not the other way around. For example, with OWL DL, a class may not also be treated as an individual (which it can be in OWL Full); and in OWL Lite, cardinality restrictions can only have the value 0 or 1. There are many other restrictions, especially for OWL Lite.

A database schema in OWL

To see how some of these OWL capabilities work, let's look again at the example from chapter 2, where we expressed a relational database as an RDF datastore. In conventional databases, the database schema is usually split between table definitions (stored in the database itself) and a data dictionary where other information is kept, usually in text form. We'll specify the database schema in OWL.

Figure 7.9 depicts the basic data model, repeated from chapter 2.

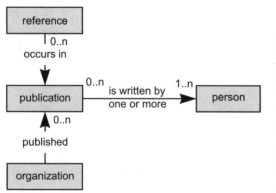

Figure 7.9
Data model for the database example, taken from chapter 2. The subject is the *reference*, which is a quotation from some published work. One or more references can occur in a given publication. A publication is written by one or more people, and an organization publishes one or more publications. Data models—also called *schemas*—much like this one can be found in numerous relational databases.

There are four kinds of things, so let's assert classes for them:

```
{owl:Class,
   {rdf:ID, Reference}
   {rdfs:label, "Reference"}
}

{owl:Class,
   {rdf:ID, Publication}
   {rdfs:label, "Publication"}
}
```

(and similarly for the other classes).

Now we can refer to our classes as `#Reference`, `#Publication`, and so on. They're automatically subclasses of `owl:Thing`, and we don't have to say so.

Suppose we want to differentiate between types of publications—say, magazines and books. We define them as subclasses of `Publication`:

```
{owl:Class,
   {rdf:ID, Magazine}
   {rdf:subClassOf, #Publication}
   {rdfs:label, "Magazine"}
}
{owl:Class,
   {rdf:ID, Book}
   {rdf:subClassOf, #Publication}
   {rdfs:label, "Book"}
}
```

Now books and magazines will get all the properties we assign to publications. We could also add a statement that says that `Magazine` and `Book` are *disjoint*, meaning that they don't share any instances. In effect, this would mean that if a publication is a `Magazine`, it can't be a `Book`, and vice versa.

Next we can create some of the relationships between the classes. In OWL, there are two kinds of properties: object properties and datatype properties. Datatype properties let you make statements about datatypes. Here we want object properties—that is, properties that apply to ordinary objects:

```
{owl:ObjectProperty,
   {rdf::ID,occursIn}
   {rdfs:label, "occurs in"}
   {rdfs:domain, #Reference}
   {rdfs:range, #Publication},
}
{owl:ObjectProperty,
   {rdf::ID, writtenBy}
   {rdfs:label, "written by"}
   {rdfs:domain, #Publication }
```

```
    {rdfs:range, #Person }
  }
  . . .
```

We now have an occurs in property for a Reference, whose values must be Publications, and a written by property for Publications, whose values must be Persons. Next, we'll assert the required cardinalities:

```
{#Reference,
  {owl:Restriction,
      {owl:onProperty, #occursIn}
      {owl:minCardinality, "1"}
      {owl:maxCardinality, "1"}
  }
}
{#Publication,
  {owl:Restriction,
      {owl:onProperty, #writtenBy}
      {owl:minCardinality, "1"}
  }
}
```

This says that Reference may have exactly one occurs in property; that is, it can only occur in a single publication. A Publication, on the other hand, has to be written by at least one person (but could be written by more than one). These restrictions are accomplished by means of owl:Restriction. Each restriction created like this applies only to the class in which it's asserted. If the property occurs in were allowed to be applied to another class in addition to Reference, the restriction that there be only one occurs in property would apply only to References. The other class could have a different restriction.

It should be clear how to proceed to build the complete database schema. We could even generate the actual database code for the tables from the schema (and populate them, if we first created an RDF datastore with the data). This schema, however, can be understood by any OWL-aware RDF application and can easily be shared.

An OWL class definition example

Working effectively with OWL requires you to get used to defining things in terms of classes and to be able to visualize the members of the classes. Often, you'll use *anonymous* (that is, unnamed) classes.

To give you more of a feel for how OWL can be used to support reasoning, let's look at an example from a thread on the www-rdf-logic mailing list. It's adapted from a post (dated March 10, 2003) by Peter F. Patel-Schneider, who is a member of the W3C working group developing OWL. We've changed the notation to the simplified version used earlier, but this doesn't change the set of statements. The thread revolved around how to specify properties of a hypothetical class called `CityOnARiver`, intended to represent cities that have a river flowing through them, so that a `CityOnARiver` would in fact be required to have a river.

Here is a set of statements about the class `CityOnARiver` that achieves the goal:

```
{owl:Class,
{rdf:ID, "CityOnARiver"}
{rdfs:subClassOf,          ⎤ Anonymous
    {owl:Restriction,    ◁—┘ class
        {owl:onProperty rdf:resource, #hasFeature }
        {owl:someValuesFrom, http://geodesy.org#River}
    }
}
}
```

This fragment assumes that a property `hasFeature` has been brought into existence somewhere out of sight in the same document, and that there is a `River` class identified by the URI `http://geodesy.org#River`. These OWL statements say that an instance of the class `CityOnARiver` must have at least one feature whose value comes from the class `http://geodesy.org#River`.[4] Let's assume that this URI really denotes the concept of a river. Then a `CityOnARiver` must have a river as one of its features (`owl:someValuesFrom` means the class in question must have at least one property of the type specified that comes from the referenced class).

This additional bit says that `Davenport` is an instance of the class `CityOnARiver`:

```
{CityOnARiver,
    {rdf:ID, "Davenport"}
    {... other statements}
}
```

Notice that this doesn't say what river it is. The OWL-aware processor could infer that `Davenport` must have a river, even though no specific river has been mentioned, and even though nothing has directly said that `Davenport` even has a river.

---

[4] To be more technical, the fragment says that there is an `owl:Class` with the `rdf:ID` value of "CityOnARiver", which is at the same time a subclass of the class `owl:Restriction`, a subclass that is used to apply restrictions to other classes. The effect is to say that `CityOnARiver` is restricted to be a subClass of some class that has a feature that is a river. In other words, a `CityOnARiver` is something that has a river. To be compete, there should also be a statement that `CityOnARiver` is a subclass of a `City`, but we have omitted it for clarity. This is an example of the rather peculiar (at first glance) maneuverings you have to go through to make sure the language can be analyzed with set theory.

Alternatively, we might have said this instead:

```
{http://geodesy.org#River, rdf:ID, "Mississippi"}

{#City,
    {rdf:ID, "Davenport"}
    {hasFeature, #Mississippi }
}
```

Assuming that the class `City` is known, this says that `Mississippi` is a river, and that there is a resource `Davenport` of type `City`, which has `Mississippi` as a feature. A processor could then infer that `Davenport` is also a `CityOnARiver`, since it meets the qualifications for the `CityOnARiver` class.

OWL's background

OWL's design has benefited from several generations of earlier ontology languages, a strong theoretical basis, and a determination on the part of many of its designers to create a language suitable for use on the Semantic Web. At the time of this writing, OWL seems poised to become the major ontology language for the Web. No doubt it will continue to evolve.

7.4.3 DAML + OIL

Earlier we said that OWL is based on an earlier ontology language called *DAML + OIL*. *DAML + OIL* itself was a merger of two independent projects called Ontology Inference Layer (OIL) and DARPA Agent Markup Language (DAML). We'll use the term *DAML* for brevity.

DAML was fairly successful as such things go. It was reported that in late 2002, there were at least 5 million DAML statements on some 20,000 web sites, not counting a number of very large DAML databases (De Roure 2003). There were certainly more in locations not reachable by the crawlers that were looking for DAML on the Web. Chapter 2 gives an example of one DAML project, Webscripter.

DAML is very similar to OWL, although some of the terms have been removed or renamed, and it wasn't divided into sublanguages. DAML is by design more restricted in its expressiveness than OWL Full.

Because DAML is so similar to OWL, we don't illustrate it here. We mention it mainly because *DAML-S*, a language for web services (see chapter 8), uses DAML. DAML-S is being reworked to use OWL, so at some point DAML will probably fade out of use. At the time of this writing, it's still possible to find interesting experimental DAML sites using leads provided by Google.

7.5 *Summary*

In this chapter, we've looked at ontologies and how they establish organized sets of concepts and vocabularies. Simpler ontologies may take the form of hierarchical lists, but in many real-world applications, more complex networks of concepts are needed.

We looked briefly at some issues that haven't been worked out fully yet, especially issues involved in using parts of one ontology with another. (For a less formal approach to the organization of vocabularies, see the browser bookmarks case study in the appendix.)

To be useful for the Semantic Web, an ontology language must do more than just define a vocabulary and place constraints on the use of the terms. It must be

- Able to reference concepts defined elsewhere on the Web
- Sharable over the Web
- Able to work with one or more languages in use (like RDF)
- Able to merge several ontologies
- Widely accepted as a standard
- Expressive enough for serious use
- Able to support kinds of logical reasoning that are found to be needed to conduct the business of the Semantic Web

OWL (especially OWL Full) scores fairly high on many of these counts. Only the last two are in question. Expert systems generally use extensive sets of rules and specialized rules processors. OWL isn't adapted for defining sets of rules (so far, there are no standardized ways for RDF to express complex rules), but work has been published suggesting how it might be possible to extend OWL so that it can support such expert systems.

As you saw in chapter 6, no one knows yet what (if any) extensions to first-order logic will be needed in the future to support all the visions people have expressed for the Semantic Web. It's still early days for ontology languages like OWL.

8 *Semantic Web services*

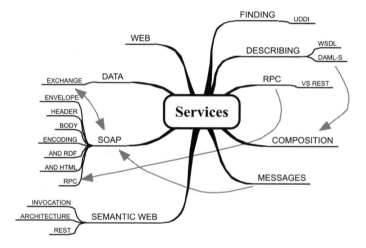

The shop seemed to be full of all manner of curious things—but the oddest part of it all was, that whenever she looked hard at any shelf, to make out exactly what it had on it, that particular shelf was always quite empty: though the others round it were crowded as full as they could hold.

—Lewis Carroll, *Through the Looking Glass*

Yesterday I ordered a book online. When it's shipped, the store will send me a tracking number. From the tracking number, I (or the bookstore) can check on the book's whereabouts as it makes its way to my house. The bookstore offered me a service: the sale and delivery of a book. The shipping company offered the bookstore a service: the physical delivery to me. A few years ago, these services would have been invoked in person or over the telephone, but yesterday the process took place electronically over the Internet.

Other services were involved in this transaction, too, although they were invisible to me. The bookstore checked and charged my credit card, and arranged the shipping details with the shipper. The bookstore's database had to be queried about the availability, price, and location of the book; and the warehouse had to be notified to ship it.

The notion that chains of services could be combined automatically is appealing because it seems to offer increased responsiveness and efficiency while reducing the amount of manual detail work that people have to do. In this chapter, we look at services with an eye toward the fit between services and the Semantic Web.

8.1 What are web services?

A *service* is a behavior that benefits someone; or, as Webster's *New World Dictionary* says, "(3) work done for others."

In the context of the Internet, we might think of personal purchases, travel services, search services, and the like. Less obvious but at least as important are services that support the more visible ones. These include, to name a few, directory services that let your software locate the services you want, services that check your credit card and authorize charges to it, and authentication services that help the parties establish who they are and whether they may be reliable to deal with.

Here's a more targeted definition (W3C 2003b):[1]

A Web service is a software system identified by a URI, whose public interfaces are defined and described using XML. Other systems may interact with the Web service in a manner prescribed by its definition, using XML based messages conveyed by Internet protocols.

8.1.1 Web pages as services

With the first definition, any web page might be a service, especially if it supplies information in response to a specific query. To illustrate, you can get a list of pages about the Semantic Web from the Google search engine by using this URL in your browser:

```
http://www.google.com/search?q=semantic%20web
```

You don't need to know anything about Google's database or the internal design of its server to get this data, just the URL and the right *query string* (the part at the end: *?q=semantic%20web*). When you know that you have to put "%20" when you want a space in a URL (and "%22" for a quotation mark), it's easy to see how to ask for any other search.

8.1.2 Beyond the plain web page

Although this example can rightly be called a web service, since it performs work for you and happens over the Internet, the notion of *web services* normally encompasses more than this. The second definition, although abstract, is suggestive of a broader scope. The usual context is that of business and commerce, involving money, delivery of tangible goods and services, legal issues, and the choreography of associated business processes that are likely to be part of the mix. *Web services,* as the term tends to be used today, covers computer-to-computer interactions that accomplish such business and commercial activities. These interactions take place over the Internet and generally use XML to carry the data. Web services can certainly be noncommercial, but much of the demand for web services, and much of their developing complexity, comes from commercial interests.

Because the use of XML is pervasive in web service technologies, they are also sometimes called *XML web services.*

---

[1] At the time of this writing, this document was still a draft and subject to change.

8.1.3 *How semantic are today's web services?*

This is a controversial question. It's clear that many people involved with the Semantic Web think that web services (speaking generically and not referring to current technology) are a good fit for the Semantic Web. Here is an example that you may remember from chapter 1:

> The semantic web promises to expand the services for the existing web by enabling software agents to automate procedures currently performed manually and by introducing new applications that are infeasible today. (Tallis, Goldman, and Balzer 2001)

However, some people argue strongly that the technologies currently being put into place for XML web services violate some basic principles of the World Wide Web—principles that played an important part in the rapid rise of the Web—and ignore Semantic Web infrastructure developments like RDF (the knowledge representation language discussed in chapter 1) and OWL (the Web Ontology language discussed in chapter 7).

There are really two different Semantic Web–related issues. The most controversial involves how a web service should be invoked, and how the related data should be handled. This is the part that is sometimes seen as violating basic web principles. The other is more of a matter of design approach. Many people involved with emerging Semantic Web infrastructures like RDF and OWL think that current XML web services could have more capability, be more flexible, and be more interoperable with agents and other software, if they were to use Semantic Web technologies instead.

In the rest of this chapter, we'll look at the main elements of web services, trying to understand the relation between XML web services and the Semantic Web, and looking at some alternative approaches that could give a better fit.

8.1.4 *Elements of web services*

The elements or components of web services can be grouped into four categories. We need to be able to

- *Exchange* data so that we can do our transactions.
- *Invoke* the service itself.
- *Describe* the service and how to invoke it, so that programmers will be able to write software.
- *Find* the right service; otherwise we'll have nothing to invoke.

Each of these categories has an XML web services mainline approach and a group of standards under development—sometimes more than one group. In several cases, alternatives are under development as well, which some think are more "Semantic Web–like." The discussion in section 8.4 covers both the description and finding of web services, since they are closely related.

8.2 Exchanging data

Data exchange involves two parts. First is the medium, which in this case is the Internet (whether wireless or not). The Internet isn't just the Web, carrying as it does many other protocols, such as email, FTP (File Transfer Protocol), and instant messaging. The term *Web* essentially means the combination of HTTP (HyperText Transfer Protocol), URLs for addressing, and hyperlinks for referring to web resources (web pages and so forth that can be accessed using web methods).

The second part is the way data is represented for transmission. This depends on the type of data. For example, today pictures are most often encoded as GIF or JPEG files for use on the Web, whereas the textual content of web pages usually uses HTML. Figure 8.1 depicts an exchange of messages requesting a service.

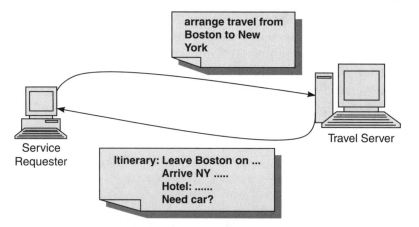

Figure 8.1   An exchange of messages that causes a service to be invoked. The computer on the left sends a message requesting a trip to be arranged. The message is received by the server on the right. When the service has made the arrangements, it sends a message back to the requestor to tell it what has been accomplished. Usually these messages travel on the Internet, but they could go some other way, such as via email or fax. With XML web services, the messages would be encoded into a structured XML format.

8.2.1 *Web only?*

There is an advantage to being able to exchange data by other means than the Web, even though the Web will no doubt get most of the activity. On the other hand, restricting data exchange to the Web would have real benefits, because you could plan to use specific features of HTTP that don't exist for, say, FTP. Also, more or less by definition, if data is exchanged without using the Web, it won't be making use of the Semantic Web.

The designers of the conventional model for web services didn't care about the notion of the Semantic Web, and they were interested in flexibility of the exchange media. They decided to make it possible to exchange data using non-Web means like email as well as by using the Web.

8.2.2 *To RDF or not?*

The second part of a data exchange has to do with the way the data is encoded. By general agreement, XML will be used (the second definition of web services given in section 8.1 says so explicitly), but XML is a framework for languages and not a data transfer language in itself. A specific markup language (or languages), based on XML, needs to be created to suit the exchange of data for web services.

From the emphasis in earlier chapters of this book on RDF as a base layer for knowledge representation, you might expect that RDF would be used together with an ontology, or vocabulary, defined using OWL or a similar language based on RDF. But not so. Instead, conventional XML web services use an XML-based language called *SOAP*. (SOAP originally stood for *Simple Object Access Protocol*, but in the newest version, the name is no longer considered to be an acronym.) SOAP was originally developed mainly by Microsoft with participation by Dave Winer, then of Userland Software. It has migrated to a new home at the W3C, which at the time of this writing is nearing completion of SOAP version 1.2. We'll look at SOAP and then at alternatives.

8.2.3 *SOAP*

Here is how the current draft of SOAP version 1.2 introduces SOAP:

> SOAP Version 1.2 (SOAP) is a lightweight protocol intended for exchanging structured information in a decentralized, distributed environment. It uses XML technologies to define an extensible messaging framework providing a message construct that can be exchanged over a variety of underlying protocols. The framework has been designed to be independent of any particular programming model and other implementation specific semantics.

SOAP provides many capabilities, the new version more than the previous one. A SOAP message is intended to be complete in itself, so that it can be sent by a variety of Internet protocols. A message consists of an *envelope* containing an optional *message header* and the *body* of the message. The header may contain information about intermediate recipients and the ultimate targeted recipient, along with a variety of details that may help a recipient process the message and may even modify the way in which the SOAP message is processed. Intermediate recipients may simply forward the message, or they may perform processing on it first. Figure 8.2[2] depicts a SOAP message with its header and body.

The specification for SOAP messages is fairly abstract, but an actual message is expressed in an XML format. SOAP is intended to be flexible and extensible, and to be able to encode information in a variety of ways, only a few of which are specified in the draft SOAP recommendation. Other ways are left to further specifications or to the service provider.

Security

SOAP can be used to transmit secure data, and SOAP messages can be digitally protected. Different kinds of security are needed depending on the nature of the message, as discussed in chapter 10. One kind might make it impossible for the senders of messages to successfully claim that they didn't send them. At the time of this writing, a number of specifications are being devised for digitally signing, encrypting, and otherwise protecting various kinds of SOAP messages.

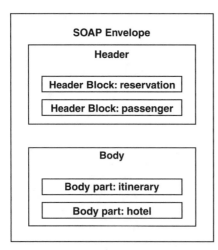

Figure 8.2
The header and body blocks within a SOAP message. The body contains the data of the message; the header, which is optional, may contain a variety of types of information. In this case, it contains reference numbers for the reservation and the passenger, which may be useful for other services that need to augment this itinerary.

---

[2] Adapted from (W3C 2003a).

8.2.4 *RDF with SOAP*

Although most current work on XML web services takes it for granted that SOAP will be used, there is no reason why RDF, let's say, couldn't be used. However, there don't seem to be any viable RDF proposals that would have any hope of supplanting SOAP, especially in the world of commercial web services—certainly not in the short term. Providing data in RDF form would offer advantages, such as established semantics, extensible ontologies, and standard processing tools.

The new version of SOAP makes it more practical to encode RDF data right in a SOAP message (Ogbuji 2002). So, it may turn out to be feasible to get the best of both worlds—routing, handling, and security provided by standard SOAP methods, and RDF providing much richer content to the messages, content that could be linked and reused much more easily than plain XML-formatted data.

8.2.5 *HTML forms*

HTML forms, with which nearly everyone is familiar, have been used to send data from a client to a server for a decade. Every book bought on Amazon, every search done on Google, every computer bought from Dell by means of a browser over the Web—all these transactions have been accomplished using HTML forms. The strictest definition of web services given earlier calls for the use of XML, which would rule out all these transactions as not being XML web services. But aren't they "web services," even if they aren't "XML web services"? After all, a service accessed through an ordinary HTML form still provides a service to a user, and it certainly makes use of the Web.

Supposing that we do require the use of XML in order to be able to call something a "web service." It's possible to send XML using an HTML form (although a form isn't ideal for the purpose). Besides HTML forms, the W3C is developing a Recommendation for advanced forms that use and send XML. It seems that perfectly good web services could be made to work using forms and the standard machinery for sending them, and it might be simpler to do so when the full capabilities of SOAP weren't needed.

Fortunately, the current version of Web Services Description Language (WSDL), a description language that describes how to connect to a web service (discussed in section 8.4), can describe service interactions using ordinary methods familiar to web programmers, as long as they send XML-formatted data.

8.3 *Invoking services*

Section 8.2 pointed out that SOAP messages can be exchanged using protocols besides HTTP, the backbone of the Web. In practice, the vast majority of web services will undoubtedly be invoked—that is, activated or made use of—over the Web using HTTP.

8.3.1 *Using HTTP for web services*

Firewalls normally allow HTTP on port 80 to pass through; otherwise, no one would be able to use their browsers (Web pages are obtained by a browser using HTTP, and port 80 is the standard port to do so). A web service isn't a web page, but if it uses HTTP on port 80, the data will go through current firewalls. So, there is a powerful incentive to use HTTP, and SOAP is designed to fit into this plan. It would probably have been more efficient to create a new transport protocol to carry the messages, but doing so would have required development of a new standard, along with new software libraries and tools; and then, a large number of firewalls would have had to be reconfigured to admit messages using the new protocol.

Although a service might use email, FTP, or instant messaging, most services will run on servers listening for HTTP messages. We need to look at how HTTP messages work, and then we can go into one of the controversial topics about web services.

8.3.2 *About HTTP messages*

An HTTP message is a relatively simple message in text format. If you intercept and print out the characters from such a message, you'll find it to be completely readable. An HTTP message from the client (such as a browser) makes a request of the server. The message states what kind of request it is, includes some extra information in the so-called *HTTP headers*, and may include some data, if there is any. It expects to receive an answer from the server that includes headers and then the body of the response, if any. When the response is finished, the connection with the server is normally ended so that each request is entirely independent of any previous one, so far as the connection with the server is concerned. The format of the headers follows a standard format used widely on the Internet.

Here's a complete HTTP request, to make clear what we've just described:

```
GET / HTTP/1.1
Host: www.cnn.com
User-Agent: Mozilla/5.0 (Windows; U; Windows NT 5.0; en-US;
```

```
rv:1.4b) Gecko/20030516 Mozilla Firebird/0.6
Accept: text/xml,application/xml,application/xhtml+xml,text/html
Accept-Language: en-us,en;q=0.5
Accept-Encoding: gzip,deflate,compress;q=0.9
Accept-Charset: ISO-8859-1,utf-8;q=0.7,*;q=0.7
Keep-Alive: 300
Connection: keep-alive
If-Modified-Since: Sun, 03 Aug 2003 00:12:44 GMT
```

This request asks the server at www.cnn.com to supply its home page. The first line states the type of request: a GET, meaning a simple page retrieval. It also states that the protocol of the request is HTTP and the HTTP version is 1.1. The lines that follow are the headers, one per line (some lines have been shortened or deleted to fit in this listing because the page isn't wide enough to hold the full headers).

The response (not shown here) likewise contains an initial line stating the protocol, the error status, and a number of header lines. A blank line comes after the last header, and then the content of the response.

You need to bear in mind the following two important points:

- *An HTTP request asks for a representation of some named resource.* The server maintains the resource, which may be a file containing HTML, a database, or something else. The web page that it might return to a browser isn't the resource itself, but just one representation of it, a snapshot of its current *state*. The state may change in the future, and the particular representation the server sends out may be influenced by additional information included with the query: If you ask for the price of a book, you don't want to see everything in the store's database (the resource here)—just the price of the one book.

- *The resource is named by a URI.* A URI (Uniform Resource Identifier) is the readable thing you type into a browser to specify what page to get; a URL (Uniform Resource Locator) is one kind of URI. It's up to the server to figure out how to get at the resource named by the URI, but the client (the browser) doesn't need to know anything about how that happens. The client doesn't even have to know where the server is. The client only has to know the URI of the resource.

GET and POST

There are only a few kinds of HTTP requests. The main ones used by browsers are known as *GET* and *POST*. A browser uses a GET request to get a page, and it uses a POST to submit data in a form:

- *GET*—Returns (GETs) data from a server. This is the most common request.
- *POST*—Applies (POSTs) data to the server, then returns data. The posted data, which comes from the client, may affect the state of the server—perhaps by debiting your account.

These are the classic HTTP request types, the ones used by most browsers. Normally either type of request is expected to return some data, most often a web page.

There is an important distinction between a GET and a POST: A GET isn't supposed to change the state of the resource, at least not in such a way that a second request would return a different result. The HTTP specification calls this kind of request *idempotent*. A POST, on the other hand, doesn't have to obey this constraint. What's the difference? Well, suppose you buy a book using your browser. If you click the Buy button twice, you will probably receive two copies in the mail and see two charges on your charge card. If you look at today's movie schedule, the act of getting the web page shouldn't cause the schedule to change—if you get it again, it should be the same (or at least, if the schedule page does change, the change isn't related to the fact that you viewed it). The schedule request is idempotent; the book purchase isn't.

Imagine: the entire Web grew up using only two kinds of requests, GET and POST. Most of the work is done using the simplest type, the GET. If you want a service, like having Google do a search, you have only to ask for the right URL—the right resource—and send enough data so the server knows what you want. Recall the Google request from section 8.1.1:

```
http://www.google.com/search?q=semantic%20web
```

Here, the search resource is /search on the server www.google.com, and the data we send to specify the search is "semantic%20web". "%20" is the way a space is encoded when a URL is transmitted. The "q=" part tells the server the name of the data we sent. This kind of URI reference is sent as a GET by the browser. An HTML form can be sent either as a GET or a POST, depending on how the web page is coded, but POST is preferred.

If you make an airline reservation, your browser probably makes GET requests to get the flight schedule and a POST request to make the reservation and send your credit card information. (A POST can be much more secure than a GET. The data for a POST can be encrypted; but for a GET, your credit card number would be added onto the URI, just like the search term in the Google example—not very secure!)

Why have we gone into this detail? Because the typical XML web service doesn't use this pattern for interactions between client and server. You might find this surprising, given the success of the Web to date, but the developers of web services saw things differently. They designed XML web services around the *remote procedure call* (RPC).

8.3.3 *Remote procedure calls*

When SOAP was first developed, it was seen mainly as a way to perform RPCs. Most distributed systems in the past (that is, before the Web) used an RPC style of interaction, and an RPC approach seems natural to many programmers. RPC tries to emulate typical programming techniques—that is to say, function or method calls. A *method call* is a function call belonging to a programming object. A *function* is a procedure that computes something. It may require data in the form of one or more input parameters. A function to compute the interest on a loan might be invoked this way:

```
interest = computeInterest(rate, period)
```

Here, computeInterest is the name of the function, rate means the value of the interest rate, and period means the period of time to compute the interest for. Note that you don't necessarily need to know how the function does the computation. You just need to know how to call the function (to *invoke* it, to cause it to perform the calculation). A function is expected to return the computed value, which is normally of a known datatype.

In the RPC style of interaction, a remote computer, or client, sends a message to a server—or to an object on the server—asking it to execute a particular function using specified values for the parameters. The server sends an answer in due course, or possibly a message announcing that an error occurred. To a programmer, this looks much like an ordinary function call, as if the remote server were part of a program running on the local computer. However, the server isn't part of the local program and isn't under its control. The complexities of communicating with the server, and of interpreting and transmitting the messages, are generally hidden from view by programming toolkits.

This style of interaction is very controversial among some proponents of the classic Web style of interaction.

8.3.4 *The Web versus RPC*

There is a purist view of how the Web works, or how it ideally should work. Although the Web is messy and accommodates a tremendous variety of programming techniques and interactions, the purists believe that definite principles underlie its success, principles that allow it to function even after it has grown to such an enormous size. Roy Fielding is closely associated with this view; he coined the name *REST*, meaning *Representation State Transfer.*

In the REST model, the key point is that a web server has a set of resources, as discussed at the start of section 8.3.2. The resources are identified by URLs, and only representations of those resources are exchanged or transferred. The interactions between client and server are accomplished using a small set of request types, which function as verbs (such as GET and POST). Every web server in the world understands GET and POST, and their semantics are well known. Thus their behavior is predictable. If you see a GET message asking for a particular URL, you know, the server knows, and a firewall knows, that the server isn't expected to change the state of the resource, and that the server is expected in due course to return a response, such as a web page, a block of XML, a sound track, etc. If you see a POST-type request, you know that the state of the resource is liable to be changed.

The server, in some cases, may create a new resource and inform the client where it is. If you order an airline ticket and are taken to a new page that has your itinerary on it (which you can print or bookmark), that's what happened. Note that this new resource is also part of the Web—it can be linked to by anyone who knows the URL and has the right credentials to get it. This is amazing—your itinerary has become a real resource, a collection of data accessible to other programs as well as to other people. Your travel agent could use it to plan other parts of your trip. Your spouse could print it out.

With this mental model, the point of making a request is to transfer a representation of the state of a resource, possibly after asking that the resource be modified. In the RPC mental model, the point is to make a calculation and return its results (the calculation may be as simple as retrieving the text of a document, or it may be extremely complicated). The results may also include changing something at the server, like the data in a database.

For XML web services (when the RPC style is used), the URL of the service identifies the server and the service, but no resource is involved. An object on the server is asked to execute a function. The SOAP message is sent to the server using (typically) a POST request, but the use of a POST is just a device to get the SOAP payload to the receiving program. The URL of the service doesn't identify a resource; instead, the desired action is specified in the content of the SOAP request. You don't ask for the data in the SOAP message to be applied to a resource, or use it to create a new one. Instead, you ask for a calculation to be performed and you get back the result, generally as another SOAP message.

Here's an example of a SOAP RPC-style request message (you don't need to understand all the technical detail—it's only included to give you a sense for the relative complexity of the message). This example is included with the programming kit that Google distributes for working with its query service:

```
<SOAP-ENV:Envelope
   xmlns:SOAP-ENV=
  "http://schemas.xmlsoap.org/soap/envelope/"
   xmlns:xsi="http://www.w3.org/1999/XMLSchema-instance"
   xmlns:xsd="http://www.w3.org/1999/XMLSchema">
  <SOAP-ENV:Body>
    <ns1:doGoogleSearch xmlns:ns1="urn:GoogleSearch"
      SOAP-ENV:encodingStyle=
      "http://schemas.xmlsoap.org/soap/encoding/">
      <key xsi:type=
      "xsd:string">00000000000000000000000000000000</key>
      <q xsi:type=
         "xsd:string">shrdlu winograd maclisp teletype</q>
      <start xsi:type="xsd:int">0</start>
      <maxResults xsi:type="xsd:int">10</maxResults>
      <filter xsi:type="xsd:boolean">true</filter>
      <restrict xsi:type="xsd:string"></restrict>
      <safeSearch xsi:type="xsd:boolean">false</safeSearch>
      <lr xsi:type="xsd:string"></lr>
      <ie xsi:type="xsd:string">latin1</ie>
      <oe xsi:type="xsd:string">latin1</oe>
    </ns1:doGoogleSearch>
  </SOAP-ENV:Body>
</SOAP-ENV:Envelope>
```

This SOAP message requests that Google perform a search for the string "shrdlu winograd maclisp teletype".[3] The specific function being requested is doGoogle-Search. In addition to the words to be searched for, the message asks for no more than 10 results to be returned, as well as a few other miscellaneous restrictions. It also includes a key (which is all zeros here)—each user of the API is issued a code that authorizes them to use the service.

The SOAP message does the same basic job as the simple GET message described earlier, which is repeated here, modified to use the same search terms:

```
http://www.google.com/search?q=
shrdlu%20winograd%20maclisp%20teletype
```

You can type this URL into a browser's address box and get back three pages of search results—although not in XML format, which would be more useful for

---

[3] This search string seems bizarre, but it isn't a joke. Try it for yourself.

machine processing. Obviously, the SOAP RPC request is much more complex, although it contains more search specifications than the GET message does. In terms of server resources, the resource being requested by the GET message is the basic URL, http://www.google.com/search. In effect, Google's *search* resource is being asked to provide a view of itself that is limited by the search terms. By contrast, the SOAP RPC-style message doesn't address a resource at all. Instead, it requests the Google server to perform the doGoogleSearch function.

In the RPC style, a firewall that tries to protect the server must have much more specialized knowledge about the messages, because each service has unique parameters and functions. Protective software and routing software that want to inspect an incoming request need to know what all these functions are and whether they're safe to allow through.

In a way, you can think of the difference between the two styles as the difference between working with a database (resources) on the one hand and specifying a work procedure (RPC) on the other. The data will remain in much the same form long after the work procedures have been changed many times over. Table 8.1 boils down the distinction between the two in an informal way. The first row contains natural language translations of a REST-style request and an RPC-style request. The second row describes what the server is being asked for.

Table 8.1 Contrasting REST-style requests with RPC-style procedure calls. Their essential meanings are paraphrased in natural language terms.

REST style	RPC style
"Show me what you know about the account balance for account 'ABC1234' and give me the results in an HTML web page."	"Look up the account 'ABC1234' in your accounts ledger, get the balance, format it according to this specification: (...), and return it to me in a SOAP message."
Asks the server for a *representation*—essentially, a view—of certain data. The server decides how best to do this.	Asks the server to execute a specific function using specified data values supplied by the RPC request. The requester and server jointly decide what the server is supposed to do.

8.3.5 *The RPC controversy*

Now you can see why there is a controversy. Even though a SOAP message, using RPC style, gets to the server using a POST, the rest of the interaction isn't very REST-like.

The semantics of GET and POST are widely known, but the semantics of an arbitrary RPC request are known only to specialized software:

- Proper REST-like interactions address resources by URLs, and cause resources to be retrieved, queried, modified, or created. This is very familiar to any database designer, who would think in terms of *CRUD—C*reate, *R*ead, *U*pdate, *D*elete. Modified and newly created resources automatically become part of the World Wide Web and are available for wider use. SOAP RPC messages aren't identified by a URL or any other global identifier, and they don't become part of the Web.

- Historically, programs that have been connected by RPC-style techniques have tended not to adapt to change well, since many programming details must be known to both ends of the transactions. The Web has proven to be very robust in the face of change.

- RPC-style techniques haven't been shown to scale up to widespread use. The Web is one of the few systems that has proven itself adaptable to life on a huge scale (email is one of the few other examples, and it has likewise prospered partly because of widely understood addresses, a small and universally understood selection of verbs, and the use of simple text formats).

REST proponents say that web services should use the principles proven by the success of the Web, whereas the advocates of RPC-style web services say that the needs of commercial services require a great many more capabilities, for which RPC-style SOAP messages are more suitable.

One relevant point hardly ever comes up in these arguments of REST versus RPC. For several decades, the design of business software has been moving to a "data-centric" orientation and away from a "procedural" orientation. This is because we've come to realize that the data of a business is fundamentally more important than the processes that create it. The processes come and go, they change, but the data—say a sales record—persists. Software designed with this focus tends to be more reliable and adaptable than software designed from a procedural point of view. The REST versus RPC controversy can be seen as a continuation of this data-centric versus procedural dichotomy.

Taken to an extreme, you could argue that XML web services aren't actually *web* services at all, since they don't make use of the most characteristic aspects of the Web. Of course, you could also argue that they normally do use HTTP, which is the Web protocol—so of course they are "web" services.

Now, why should readers of this book care about this controversy? The Semantic Web could potentially be useful for web services in many areas, including invoking services and exchanging their data (as you saw in section 8.2). For this to happen, services must use techniques that lend themselves to both semantic enrichment and to Web-like linking; and for this, the REST style is more suitable.

The original developers of XML web services have shown a pronounced disinterest in all things smacking of the Semantic Web; in the commercially oriented projects that are developing most of the technologies for web services, the Semantic Web tends to be regarded as an impractical, idealistic fantasy. Fortunately, REST proponents have argued hard and clearly enough that the latest versions of SOAP (and WSDL, discussed in section 8.4) have been broadened to support REST-style service invocations. Whether the next generation of web services will follow the REST or the RPC path is unclear at the time of this writing, but at least the potential is there.

8.4 *Describing and finding services*

Services need to be described so that programmers can know how to program for them, users can know how to use them, and service-construction toolkits can find out how to do their service-constructing. The word *description*, though, covers a wide range. On the lowest level, we need to describe how to connect to a service and what format to expect for its data. On a higher level, we need to describe a service in a manner that allows it to be found and evaluated—in other words, "What will this service do for me?" On a more detailed level, we would like to be able to describe how a service works, so that we can write software to utilize it and allow different services to cooperate.

These kinds of descriptions are very different from each other. Each of them could be handled by the knowledge-representation technologies covered earlier in the book, such as RDF for representing data and OWL for ontologies. In each case, the main line of development currently doesn't use these technologies, although some alternatives are in development.

8.4.1 *Connecting to services*

In the Google example at the start of section 8.1.1, we could easily learn how to invoke the service by having someone tell us what URL and query parameter to use (such as the words to search for), or we could examine the code in the web page to find out. For widespread web services to work, there must be a better way, something more systematic that can be used both by people and (especially) by computers. This is important because typical XML web services are more complex than our simple example. Web Services Description Language (WSDL) has come into use for this purpose.

What is WSDL?

WSDL is an XML-based language that describes key technical data needed for connecting to a service. Thus a WSDL file includes the network name of the server that supplies the service along with the connection means, such as HTTP GET or SOAP. WSDL can also describe the kinds of messages to be sent or received, and even their structure or datatype. WSDL is *extensible*, meaning that new protocols, message types, and so forth, can be added. An example of a WSDL file is discussed in the next subsection.

WSDL is now being extended by the W3C. Version 1.1 was approved in 2001, and version 1.2 is in draft status. WSDL can be extended to cover new service types and connection types because it uses an abstract model of messages, input and output ports (abstract network end points), and allows operations for those ports. In fact, a service is considered to be a collection of ports. Presumably, the collections are closely related; otherwise, why would they be together in a single service?

For practical use, these abstractions need to be connected with real networks and real computers at actual addresses. *Bindings* provide these connections. There is a binding for SOAP, and others for HTTP GET and POST. New bindings can be added as WSDL is extended to cover new protocols and message types.

Figure 8.3 depicts this WSDL model of a service. A WSDL document contains parts describing each of these components. One WSDL set of definitions can describe multiple operations, messages, and ports.

You can see that WSDL describes services in a narrow way: It only describes the technical points needed to make requests of a service and receive responses. Even though there are operations, they are known only by their names. WSDL contains no description of what those services are intended to do.

A WSDL example

Let's look at an example of a WSDL service definition (see listing 8.1). It's a simple one, and I've simplified it more since it's just an example. This version defines a service that uses HTTP GET, whereas the original also defines services using HTTP POST and SOAP. I also removed the namespace declarations to make the example shorter and easier to read, so this example isn't quite correct XML.

The primary purpose of this example is to see how much semantic information it contains. The semantic content turns out to be narrowly focused on the mechanics of sending messages. This is efficient for its purpose but leaves little ability for semantic enrichment. For example, it might be useful to refer to one operation in a WSDL file and, using RDF, say more about this operation,

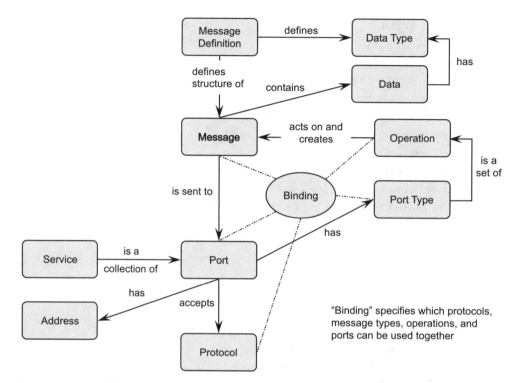

Figure 8.3   The WSDL model of a web service. WSDL defines four abstractions: *message*, *port*, *protocol*, and *operation*. Ports accept certain types of messages and provide certain operations. A service is a collection of ports. To use a service, these abstractions must be made real, or concrete. The binding says how this is to be done. It *binds* abstract operations to real addresses and real network protocols. Messages are normally encoded in XML, usually with SOAP.

or to classify it so that it could be found more easily in searches, but doing so isn't practical.

This WSDL document is available from its web site.[4] Its description reads "Look up ATM Locations by Zip Code." Apparently, we're supposed to supply a Zip code in the form of a string of characters and get back a list of ATM machines located in that Zip code.

You can skip the technicalities of the listing if you like and pick up again at the next subsection, "Semantic content of a WSDL file." If you look through the

---

[4] Web service web sites tend to come and go frequently. This WSDL file was obtained from http://ws. serviceobjects.net/gc/GeoCash.asmx?WSDL, but by the time you read this, it's possible that the page will no longer be available.

listing, you should be able to recognize parts of the model from figure 8.1, such as *message*, *port*, and so on (boldfaced to help you pick them out). The key points are discussed after the listing.

Listing 8.1 A WSDL service definition

```
<definitions>
<!-- Namespace declarations have been omitted
     to shorten this example -->

  <types>      ←①  Defines datatypes
    <s:schema elementFormDefault="qualified"
      targetNamespace="http://www.serviceobjects.com/">

      <s:complexType name="ATMLocations">     ←②  Defines ATMLocations type
        <s:sequence>
          <s:element minOccurs="0"
             maxOccurs="unbounded" name="ATM" type="s0:ATM" />
          <s:element minOccurs="0"
              maxOccurs="1" name="Error" type="s:string" />
        </s:sequence>
      </s:complexType>

      <s:complexType name="ATM">     ←③  Defines ATM type
        <s:sequence>
          <s:element minOccurs="0" maxOccurs="1"
             name="Bank" type="s:string" />
          <s:element minOccurs="0" maxOccurs="1"
              name="Address" type="s:string" />
          <s:element minOccurs="0" maxOccurs="1"
             name="Location" type="s:string" />
          <s:element minOccurs="0" maxOccurs="1"
             name="City" type="s:string" />
          <s:element minOccurs="0" maxOccurs="1"
             name="State" type="s:string" />
          <s:element minOccurs="0" maxOccurs="1"
             name="Zip" type="s:string" />
          <s:element minOccurs="0" maxOccurs="1"
             name="Latitude" type="s:string" />
          <s:element minOccurs="0" maxOccurs="1"
             name="Longitude" type="s:string" />
          <s:element minOccurs="0" maxOccurs="1"
             name="Notes" type="s:string" />
        </s:sequence>

      </s:complexType>

      <s:element name="ATMLocations" nillable="true"     ←④  Defines
         type="s0:ATMLocations" />                             ATMLocations
    </s:schema>                                                element
  </types>
```

```
<message name="GetATMLocationsHttpGetIn">      ⟵❺  Defines incoming
  <part name="strInput" type="s:string" />          message
  <part name="strLicenseKey" type="s:string" />
</message>
<message name="GetATMLocationsHttpGetOut">     ⟵❻  Defines outgoing message
  <part name="Body" element="s0:ATMLocations" />
</message>

<portType name="GeoCashHttpGet">     ⟵❼  A port
  <operation name="GetATMLocations">
    <documentation>Please use our services at
        http://ws.serviceobjects.net</documentation>
    <input message="s0:GetATMLocationsHttpGetIn" />
    <output message="s0:GetATMLocationsHttpGetOut" />
  </operation>
</portType>

<binding name="GeoCashHttpGet" type="s0:GeoCashHttpGet">   ⟵❽  Binding
  <http:binding verb="GET" />     ⟵❾  HTTP GET operation
  <operation name="GetATMLocations">
    <http:operation location="/GetATMLocations" />
    <input>              ⟵❿  Defines encoding style
      <http:urlEncoded />        of input message
    </input>
    <output>   ⟵⓫  Defines encoding style of output message
      <mime:mimeXml part="Body" />
    </output>
  </operation>
</binding>

<service name="GeoCash">   ⟵⓬  Service definition
  <port name="GeoCashHttpGet"
     binding="s0:GeoCashHttpGet">
    <http:address
       location=
       "http://ws.serviceobjects.net/gc/GeoCash.asmx"/>
  </port>
</service>
</definitions>
```

❶ Datatypes are defined using XML Schema, but you don't need to understand the details for our purposes.

❷ A type ATMLocations is defined. It can contain any number of ATM elements and also an Error element that will presumably contain any error information.

❸ This is the definition of the ATM type, which contains a bank's name, address, and so on.

❹ The schema defines an element also called ATMLocations, and its type is stated to be ATMLocations (it's legal to name an element and a type the same thing). This element will turn out to be what is sent back in reply to a request.

❺, ❻ Two messages are defined, for the incoming message (the request) and the outgoing message (the response). The messages could be named anything, since the names are only used for reference within the WSDL document. The names are usually chosen so people can get an idea of the messages' purpose. The request message is called GetATMLocationsHttpGetIn; the HttpGetIn part of the name suggests that this message applies to HTTP GET type requests. The outgoing message defined at ❻ uses the ATMLocations type defined at ❷.

The name of each part element is the name of the parameter that will be supplied as part of the GET request. Notice that there is a strInput, apparently for the Zip code, and a strLicenseKey, apparently for an authorization code. These parameters would be appended to the URL for the service. Notice that word, *apparently*—the WSDL file itself has no way to tell us, let alone our computer, what values to use for these parameters. We'd have to read something else, or be told by someone, or guess based on the names, as we've done here.

The URL for this particular operation of the service is built up from values given at ❾ and ⓬. You could invoke the service for Zip code 12398, license key (totally fictitious in this example) XXX-YYY-ZZ, with this URL (wrapped onto two lines because it's too long to fit across the page):

```
http://ws.serviceobjects.net/gc/GeoCash.asmx/
/GetATMLocations?strInput=12398&strLicenseKey=XXX-YYY-ZZ
```

Notice that the request datatype is a string, which is about the only thing you can send with a GET-style request. The response is supposed to be an XML document with an ATMLocations element that contains a number of ATM locations in ATM elements.

❼ This is a port. A port is a connection point, and in WSDL it's an abstract connection rather than a physically real one. Notice that the port consists of an operation (it could have more than one, but not in this simplified example) and an input and output message. These messages are related back to the messages defined in ❹ and ❺.

❽ Now we connect the abstract messages and ports with real network entities. The binding is connected to the operation defined earlier and to the HTTP GET operation at ❾.

❿, ⓫ The encoding style of the input and output messages is specified. Based on this, we expect to receive an XML message in the response.

⑫ This is a service definition (WSDL documents can define more than one). Notice that the service is represented as a collection of ports (just one in this case), as we said earlier. The .asmx is one of the signatures of a web service developed using the Microsoft .NET software development system, but the WSDL file, and the service, can be used by anyone using any programming system.

Trying it out, we don't have a valid license key, so we should receive an ATMLocations element (as specified at ⑥ above) with an Error element containing an error message. That's just what we get:[5]

```
<ATMLocations xmlns:xsd="http://www.w3.org/2001/XMLSchema"
    xmlns:xsi="http://www.w3.org/2001/XMLSchema-instance"
    xmlns="http://www.serviceobjects.com/">
  <Error>Please provide a valid license key. </Error>
</ATMLocations>
```

Semantic content of a WSDL file

What's the point of this somewhat lengthy example? It illustrates the kind of semantic content WSDL can specify and suggests where you have to make use of your own special knowledge of the system. The service is completely defined by the WSDL file, so far as the technical aspects of making the request are concerned. It's hard to read through the WSDL and keep all the parts straight, but conceptually they're cleanly separated.

Software can be (and has been) written that will write the code to implement the specifications in the WSDL automatically. Toolkits like the one in Microsoft's .NET Studio, for one, can generate such code. That code can make a correct request of a server, or can let the server understand that a request is asking for this particular service and send the request parameters to the processing code. But what values do we use for those parameters, like strInput and strLicense-Key? WSDL doesn't tell us.

That is, it doesn't tell a computer what should go into the request. A person can guess from the names, like strLicenseKey, which suggests an authorization code, or Error, which of course suggests an error message. So from the point of view of semantics, the meaning of things, WSDL is an empty vessel outside of its narrow purpose. This may not be a bad thing, since it keeps the WSDL clear cut and, if not simple, at least as simple as possible. But how can we get computers to

---

[5] Using the GET operation instead of POST or a SOAP message is easy, because you can type the URL into a browser's address box. To send a POST version of the same thing would be a little harder because you'd have to create an HTML form to send from a browser, or do a little programming. A SOAP version would be much more difficult because the SOAP message would be more complex to construct.

know what data to supply for these messages, or what the service is about in the first place?

WSDL could have been written in a knowledge representation language like RDF. With such an approach, adding semantic information would have been fairly easy, provided a suitable ontology had been designed, and the whole thing would be machine-usable. This would give you access to a wide range of tools and programs for working with rich semantic information, which ought to be quite valuable.[6] You'd be able to tie a service description to a process description for it, to user ratings of its quality, to a set of search terms that would let you discover similar services, and a host of other possibilities would be available.

As things are now, none of that is directly possible, and it takes additional knowledge to use a service described by WSDL. Many sites that offer a WSDL file also have a human-readable file explaining how to use the service and, sometimes, what the parameters and responses mean. An automated toolkit can construct the code to connect with the service and exchange messages; but to do anything useful with the result, programmers must write more code based on what they've read in the extra, human-readable file.

Is it good or bad (from the point of view of automated use) that WSDL is so narrowly focused on the technical connection details? Well, it isn't hard to translate WSDL into RDF.[7] The RDF can be queried to extract the connection details automatically, just as well as a WSDL file. So, it wouldn't be hard to shift to an RDF-based WSDL replacement. The way would be open to add any amount of enrichment and semantic information. On the other hand, the whole area of the classification and "meaning" of services is large and entails more than first meets the eye. It ties into the problem of finding and advertising services. It might be better to keep these connection-oriented service descriptions simple by keeping them narrowly focused.

The developers of XML web services chose to put finding and classification into another standards effort called Universal Description, Discovery, and Integration

---

[6] As Uche Ogbuji said in an article on WSDL modified to also be in RDF format, "If you were to feed this into an RDF processor, you would get a huge wealth of information that neatly maps out the qualifications and relationships that make up the WSDL description."
(See www-106.ibm.com/developerworks/library/ws-rdf/?dwzone=ws.)

[7] The W3C web site has an example, done by Eric Prud'hommeaux, at www.w3.org/2002/02/21-WSDL-RDF-mapping. Uche Ogbuji has published another example at http://www-106.ibm.com/developerworks/library/ws-rdf/?dwzone=ws#11. The current Working Draft of the W3C Primer for WSDL 1.2 contains a placeholder section to discuss how to map between RDF and WSDL.

(UDDI), which is discussed in the next section, and also to put process description into other standards. The semantic information that might have been mixed into WSDL has been kept out and reserved (with this approach) for UDDI. DAML-S, an RDF-based language for process description, has taken the opposite approach and attempts to provide for connection, discovery, and process description all in one language. We'll look at UDDI in the next section and at DAML-S in section 8.4.3.

8.4.2   Discovering services

Although there is a relationship between the discovery and the description of services, we've chosen to split them for separate discussions. This section is about the discovery part, and section 8.4.3 covers the description of services.

Yellow pages and business directories

In the old days, before the rise of the Internet and widespread distributed systems, there were yellow pages, which were centrally published but open to businesses who paid for placements. There were also business directories, like the Thomas Register; these too required a fee. Then there were industry-specific directories, which tended to be open to those in the right business or trade association.

Yellow pages provide information on how to contact a business—phone number, address, and so on—along with guidance that helps the user find the right service. Businesses are listed by category and sometimes within a category by location or specialty as well. This additional information is really meta data about the companies and their services. Yellow page entries also serve to advertise a service or company.

Centralized or not?

Web services need to be advertised and found, too. The job is harder because the scope is larger and because the directory needs to be computer-readable. Before the rise of the Web, there would probably have been a closely controlled, central repository of information about business services. Today, though, you'd expect to see a more open, distributed network of repositories of information about business services.

UDDI

Universal Description, Discovery and Integration (UDDI) is being developed (primarily by large businesses including IBM, Sun, Hewlett-Packard, and Microsoft) to play the role of a directory system. UDDI is a large and complex system that aims to be a framework for creating networks of repositories that contain searchable information about services. From a presentation at uddi.org, it's about

- Standards-based *specifications* for service description and discovery
- Shared *operation* of a business registry on the Web
- Partnership among industry and business leaders.

Also according to uddi.org, the "vision" of UDDI is

> a "meta service" for locating web services by enabling robust queries against rich metadata.

UDDI is complicated to such an extent that we won't try to get into its details. It's based on an abstract model, and messages to and from a UDDI system are in an XML format.

UDDI includes an data model, a network or aggregation model, a messaging model, a security model, a policy model (policies are defined this way in the UDDI specification: "Certain behaviors, as identified in Chapter 9, *Policy*, that are permitted to vary from registry to registry or even from node to node within a registry"), and a set of generalized programming interfaces. It's the kitchen sink of specifications.

The information model contains the entities `businessEntity`, `businessService`, and other, more technical-sounding structures. Most of the information is connected to or found by *keys*, and the keys are generally found in the registry nodes. With authorization to access a registry and knowledge of the right keys, you can track down any information about a service or a type of service. The keys can be found by a number of search mechanisms, including searching by name, type of service, location, or key type and value. In the latest version, UDDI 1.3, keys can be ordinary URLs, which wasn't the case previously. In previous versions, the UDDI operator assigned the identifying keys; they were the only practical way to extract information from the repository. Also, the keys weren't very readable. Now, service owners assign URLs that belong to their domain and can be considerably more readable. This is a real improvement.

Ontologies can be used to help with searches. They can be registered or not. The ontology support in UDDI is somewhat weak, consisting mainly of terms or pointers to terms in particular ontologies. They are nowhere near as flexible and general-purpose as the ontology systems discussed in chapter 7, but at least UDDI ontologies may support additional capabilities (outside of UDDI per se). UDDI has a small built-in ontology of its own.

Once found, the registry may contain technical information on how to invoke the service, such as a pointer to a WSDL file (see section 8.4.1). WSDL (see the previous section on describing services) isn't part of UDDI, but the two can be used together.

UDDI repositories may be standalone or connected in federations. They may be open to anyone or closed except for subscribers.

UDDI isn't in widespread use yet. A recent search on Google for "UDDI Repository" turned up a number of demonstration repositories. Presumably, networks of UDDI repositories (either public or private) will develop as more web services are offered. However, there is no indication, as this is written, whether the technology will succeed on a large scale. Some people think it will be fine within corporations but won't work well on the worldwide scope of the Web.

Just as with WSDL, UDDI developed without adopting a semantically aware framework such as RDF. And, as with WSDL, conversion of UDDI data into RDF would be relatively easy.

Google-enhanced service discovery

Search services like Google can be amazingly effective, especially when they're enhanced by targeted semantic information, as the TAP project has shown. TAP (described in chapter 5) analyzes a search request before it goes to the search engine. It has a database of semantically related information. When the TAP processing finds items in the request that it recognizes, it consults its database to find appropriate categories (such as music, Europe, and so on). TAP also knows which data sources are the best for those categories, so it can issue a series of efficient requests to promising search sites and databases. The results are reportedly much better focused and useful than those obtained from ordinary searches.

Thus it has been proposed that numbers of simple repositories, which would be indexed by Google and similar search sites, would be at least as useful as a few large UDDI repositories, and probably much more effective. The technical difficulty and cost associated with such simple repositories would be far less than for large repositories. It might even turn out that repositories weren't needed—Google or other search engines might be enough to find useful web services—but it seems more likely that TAP-like semantic search enhancement would be desirable.

WSDA and other grid computing discovery projects

Grid computing is a fairly new concept for distributing computing services and resources across a large network. Grid computing has been described this way (Foster, Kesselman, and Tuecke 2001):

The term "the Grid" was coined in the mid 1990s to denote a proposed distributed computing infrastructure for advanced science and engineering....

The real and specific problem that underlies the Grid concept is *coordinated resource sharing and problem solving in dynamic, multi-institutional virtual organizations*. The sharing that we are concerned with is not primarily file exchange but rather direct access to computers, software, data, and other resources, as is required by a range of collaborative problem-solving and resource brokering strategies emerging in industry, science, and engineering. This sharing is, necessarily, highly controlled, with resource providers and consumers defining clearly and carefully just what is shared, who is allowed to share, and the conditions under which sharing occurs. A set of individuals and/or institutions defined by such sharing rules form what we call a *virtual organization* (VO).

The term *grid* seems to have been motivated by an analogy with a utility grid—think of the electric power system, which connects homes and businesses with a grid of wires that supply electricity. In a computing grid, computing services would replace electricity, and the computer networks would replace the electrical wiring.

As the previous quotation makes clear, an important part of the grid concept is that its resources are highly dynamic. At one moment, computer A can take on your computing task; at another, it will be computer B (A being busy on another task). So, to make a grid system work, dynamic and automatic discovery of computing services on a large scale must be possible. Clearly, this need is similar to the need for discovery of web services. In fact, discovery for grid computing needs to be far more dynamic and complex than for the commercial web services we've been discussing under the heading of XML web services. Perhaps solutions to the grid discovery problem could be useful for ordinary commercial web services.

Several projects have proposed powerful and well thought out discovery systems for distributed grid computing services. Two notable proposals are Web Services Discovery Architecture (WSDA) (Hoschek 2002) and Open Grid Services Architecture (OSGA) (Tuecke et al 2002). WSDA seems especially simple and powerful. WSDA uses many of the Web standards we've discussed, including HTTP and XML. It's compatible with SOAP, WSDL, and UDDI, although at the same time it's simpler, more flexible, and more powerful than UDDI and WSDL.

We can't be sure, but grid computing may supply better technologies for description and discovery of web services than the current mainstream approaches. These approaches look like they will lend themselves more readily to semantic technologies for the Web, as well.

8.4.3 *Describing web service processes*

Services will often need to be combined. The purchase of a book might require a sequence of services, including looking up credit card information, verifying the Zip code for delivery, creating a shipping order for the warehouse, and so on. Each of those parts might involve a sequence of other services. A certain flow of work must be followed, and conditions must be met. If the credit card charge fails, the other services aren't invoked. If the book isn't in the warehouse, other warehouses have to be checked. These steps need to be monitored.

For all of this to happen, a service's design needs to be described in some detail. If this is done well enough, the hope is that a series of services could be put together automatically, maybe even for a particular transaction. Even if this is too hard for the time being, a good process description is needed for software to be written to perform it. With a sufficiently good description that a computer can understand, the program could perhaps be written automatically.

Naturally, a number of projects are working on process description languages. Here, we only look at DAML-S, which uses RDF and DARPA Agent Markup Language (DAML; and, in the near future, will switch from DAML to OWL) to define a vocabulary for process descriptions. DAML-S is still in draft form at the time of writing, but it's close to a version 1.0 release. We'll look at it here because DAML-S is clearly a candidate Semantic Web technology, possibly the leading one for web service description. Bear in mind that other projects may succeed instead of DAML-S; you should regard it as an illustrative example of a language that may or may not turn out to be expressive enough for the purpose.

Here's a quotation by Bryson et al (2002) that provides a glimpse into the power that Semantic Web technologies could bring to web services. It talks about *agents*—agents that might be desired to use web services on our behalf:

> In this paper, we review the fundamentals of constructing an intelligent agent. We focus on modular, reactive approaches to agent design, because they are conducive to the highly distributed, complex nature of Web intelligence. We then examine how to implement our proposals in DAML-S. Using the DAML-S process ontology formalism means that reasoning and proof-checking can be applied by concerned agents over the outcome of extending their design via Web services.

DAML-S

DAML stands for DARPA Agent Markup Language, as we discussed in chapter 7; it's also used as shorthand for *DAML + OIL*, the combination of two similar ontology framework projects. You may recall from chapter 7 that OWL developed from DAML (really DAML + OIL). The *S* in DAML-S stands for *Services*. DAML is basically a description logic language (see chapters 6 and 7), and it imposes limitations on the language in the interest of ensuring that results can be computed. Like DAML and OWL, it's based on RDF, and it defines additional models, concepts, and terms beyond those supplied by DAML or OWL. At the time of this writing, DAML is giving way to the newer OWL, and DAML-S will begin using OWL instead of DAML in the relatively near future.

The DAML-S web site (www.daml.org/services/) characterizes DAML-S this way:

> DAML-S supplies Web service providers with a core set of markup language constructs for describing the properties and capabilities of their Web services in unambiguous, computer-interpretable form.
>
> DAML-S markup of Web services will facilitate the automation of Web service tasks including automated Web service discovery, execution, interoperation, composition and execution monitoring.

Notice that DAML-S covers the same ground—and more—as WSDL and parts of UDDI. It doesn't cover the construction and operation of repositories per se, which is a large part of UDDI. Instead, it concentrates on providing modeling concepts and an ontology for the definition and use of services. The term *composition* in the quotation hints at this, for most transactions will involve a number of steps, each one of which could be considered a service in its own right. *Composition* refers to the combination of the individual services into an overall transaction. To buy a book, you might first use a book-finding service, then a purchase service (both probably would be part of a larger Bookstore service). The purchase service might use a credit-card verification service. Finally, the seller might use a shipping service. See figure 8.4 for a graphical depiction of such composition.

DAML-S can describe each of these processes. Since DAML-S is an application of DAML + OIL, which in turn is written in RDF, DAML-S datastores are amenable to processing by all kinds of RDF-capable software. DAML-S models a service as something provided by resource, that has a service profile (what the service provides), a service model (how it works), and a service *grounding* (how to access it). Since the profiles and models are represented by classes, the DAML-S model of a service automatically entails its classification and all the benefits for searching and processing that classification can bring. You can see that DAML-S proceeds from the viewpoint of knowledge modeling and classification, rather than from more conventional information technology (as UDDI and WSDL do).

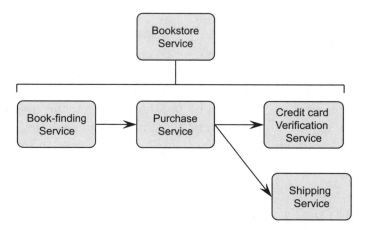

Figure 8.4 Illustrating the composition of services. A realistic service usually needs to use a number of subordinate services. These services must be composed into a whole. In this illustration, a bookstore service needs to find the requested book and then purchase it. The purchasing service needs to use a credit card service and a shipping service. These services must be invoked in the right order, since the results from one are needed for later services.

DAML-S also supports the advertising of services (in the sense of announcements of its availability), as the following quote from a DAML-S example makes clear:

> DAML-S has been designed to enable automated Web service discovery by providing DAML + OIL descriptions of the properties and capabilities of a Web service, typically used to locate or select a service. These descriptors can be used to populate a registry of services, to provide better indexing and retrieval features for search engines, or they can be used as input to a match-making system.[8]

Like WSDL and UDDI, DAML-S is based on abstract models that attempt to keep a clean separation between different kinds of concepts and between abstract foundations and actual implementations. This approach represents good, modern design practice. However, as you've seen, the way the models are developed differs between DAML-S on the one hand and WSDL and UDDI on the other. The former relies heavily on classification and class properties, so that a DAML-S document defines the relationships between the entities and properties. The latter uses a kind of object- or database-centered approach in which the relationships

---

[8] Version 0.6 of the DAML-S walk-through: www.daml.org/services/daml-s/2001/10/DAML-S-0.6-walkthru.ps.

must be implemented by the software that processes the data. The DAML-S approach is far more open, adaptable to change, and usable by more general software. The WSDL and UDDI approach may lend itself to more efficient special-purpose software.

DAML-S probably won't survive in its current form. DAML + OIL is being replaced by the W3C's OWL, and DAML-S is being converted to use OWL. Topic Maps (chapter 3) could model the same concepts as DAML-S.

The Foundation for Intelligent Physical Agents (FIPA), a framework for intelligent agents covered in the next chapter, also has extensive models for services and how agents could interact with them. The models are somewhat different but are again based on a set of abstractions that could be related to either DAML-S or WSDL and UDDI.

Because WSDL messages can easily be translated to and from RDF, and the database-like structure of UDDI can also be translated to and from RDF, it seems that RDF/OWL/DAML-S or something similar could help integrate frameworks like the currently favored XML web services into a future Semantic Web.

8.5 Will web services converge with the Semantic Web?

Because commercial services require so many features, there are many projects to develop specifications to cover a myriad of technical capabilities. For example, Microsoft and IBM with some partners have been developing a family of specifications known as Global XML Web Services Architecture (GXA). These are intended to be relatively small, simple, modular specifications that can work together. A partial list of their titles will give you an idea of what they cover:

- WS-Addressing
- WS-Coordination
- WS-Inspection
- WS-Policy
- WS-Referral
- WS-ReliableMessaging
- WS-Routing
- WS-Security
- WS-Transaction

Each of these specifications uses XML to structure its data. Each addresses a specific capability seen as necessary for commercial web services. For example, WS-Inspection provides a simple language for inspecting a web site to see what services it has to offer. A WS-Inspection file can contain keys for UDDI directory entries, pointers to WSDL files, and other useful meta data. An examination of all the developing specifications would be lengthy and wouldn't shed much more light on the relationship between web services and the Semantic Web.

The web services "mainline," which includes WSDL, SOAP, the WS-* specifications listed earlier and others, and UDDI, is being promoted by a number of large companies like Microsoft and IBM, so the effort has a lot of momentum. REST proponents, though, have been able to influence the web services work being done by the W3C, including SOAP and WSDL, two of the backbones of mainline web services. Furthermore, there is strong support for Semantic Web principles because of its leader, Tim Berners-Lee, who has been promoting his vision of the Semantic Web for a long time. These efforts have led to the reworking of SOAP to be more amenable to REST-style approaches, which may in turn make them more amenable to making use of Semantic Web technologies.

The real questions are still to be answered. With all the effort being put into developing commercial web services, will they be too complicated and expensive? Will they be accessible only to large companies with many resources? Will they require centralized registries? Will they be able to scale up to the scope of the Web, and do they need to? Will they benefit from semantic enrichment? Will they be accessible to smart agents and search sites? In a word, will the Semantic Web have a role to play in the world of commercial web services? These are good questions that can't be answered now.

8.6 *Summary*

A web service is a software system identified by a URI, which provides some value to its users. Other systems may interact with the web service, according to its design. A great deal of work—and hype—is going into the development of standards and frameworks for web services because there is a perception that large amounts of commerce will begin using web services on a large scale.

You've seen that the current XML web services approach, based primarily on WSDL and UDDI, isn't oriented toward Semantic Web–style functionality, except inasmuch as it will be possible to find and invoke services over the Internet. You've also seen that there are good possibilities for adapting services, possibly with RDF. DAML-S, an alternative approach to describing web services, uses an ontology/knowledge representation approach.

It's clear that describing, locating, and using services on the Internet is far more complicated than simply publishing web pages. XML web services toolkits attempt to hide some of this intricacy from the programmer, but underneath it's a complex affair. The REST advocates (see section 8.3.4) think the whole process would be much simpler if the pure principles of the Web (as they see it) were followed. The mainline proponents say that the REST approach is incapable of efficiently and securely supporting the needs of commercial web services.

Most, if not all, of the developing standards—WSDL, UDDI, and the rest—can probably be translated into an RDF form. It's therefore possible that ways could be worked out to combine Semantic Web technologies with future versions of XML web services. You've seen that this will be more feasible if service providers move toward a REST-like approach, because the Web is about the widespread interconnection of resources, and a REST-like approach turns the stages of web services into resources. The latest version of UDDI can use URIs as identifiers for the information stored in UDDI repositories, which is a step toward opening up this system to the Web, and which also puts control of those identifiers back into the hands of the service owners instead of the repository owners.

Even if mainline XML web services become widespread according to the design of the first generation of XML web services, which is possible since they have so much momentum behind them (and, to be candid, the new semantic technologies require a different way of thinking that is unfamiliar to most programmers), something like DAML-S could spread as a grass-roots phenomenon. Such spreading has been happening with Rich Site Summary (RSS; a format for publishing news summaries, described in chapter 2), for one, so there is a precedent.

As you can see, the direction for future evolution of web services is an open question. Will it become dominated by a few large players who maintain tight control of the information in the repositories and charge for access to it, or will it move to a free and open model? Can the two outcomes co-exist? Can there be other outcomes? Will Semantic Web technologies be able to play a role?

Stay tuned.

9

Agents

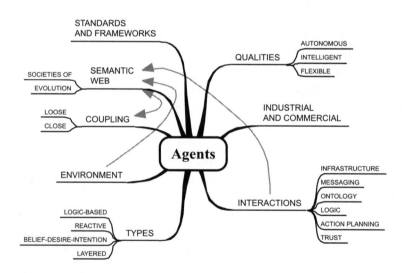

This is ridiculous! Anybody in this room could win a race with a turtle, you know, and we're not great heroes and athletes. Even, for example, some old, very dignified person, like Bertrand Russell, he could win a race with a tortoise. And if he couldn't win it, he could outsmart it!

—Severn Darden, *Lecture on Metaphysics*

"What is it you want to buy?" the Sheep said at last, looking up for a moment from her knitting.

"I don't QUITE know yet," Alice said, very gently. "I should like to look all round me first, if I might."

—Lewis Carroll, *Through the Looking Glass*

In daily life, an agent is a person who acts on your behalf. One agent may buy groceries, while another may negotiate an agreement for you. The metaphor is obvious—a machine that acts on your behalf, with some degree of autonomy, is an agent. There is more to it than that, though. For one thing, the definition would cover some simple mechanisms, like thermostats, that we don't normally think of as agents. For another, an agent has to operate in some environment, and with our interest in world-wide data that's accessible to computers, that environment will be a distributed, networked system.

Agents are often mentioned in connection with the Semantic Web. It's said that agents will perform tasks, find services, and even negotiate schedules for us.

Many people think—or hope—that more or less autonomous software entities will carry out many of the tasks of the Semantic Web. Obviously a small, closed system of agents, all written in the same language and all understanding the same commands, will be much easier to create than a broad, heterogeneous, open system where the agents use many different vocabularies and have little control over their environment. This chapter covers the basics of agents, not in a detailed or theoretical way, but with an eye to the potential use of agents on the Semantic Web.

9.1 *What is an intelligent agent?*

If you look back at the two scenarios in chapter 1 and see how the personal digital assistants behaved, you'll notice that they showed adaptability and initiative, even to the point of negotiating a common understanding of a new word. The term in use is *intelligent agent*. In this context, *intelligent* refers to flexible, autonomous behavior, in which an agent reacts to its environment appropriately and may take initiative to meet its goals. The term also indicates some kind of social capability, so that the agent may interact effectively with other agents and, from time to time, with people.

In this chapter, then, we're concerned with autonomous, intelligent software packages that operate in an environment outside their control, seek to reach goals, and can interact with other agents in pursuit of their goals. Naturally, being "autonomous" and "intelligent" are relative terms, and we expect these agents to be given their goals by people and to ultimately be controllable by people. Our agents by and large won't operate in isolation, but will interact with a variety of others.

The definition of an agent isn't universally agreed on, but the key points we've mentioned will serve well enough. Besides being a kind of software, agents can be thought of as a new approach to creating complex software systems. In software engineering, *close coupling* refers to software modules that are designed to work closely with certain other modules, often invoking internal functions whose details they are familiar with. An *agent system*, by contrast, is a very *loosely coupled* system. (See McGrath and Murray [2003] for a good discussion of loose coupling in the context of web services.)

Close coupling can be likened to the legal system. To interact with the legal system, you need an expert (an attorney) who interacts with the court system in highly specific and constrained ways according to detailed rules. Loose coupling can be likened to a soccer team. The team members share certain kinds of equipment and use it in much the same way, but the manner of play adjusts itself according to the situation of the team members at any particular time, and the team members interact in a flexible rather than a rigid manner.

Close coupling can lead to high-speed operation and many efficiencies but makes it hard to extend or modify a design and to adapt it to operate in an open, distributed environment. A closely coupled system can be like a jigsaw puzzle where the parts fit together tightly and can fit only one way. A loosely coupled system interacts in more general ways, usually by exchanging messages that can be understood by a range of software with different design and construction. In this way, a program in a loosely coupled system needs to know far less about the detailed workings of the rest of the system than is the case for a program in a closely coupled system. This approach brings the possibility of flexibility and openness, at a cost of lower operating efficiency. It also requires considerable standardization to allow the loosely coupled, separately designed parts to work together.

The current Web is loosely coupled, which allows a wide range of programs, designed independently from each other, to operate together. A system designed using an agent approach, if it's very loosely coupled, could fit in well.

9.2 *Agents at work*

Agents have been used in commercial service for several years, although they may not meet all the criteria mentioned above for intelligent, autonomous, distributed agents. Some industrial process controllers have many of the characteristics of agents; but they tend to be closely tied to the exact industrial process they run, and they certainly aren't open to relatively uncontrolled environments and the requests of other unknown agents. Still, these agent systems have had to solve many of the same problems as agents on the Semantic Web.

In developing a complex design, the designers always have to make tradeoffs between the weight, bulk, power consumption, and function of the components and subsystems. It can be difficult to find a good solution. For example, in airplane design, the tradeoffs are weighted by imposing a cost for each unit of weight. Each pound of excess weight of a component might be assessed a penalty of, say, $100.

An agent system is especially well suited for representing independent tradeoffs with well-defined costs. Each agent could represent a different component. Agent systems have been used to solve such tradeoffs during high-level design: Each agent negotiates with the others, based on costs assigned by the designers. Eventually, a solution is reached; and, often, that solution is reached more quickly and is better than can be achieved with conventional approaches. Scheduling and planning are similar in concept, and agent systems have been used for shop and machine tool scheduling in manufacturing plants. For example, agents have been used in automotive plants to schedule paint booths and stamping shops. Agent systems have been reported to increase the uptime of complex transfer lines from 50% to 90%. ([Weiss 2000], p. 397)

In general, any system that can be modeled as a series of tasks interacting with each other and with a common environment may be a candidate for an agent approach, if the tasks can be defined well enough and if costs that make sense can be assigned to weight the results. Real-time control problems fit into this category.

9.3 *Basic agent types*

The classic Artificial Intelligence approach to autonomous entities was to build a logical reasoner that would take data from sensors, such as photocells or cameras, consult a store of facts and rules, and attempt to compute how to behave. These attempts never worked well; in response, many alternative approaches have been developed. Some of this work has carried over to research on agents.

One classification scheme (Weiss 2000) classifies agents into four categories:

- Logic-based agents
- Reactive agents
- Belief-desire-intention agents
- Layered architectures

We'll look at each of these types. Logic-based agent types probably fit best with much of the current Semantic Web development work—which is based on ontologies supporting logical inferences using information in knowledge bases, as you saw in chapters 6 and 7 on ontologies and logic. But it isn't the style of agent that determines how it could fit into the Semantic Web; rather, this depends on its method of interaction with other agents and resources on the Web. Any of these agent types could be used in both Web and non-Web environments if designed accordingly.

9.3.1 *Logic-based agents*

Logic-based agents represent the classic AI approach mentioned earlier. In essence, agents contain a system for logical deduction and proving theorems, together with sets of rules and procedures and a theory of their world and how to behave. Based on input from sensors, an agent tries to prove theorems by logical reasoning. If a theorem can be proved, the agent carries out the action defined for that theorem. A theorem might be that an airplane is in normal flight, based on its altitude, speed, rate of heading change, and angle of attack. If the aircraft agent can prove this theorem at one particular moment, it can consult its rules to see what to do next.

This hardly seems like a "theorem" (it's more like a simple formula), but the theorems can be much more complex and require intermediate deductions and inferences. Theorem-solving software has been in use for many years. One drawback is that there is no way to guarantee how long an arbitrary theorem will take to solve, or even if it can be solved. This wouldn't be good for real-time control agents.

Another difficulty is in providing for flexibility and suitable behavior in unexpected situations. Also, representing the environment is difficult: It must be turned into a symbolic representation, and such representations aren't highly developed. Representation of a visual environment, for instance, isn't well developed, at least not compared with the vision of living creatures like birds and humans.

In general, purely logic-based approaches didn't work well in classic AI, and the same problems carry over to agents. Still, in restricted environments with well-understood tasks, a logic-based approach may succeed well.

9.3.2 *Reactive agents*

The reactive approach is virtually the opposite of the logic-based approach. There is no symbolic reasoning, no logical deduction, no overall view of the agent's situation and goals. Instead, the agent reacts to specific changes in its environment directly via specific local behaviors. These behaviors are something like reflexes. If you lose your balance, reflex responses from your nerves and muscles restore it with no conscious action. You have reacted directly to changes in your environment, which includes information on the position of your body parts and their motions.

Because different aspects of the environment change separately, many combinations of specific responses can arise. Some behaviors can inhibit, or take precedence over, others. The agent's overall behavior emerges from these combinations. Ants probably fall into this category of reactive agents. Individual robots have been built with this approach (including insect-like robots that discover how to stand up and walk without that behavior being programmed in), showing that complex and flexible behavior is possible with this model.

9.3.3 *Belief-desire-intention agents*

Belief-desire-intention (BDI) agents have been the most successful pattern so far. BDI is sometimes said to use *practical* reasoning. Beliefs correspond to knowledge about the world, desires to goals, and intentions to plans. A degree of inferencing capability is built in. Intentions and even desires can be in conflict and may need to be reconciled, just as often happens with people. An agent's intentions may change over time, as might be appropriate if a plan is found to be unworkable or if the priorities are changed.

One challenge is balancing desires against beliefs and intentions. If intentions are changed too often, nothing effective ever gets done; but if they aren't revised according to newer information about the environment and the state of desires, inappropriate plans may continue to be executed. A good balance depends on how fast the environment—that is, the rest of the world—changes.

9.3.4 *Layered architectures*

Although layered architectures have been mentioned as one category of agents, to some extent a layered approach could apply to any kind of agent. There are two approaches to layering, sometimes called *horizontal* and *vertical*. With horizontal layering, each layer processes one kind of (usually sensory) input from input to output. The results of each layer must be balanced to produce a coherent result.

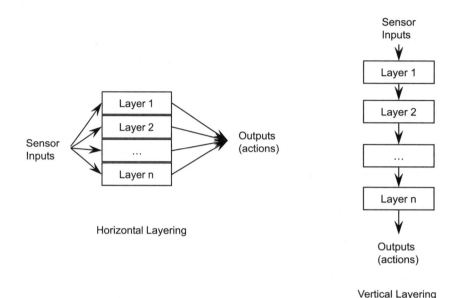

Figure 9.1 **Horizontal and vertical layering in agent architecture. In the horizontal design, the layers process sensory inputs in parallel (although the layers may communicate with each other as well). In the vertical design, inputs flow through one processing layer after another, although again the layers can communicate during this process.**

With vertical layering, different kinds of processing take place in different layers, such as planning, reacting, and so on. Processing usually takes place in one layer after another, although some or all of the layers may receive input from all the sensors. See figure 9.1.

9.4 *Agent interactions*

The potential number of kinds of interactions between agents is huge. Most agents will need to communicate in order to coordinate their activities, jointly plan actions, negotiate, maintain a shared state (such as beliefs or goals), request actions of other agents, and change their plans based on the actions of other agents. Agent systems operating on the Semantic Web will also need to be able to establish the credentials and trustworthiness of other agents, work with agents that haven't been designed as part of the same project (and thus don't necessarily share goals), and operate in the largely uncontrolled environment that the Web inherently brings with it.

Agent interactions will take place on several levels:

- *Common infrastructure*—On the most basic level, agents need a common infrastructure to be able to communicate. Agents that exist in the memory of a single computer can communicate by using a form of shared memory or other standard interprocess communication method; but for the Semantic Web, agents will presumably use the Internet (or private intranets, in some cases). Some people see agents as being similar to advanced services. According to this view, agents would communicate by exchanging message payloads much like payloads for services, and most likely using the same protocols.

- *Messaging*—Up a level, an agent needs to be able to decipher the messages it receives. This requires standard message structures and message types, along with a standard language to express the messages.

- *Ontology*—Up another level, an agent needs to understand the vocabulary used in the messages it receives. This is the domain of Ontology. If an agent doesn't know the ontology used in a message, it will either have to find and import it and reconcile the new vocabulary with the ones it already knows about, or it will have to reply and say that it's unable to work with the message.

- *Logic*—The scenarios in chapter 1 had the personal assistant agents explaining their reasoning to their owners. Agents may also have to explain their reasoning to other agents. In addition, they may have to send logical prescriptions and formulas to other agents, so most likely a language for interchanging logical formulas and reasoning will be needed too.

- *Action planning*—The languages just mentioned may be enough to support mutual planning and agreements for action, with the addition of more message types and an appropriate ontology. Otherwise, another language or language extension would be needed.

- *Authorization and trust*—Agents will need to be able to interchange credentials that establish their provenance, trustworthiness, and authority to take certain actions (like charging a credit card, for instance). In chapter 10, you'll see that an agent will need to be able to assert and prove that it has the authority to act for its owner and to commit resources (such as paying for services). Because one agent will generally interact with several others, it will presumably have to be able to pass some of that authority along the line to other agents. How this can be done safely and reliably is a large and, as yet, unanswered question.

9.5 Agents on the Semantic Web

The theory and design of agents can get very complicated. The agents themselves may not be that complex, considered as individual pieces of software; however, their interaction with other agents and the environment can become intricate. One striking point is that an agent has no overall view of the system or the system's goals. It knows only its own goals and environment.

When many agents have to cooperate—for example, to perform scheduling or control traffic—the system won't perform in a completely predictable way, although if it's well designed it will usually arrive at a good solution. Unexpected behaviors can also arise—so-called *emergent* behaviors—and they become more likely as the number of possible behaviors and interactions increases. We have to hope that the unexpected aspects can be dealt with through tuning and design changes during development and testing.

9.5.1 Beyond factory agents

It isn't hard to picture a society of agents working in a factory setting or other controlled environment. Agents like that would have well-defined goals and would only interact with other agents designed as part of the same system, which would be well authenticated and trustworthy. The ontologies and methods of reasoning would be restricted and known to all agents.

Contrast this with the rather futuristic scenarios from the first chapter. There, the personal assistant agents interacted with other agents and a variety of information sources on the Web. Terms from other ontologies had to be imported and used appropriately, and the goals that motivated those actions were not all that clear cut. A variety of reasoning methods had to be applied. The totality of these scenarios is far beyond today's factory agent systems.

Remember from chapter 6 that the Semantic Web will be a so-called *open world*. This means that some information may turn out to contradict other data and that some resources may not always be accessible. Moreover, malicious agents are sure to try to masquerade as trustworthy allies from time to time.

You can see that a society of agents that must operate on the Semantic Web will be much more complicated than a group that operates in a relatively private environment like a factory. But it's unlikely that a full-blown, complex agent system could come into widespread use all at once. The original Web started from small-scale, simple beginnings and evolved from there. Agents will have to do the same, although the starting point will of necessity be more complex.

9.5.2 *Agent evolution*

The simplest possible agent would be charged with a single task: gathering information. Single-task, information-gathering software has been in use for years. A so-called *spider* searches web sites to discover and index all their linked pages and then searches those linked sites as well. Some software packages retrieve weather or stock information from a variety of sources. This kind of software hardly counts as an agent according to this chapter's point of view, since it doesn't cooperate with different kinds of agents and doesn't exhibit flexible, intelligent behavior. Still, it's a start.

Most likely, simple agent systems will be developed that are deployed by a few people or companies—systems that have limited abilities and for which trust and security questions will be of low importance. Perhaps they will be offered with PDA-style pocket computers. As standards evolve (whether officially recognized or de facto), more capabilities will be tried out. Vocabularies will be developed, and ways will be devised to discover their location when they're needed. Practical and useful reasoning methods that can deal with the uncertainty and openness of the environment of the Web will be devised and come into broader use. Two or more groups will cooperate to make their agents work together. Little by little, more capabilities will come into common use. At some point, agents may become flexible and complex enough that useful behaviors may arise (more or less spontaneously), depending on their experience rather than being specifically programmed in detail. At this point, the advanced scenarios from chapter 1 will look more feasible.

This process is already underway.

9.6 *Frameworks and standards*

This section looks briefly at some developing standards for agents on the Semantic Web. It doesn't cover academic systems and agent programming languages that have been published, or systems used in industrial applications. These standards may become the basis for Semantic Web agents, although that's far from certain.

9.6.1 *Foundation for Intelligent Physical Agents*

The Foundation for Intelligent Physical Agents (FIPA) is a consortium with member companies world wide. Its goal is to produce "standards for the interoperation of heterogeneous software agents." FIPA supports work on ontologies, semantics, services, scheduling, and security, to name the most prominent goals.

FIPA has created a fairly comprehensive framework of specifications that attempts to cover the entire range needed to specify agent command, control, and interactions. These specifications are in different states of development; some are placeholders, and others are mature. FIPA has tried hard to make sure that each specification is carefully focused on a limited area. The FIPA specifications are, for the most part, quite abstract. For example, the ACL Message Structure Specification defines the structure and contents of messages, but independently of any interchange format. Actual agent messages could be constructed using XML, RDF, or a wide range of other approaches. There is also an ACL Message Representation in XML Specification that specifies how to express FIPA messages using XML. This abstract approach is powerful and separates the essential design features from considerations required for practical implementation.

To give you a feel for the extent of FIPA's coverage, and also to illustrate the wide range of technical areas needed to develop and deploy agents, here is a partial list of FIPA specification titles:

Abstract Architecture Specification

ACL Message Structure Specification

ACL Message Representation in XML Specification

Agent Software Integration Specification

Communicative Act Library Specification

Content Language Library Specification

CCL (Constraint Choice) Content Language Specification

KIF Content Language Specification

RDF Content Language Specification

SL (Syntax and Lexical) Content Language Specification

Nomadic Application Support Specification

Query Interaction Protocol Specification

Request Interaction Protocol Specification

Request When Interaction Protocol Specification

Device Ontology Specification

Ontology Service Specification

Personal Assistant Specification

Personal Travel Assistance Specification

Looking through this list, it's obvious that FIPA has taken a thorough approach to covering its chosen field. The use of RDF is accommodated (and also XML, although it isn't included in our partial list). Also notice the specifications related to ontology: The Ontology Service Specification provides a framework for agents to share ontologies, which will be extremely important when a range of separately designed agents needs to work together. Agent Software Integration is another forward-looking specification; it attempts to provide a way to wrap or integrate existing or non-FIPA software so that it can participate in a FIPA-compatible agent society.

The first specification in the list specifies an abstract architecture. This is an effort to make sure that an agent system is designed with certain kinds of features. For example, the Abstract Architecture says this, in part, about agents (www.fipa.org/specs/fipa00001/SC00001L.html#_Toc26668620):

> An *agent* is a computational process that implements the autonomous, communicating functionality of an application. Typically, agents communicate using an *Agent Communication Language*. A concrete instantiation of *agent* is a mandatory element of every concrete instantiation of the FIPA Abstract Architecture.

It goes on to list the relationships between an agent and other elements of the abstract architecture.

The abstract architecture was added to FIPA some time after the first version of the framework was made available. Thus, some implementations follow it and some don't.

9.6.2 *FIPA-OS and other FIPA implementations*

The FIPA specifications don't tell you how to write software that can analyze beliefs and uncertainties and arrive at assessments of trustworthiness. But if you can do that, the specifications give you a framework for interacting with other agents. The FIPA-OS open source project (www.emorphia.com/research/about.htm) provides a programming toolkit for developing FIPA-compliant agents.

FIPA-OS is an open-source effort, meaning that the source code is freely available. Some 30 companies are said to have contributed code to the project. The toolkit, which is coded in Java, gives you an implemented framework (of course, it's still a work in progress) for both agents and agent communications, but you still have to design the agent interactions, the logic of the programming, and the means by which the agents can assess their actions and interact with any central control or agent that may be needed for overall direction. FIPA-OS comes with simple examples of agents to give you a starting point.

The current crops of FIPA implementations and frameworks fall into two groups: those that implement the FIPA Abstract Architecture and those older ones that don't. FIPA-OS is one of those that doesn't implement the FIPA Abstract Architecture Specification.

Other implementations and frameworks

Other implementations are available, such as Zeus (http://more.btexact.com/projects/agents/zeus/) and the Java Agent Development Framework (Jade; http://sharon.cselt.it/projects/jade), both of which are open source projects. At the time of this writing, they also don't implement the Abstract Architecture Specification. These frameworks are being used in research projects, such as Knowledge On Demand (KOD; http://kod.iti.gr/). Figure 9.2 is a diagram of KOD, showing the prominent role agents play. This system is built with Jade.

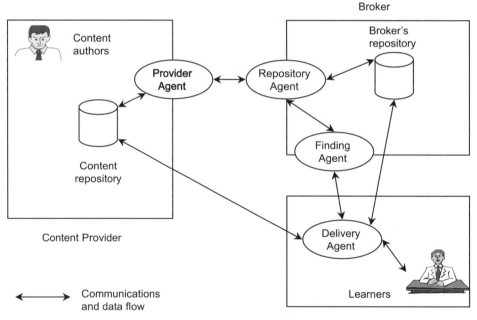

Figure 9.2   Architecture of the Knowledge On Demand system (adapted with simplifications from KOD). The agents are built using the Jade agent framework. Agents act for users in finding, storing, and obtaining information. Not shown is software that packages the data and meta data before it's exchanged between agents.

9.6.3 *Java Agent Services*

FIPA provides a comprehensive set of specifications for agents and agent interactions. FIPA-OS, Jade, and Zeus are toolkits or implementation frameworks. None of these defines a standard programming interface. In other words, you have to learn different programming commands and structures to use each of the toolkits. A standard programming interface is probably essential for businesses to begin using agents on a large scale.

The Java Agent Services (JAS) project (www.java-agent.org) is developing a Java Application Programming Interface (API) and a reference implementation of that interface. Unlike the older FIPA-based frameworks we've mentioned, JAS will be an instance of the FIPA Abstract Architecture. The goal is for JAS to become a standard interface for FIPA agents. With such an API, you can write code that will work with any number of implementations and toolkits, as long as they use the JAS API. At the time of this writing, the JAS project has released version 1.0, a package that includes both the specification and a reference implementation.

9.7 *Summary*

This chapter has covered the basics of intelligent networked agents, at least as far as their infrastructure is concerned. We consider an agent to be a software component that acts for people with some degree of autonomy. By *intelligent*, we mean the agent has some awareness of its environment and can adapt its behavior to changes in that environment and to the responses of other agents.

You've seen that agents represent a way to build loosely coupled systems, which is necessary for systems that need to be flexible, adaptable, and able to scale up to the scope of the World Wide Web. Intelligent, networked agents will use all the other layers of the Semantic Web—knowledge representation languages, interoperable ontologies, logic processing, services, searching, the whole works. Solving the issues of trust, identification, and authorization so that autonomous agents can be used on the Internet with confidence for sensitive tasks such as business transactions will obviously be challenging. So will the design of intelligent behavior. Nevertheless, agents on the Internet are starting to come into use, and their capabilities will continue to evolve.

The FIPA (Foundation for Intelligent Physical Agents) specifications are a general set of specifications for agent infrastructure. JAS is a developing set of programming interfaces for programming FIPA-based agents in the Java programming language. These are the most-developed frameworks that are commonly available for creating agents that could be used on the Web, so Semantic Web agents may eventually be based on them.

10

Distributed trust and belief

"You!" said the Caterpillar contemptuously. "Who are you?"

Which brought them back again to the beginning of the conversation. Alice felt a little irritated at the Caterpillar's making such very short remarks, and she drew herself up and said, very gravely, "I think, you ought to tell me who you are, first."

"Why?" said the Caterpillar.

—Lewis Carroll, *Alice's Adventures in Wonderland*

Who are you going to believe, me or your own eyes?

—Groucho Marx

The Sphinx was a twisty character, she tricked me into saying it!

—Severn Darden as Oedipus Rex

When I needed to travel to Thailand, I applied for a passport. I took my birth certificate to the Post Office, where the passport clerk inspected it and signed a form, and in due course I received a passport. My birth certificate vouched for my identity. The United States government trusted that I am who I claimed to be. A commonplace event, yet how strange. My birth certificate is a piece of paper, and it isn't even stamped with the seal of a hospital or court. It's obviously old and looks its age, but aside from its being in my possession there is no way it can identify the human being who presents it as being me. What if it had been stolen?

I visit the web page for a piece of software that claims it can virtually eliminate spam from my email. I trust the page in the sense that I accept that it represents the software company, and I trust the company not to put my credit card information to unauthorized use. But should I believe that the software will perform as claimed?

These kinds of questions are ancient: "Why should I believe you are who you say?" and "Why should I believe what you say?" The rise of commerce over the Internet has raised the stakes because there is no personal contact, just anonymous electronic activity. Today, questions of identity and security on the Web are largely handled by encryption and security certificates. But the Semantic Web will bring deeper and more complex issues; it will also bring other ways to deal with them.

10.1 *The territory*

Any police procedural novel captures the essence of the matter. Witnesses have to be reliably identified and their biases discovered. Each piece of evidence has to be placed in context. Each statement by a witness or suspect must be evaluated as to how much confidence should be placed in it. The Semantic Web will bring new dimensions to the puzzle. The facts and opinions will be aggregated, without much human intervention, from sources distributed all over the Web. Software agents, as discussed in the last chapter, add another dimension to this matter. How can an agent establish that it's authorized to act for you? Even if one agent were to inform another that it had proper authorization, how could a data supplier be sure that the first agent was truthful and be assured that its data would only go to the correct place?

Even the case of software agents has its analog in the pre-Web world. An agency using foreign espionage agents must face many of the same problems. A foreign agent may be masquerading as your agent but really be operating for someone else. A foreign source may supply information of dubious reliability. Even with a trusted agent known to obtain correct information, the reports must be placed into the right context.

The territory of trust and belief, then, covers these areas at the least:

- Trust
    - Identity: Who are you?
    - Why should I trust you?
    - Who else trusts you?
    - How much should I trust you?
    - How can I know that you said what you've claimed to have said?
- Belief
    - How much confidence should I place in what you say?
    - What should I believe when different "facts" don't agree?
    - How much should my prior beliefs influence my confidence in what you say?
    - How can I establish the correct degree of belief for a given set of information?

Of course, the word *you* might refer to an agent, to any other source of information or services, or to any entity that vouches for another's identity.

You might think that *Trust* could be subsumed under *Belief*, on the grounds that, for example, trust in a person's identity amounts to a belief that the claimed identity is the actual identity. Thus, the one can be seen as a special case of the other. There is merit in this notion, and you'll see that some of the approaches to dealing with the issues are likely to be similar for the two. Yet there is a qualitative difference, in that *Trust* tends to be about quasi-official information—identity, responsibility for statements, and the like—while *Belief* tends to be about meta data, alleged facts, and opinions. According to WordNet (www.cogsci.princeton.edu/~wn/), trust (as a verb) means "to have confidence in," whereas belief is "cognitive content held as true." Obviously the boundary is fuzzy, and the terminology in use isn't yet consistent.

10.2 *Tools of trust*

On the Web today, the area of *Trust* is largely confined to *Identity* and *Who else trusts you?* Identity is usually established by means of digital *certificates*. Certificates depend on a version of so-called public key cryptography. In this connection, a *key* is a string of digits or characters that can be used to encrypt or decrypt a message. Entire messages may be encrypted to keep them secret, but often all that is necessary is to ensure that a message hasn't been changed. In that case, it's enough to encrypt a short summary, or *digest,* of the message. A *digital signature* amounts to a specially encrypted digest of a message that allows you to verify who signed it. You'll see how keys, digests, and signatures work shortly.

Certificates supply a degree of authentication of identity, but of course they're only as good as their issuer. In practice, one issuer of a certificate is vouched for by another in an interlocking set of hierarchies, sometimes called a *Web of Trust.*

We won't spend much space on this system because it's in operation today and will continue regardless of whether the Semantic Web comes into being. However, other trends may bear on how trust and confidence are established in the future, and these relate more closely to the Semantic Web.

What follows is a simplified sketch of the interaction of keys, digests, and certificates.

10.2.1 *Private keys*

A *private* key is a key known only to you. You use it either to encrypt data or to decrypt it. As long as you keep the key safe, no one else can encrypt or decrypt messages with it. If only you possess the key, though, how can anyone else ever decrypt any message you encrypted? And how can anyone else encrypt a message for you to decrypt and read? One way is to share the key. This wouldn't work well on a wide scale—because a secret widely shared is soon not a secret—but there are better ways. These involve *public* keys.

10.2.2 *Public keys*

It turns out that it's possible to use your private key to encrypt a message that can be decrypted using a *different* key. If you give this second key to someone, and they succeed in decrypting a message with it, they can be assured that the message was encrypted using your private key. This is almost the same thing as saying that it came from you.

Conversely, it's possible to have a key, different from your private key, that anyone else can use to encrypt a message but that only your private key can decrypt. In this way, a message meant only for you can remain a secret to everyone else.

This second key can be the same for both cases. It can be given out safely to any number of others. Therefore it's known as a *public* key.

10.2.3 *Digests*

A *digest* is a summary; in the world of cryptography and security, a digest is a special summary of a document or message that can't be reversed into the original. No key is involved. Suppose I compute a digest of a document, and you compute a digest of some document using the same algorithm. Then if the digests are exactly equal, the two documents are identical; and if the digests differ at all, the two messages aren't identical. Slightly different messages generally produce very different digests, so the similarity between digests can't be used to predict the similarity between the two messages.

The value of this approach is that you can compare messages without disclosing their contents simply by comparing their digests. Digests can also be encrypted using a private key. An encrypted digest can be used as a *signature* that authenticates a message: The signer's identity is established by decrypting the signature with a public key, and the message's content is authenticated by comparing its digest with the digest decrypted from the signature.

10.2.4 *Public Key Infrastructure*

Public Key Infrastructure (PKI) is a common system that makes use of both private and public keys to safeguard important communications. PKI is by far the most common such system used today.

Here is how you can be sure that I am me. You have to know my public key. You send me a message; any message will do. I encrypt it with my secret key and send it back to you. You try to decrypt it using my public key. If you get back the same message, you know that my private key must have been used.[1] But how do you know the public key you used is really mine? Maybe someone else slipped you theirs, instead.

The solution that is in widespread use is the *digital certificate*. A certificate is issued by a *Certificate Authority* (CA), which is an organization that is supposed to be trustworthy. Verisign is perhaps the best-known Certificate Authority. Just as a government agency issues a driver's license that is good for most identification purposes, Verisign issues digital certificates that are good for most digital authentication purposes.[2] Verisign uses its private key (what else?) to sign a digest of my public key. Using Verisign's public key, you can make sure that my certificate was issued by Verisign and that it was issued against my key.

A certificate may be issued by some entity that isn't as well known as Verisign. How can you trust it? Aha: It has its own certificate, signed by another CA. There may be an entire chain of certificates, reaching up to some relatively unimpeachable authority. The PKI system provides protocols to allow authenticating software to traverse the entire chain, if necessary, until a satisfactory authority is reached. For example, a university could set up its own CA for its research labs. The labs could then share data and reports using certificates for authentication while keeping them from unauthorized eyes. Figure 10.1 depicts several such chains of trust. Notice how separate chains can cross-certify each other; this can be accomplished by having each CA cross-sign the other's public key. The CA at the top of each chain, or hierarchy, is called the *root CA*. A root CA has the controlling authority over the CAs lower down.

There are two problems with this scheme. First, if the private key of a root CA is compromised, then its entire chain is rendered untrustworthy, since anything it authenticates would be suspect. But at least the other hierarchies could continue to operate as long as they don't try to use the compromised chain.

---

[1] In practice, I'd probably compute the digest of your message and encrypt that, rather than the message itself. You'd then decode the digest, compute the digest yourself, and make sure the two digests agreed. That way no one else could know the contents of the original message. This is a good thing.

[2] CAs like Verisign generally offer certificates with different degrees of authentication (and cost). The certificates offered over the Internet for a low or zero annual cost are issued with no real evidence as to your identity. This may be sufficient for you to authenticate your email to friends or to get familiar with the workings of digital signatures. Each CA establishes a policy, or set of policies, that set forth the requirements for issuing a certificate. This topic is also discussed further later in this section.

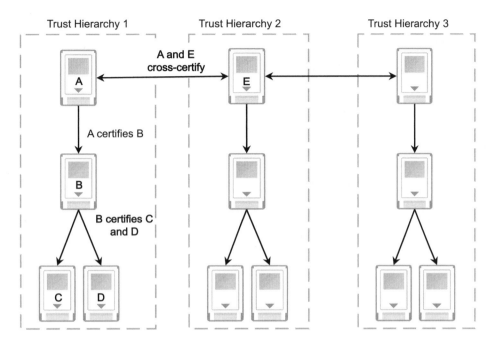

Figure 10.1 Three trust hierarchies, or chains. Each server represents a Certificate Authority (CA) that is authorized to sign and authenticate other certificates within its hierarchy. In each one, the top CA is called the *root* authority. Each CA can certify CAs below it, and two hierarchies can cross-certify each other. This allows members of one hierarchy to be authorized to access members of the other.

Second, as the number of cross-certified chains grows larger, the number of cross-certifications becomes unmanageably large. Figure 10.2 illustrates this situation, which will never do for operations on the scale of the Web. Another approach must be used: the current solution is the *bridge CA*.

Figure 10.3 illustrates how a bridge CA can bring a measure of sanity to the numbers of trust hierarchies that need to communicate. It does so by drastically reducing the number of interconnections.

The administrative and configuration issues involved in maintaining proper control are considerable, as is the technical design of the bridge itself. Another issue is that different trust hierarchies generally set different policies that bear on the trustworthiness and identity of their members. For example, what level of proof is needed to establish your identity before you're allowed to be certified? Harking back to the beginning of this chapter, this is analogous to having a policy that a birth certificate can be used to get a passport or a driver's license. In the process of determining identity and authorization, the authenticating authority

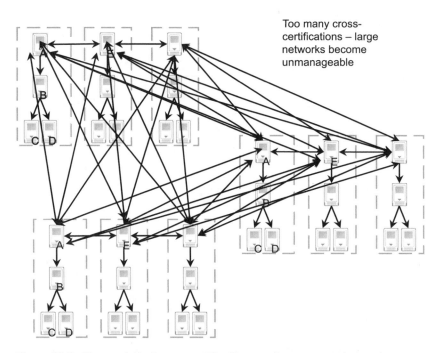

Too many cross-certifications – large networks become unmanageable

Figure 10.2 **The number of cross-certifications can become very large as more trust hierarchies are linked in. If every one links to every other one, the number of cross-links increases as the square of the number of hierarchies.**

must take into account not only the technical aspects of keys and digital signatures; it must also attempt to take the applicable policies into account. Sorting through a complex maze of cross-certifications and hierarchies with different policies and histories can involve intricate logical processing, which is one of the reasons the layer labeled *Trust* sits on top of the layer marked *Logic and Proof* in the Semantic Web layer cake shown in chapter 1.

If you have a certificate of your own—and at the time of this writing you can get one for about $15 (U.S.) that's valid for a year—your browser and email client can use it instead of passwords to authenticate your identity to many web sites. Of course, it's really authenticating that your computer or account or key was used, not you personally, but it's still a step in the direction of secure authentication.

This has been a very simplified account of PKI, but it gives the basics that you need.

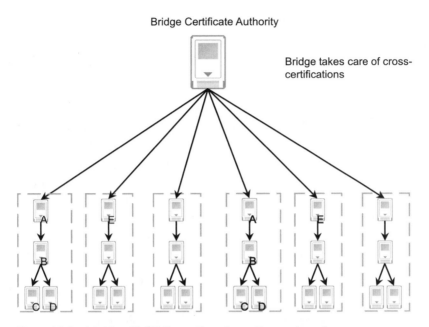

Bridge Certificate Authority

Bridge takes care of cross-certifications

Figure 10.3   A bridge CA (BCA) greatly reduces the number of cross-certifications needed for different trust hierarchies to interoperate. This approach can make large-scale systems of authentication practical, but it places a high burden on the security and trustworthiness of the BCA.

10.2.5 *Digital signing*

Besides encrypting messages, you can "sign" documents with *digital signatures* that are authenticated by CAs or CA chains. Signing is supposed to vouch for something's authenticity.

Signing whole documents

You might think that encrypting a document with your private key would establish its authenticity, since only your private key (authenticated by a CA) could have been used. Doing so might be overkill, though. It's expensive in terms of processing power to encrypt a large document; and if a large body of encrypted text were compared with an unencrypted copy, it might be possible for someone to eventually figure out your key. Furthermore, most documents that need to be signed don't need to be encrypted—the majority of contracts would probably fall into this category.

If you needed to verify that you signed a particular version of a document, you could compute its digest, which would be far shorter than the original document (the MD-5 digest algorithm produces digests that are 128 bits, or 16 bytes, long).

You would then encrypt that digest with your private key. Anyone with your public key could decrypt the digest and compare it against the digest of a candidate copy of the document to see if they were exactly the same. This process would establish both that the signed document was a correct copy and that you had in fact signed it.

Signing parts of documents

You can also sign parts of documents. There must be a way to designate which part is being signed; and then you encrypt its digest. The W3C has developed the XML-Signature Syntax and Processing Recommendation for digitally signing selected parts of XML documents. Technical details are involved that we need not go into, which handle the fact that a given XML document can have different forms after processing but still contain the identical information.[3]

A non-XML document can be signed, too; its digest is placed into a separate piece of XML, along with a URI reference to the document, the algorithms used, and the applicable public key.

Non-repudiation

For some purposes, it's important that you not be able to deny that you signed something. If your private key has been used to encrypt a message or a part of a document, it can't be denied that your key was used, as long as your public key can be found. If the time of signing were itself signed, the date would be positively established as well.

10.2.6 A trust scorecard

Let's check to see how well this infrastructure of keys, certificates, CAs, and bridges stacks up against the territory laid out in section 10.1 (see table 10.1).

The evaluation seems reasonably good, but some things are less obvious. For one thing, there is no way to assess trust—and authentication of identification—outside the interlocking hierarchies of the CAs, and the reliability of their certification depends on their policies. In a way, it's similar to a driver's license. The state vouches that you've established your identity, but it's well known that there are a lot of fake driver's licenses. Furthermore, some states are more lenient about issuing licenses than others. Thus the policies for authenticating the driver's identity aren't completely rigorous. In the same way, different CAs, and

---

[3] For example, extra spaces between elements may be removed, single quotes may be changed to double quotes, and so on.

Table 10.1 Scorecard for current PKI technology, rated by the questions asked in section 10.1.

Issue	Grade
Identity: Who are you?	Good, as long as your private key hasn't been stolen or otherwise compromised, depending on the individual policies of the applicable CAs.
Why should I trust you?	Depends on the individual policies of the applicable CAs.
Who else trusts you?	Established by the CA hierarchies.
How much should I trust you?	Subject to CA policies, with no particular provision for the degree of trust.
How can I know that you said what you've claimed to have said?	Digital signatures cover this fairly well.

different chains of CAs, have different standards, called, as you saw earlier, *policies*. And, of course, any CA is subject to human error and fraud.

In addition, this whole network of trust arrangement depends on a few trustworthy CAs at the top, which amounts to a highly centralized power structure. The interlocking hierarchies are also expensive in the aggregate. It would be better if there were more widespread, decentralized, lower-cost, alternate ways to assess identity and trust.

A related problem lies in establishing that a particular public key really represents the person it's supposed to represent. This may or may not be satisfactorily covered by a CA. If I send you a key and claim that it's the public key of Bill Clinton, it may or may not really be one of his public keys, and it may not be easy for you to definitively determine whether it really is.

Finally, there is no way to approach the question of the degree of trust to be placed in an authenticated key (a person or organization), outside of reviewing the aggregate collection of policies of the applicable CAs.

10.3 *Reliable and believable?*

The Semantic Web, you've seen, will make heavy use of data and meta data of all sorts, collected from a wide range of sources distributed across the Web. Typically we think of that information as a set of statements or assertions, collected into datastores that are somewhat like current databases but with more flexibility, and endowed with more powers of analysis and logical inference. Chapters 2 and 3 discuss possible ways these statements might be organized, and chapter 6 talks about how logic plays its role and how statements may be interpreted.

10.3.1 *All statements aren't equal*

What chapters 2, 3, and 6 don't address is the fact that all statements aren't equal. For one reason or another, one statement may not be reliable, whereas another may. A piece of information may be wrong due to a mistake, ignorance, a typographical error, or malice. It may be a guess or an opinion. We usually think of data in a database as being authoritatively correct, but this isn't possible on the Web, and it won't be possible on the Semantic Web either. The problem is, on the Semantic Web, we want our software to handle all information correctly. How can the reliability of any given chunk of data be established?

For that matter, what does it mean for data to be reliable, to deserve confidence, for me to believe in it? There are no standard means or measures, although obviously the source must have something to do with it. To complicate things, a given source may be reliable in one area but not in another. Furthermore, as you discover more about the reliability of information from a source, you're likely to revise your assessment of its reliability. You may become more willing to believe the information.

The potential unreliability of data distributed over the Semantic Web leads to two directions to follow: how to deal with such information and how to assess its reliability.

10.3.2 *Handling contradictory information*

The simplest thing that can happen along these lines is for a processor to discover a supposed fact that contradicts other information it already knows about. Depending on the design of the datastore, the contradiction might be something as simple as a different spelling of a name, a different address for the same organization, or an attribution of a quote to a different person. What should the processor do? Section 6.1 discusses this issue, pointing out that in logic, the presence of a contradiction allows anything to be proven. Our processor is liable to draw any old conclusion—the whole datastore would be poisoned, in a manner of speaking. We don't want that!

At the very least, the processor should detect the appearance of a contradiction and know what new input caused it. It could then request that the user make a decision regarding what to do. A more advanced system might be able to assess the reliability of the new information relative to the old and automatically take appropriate action (more on this possibility later).

If RDF is in use, then there is a technical problem that hasn't yet been solved. As we pointed out in chapter 2, there is no way to refer directly to any RDF statement.

Therefore, we can't store it with an annotation about its contradictory status or even its source. It's possible to do so indirectly, by the process called *reification* (also discussed in chapter 2), but this technique is clumsy and inconvenient to work with. Some RDF processors have the ability to refer to a statement as an entity for their own internal purposes, but this isn't a part of standard RDF and so can't be exchanged with other RDF processors. The easiest way to handle this kind of situation would be to extend an RDF statement so that it has four parts rather than three; the additional part would act as an identifier for the whole statement. So far, the RDF developers haven't moved in this direction. Note that Topic Maps (chapter 3) don't have this problem of being unable to refer directly to statements.

Whether or not RDF is in use, we encounter another kind of technical complication if a statement that was made part of the datastore is later removed, as it might be in the face of contradictory information. The storage of one statement can cause one or more other statements to be created. If an RDF processor encountered a statement about Bill Clinton, it might be able to determine that Bill Clinton is a person and add a statement to that effect. Now, if the original statement were to be withdrawn (*retracted* in the jargon), all those additional statements would need to be identified and withdrawn as well. For a large datastore, this task could be extremely lengthy and compute-intensive. This kind of activity is sometimes called *truth maintenance*; active research is going on in this area (for example, [Broekstra and Kampman 2003]).

10.3.3 *Dealing with information of uncertain reliability*

The outright contradiction discussed in the previous section seems like the simplest situation. Most of the time, information obtained from a source on the Web will have some uncertainty about its reliability and may possibly be from a source that's also of uncertain reliability. If the Semantic Web turns out to be unable to deal with these facts, it will be unable to approach the grandiose scenarios some have proposed, such as those presented in chapter 1. To begin exploring this subject, let's recall one of those scenarios. In it, a futuristic personal digital assistant says this:

> I checked his affiliation with university of Montana, he is cited several times in their web pages: reasonably trusted; I checked his publication records from publishers' DAML sources and asked bill assistant a rating of the journals: highly trusted.

There are several key points here:

- The assistant makes good use of the Semantic Web to gather useful data. This suggests that the route to solving this Semantic Web problem is to use its own distributed connections.

- The digital assistant has a means of combining these various assessments to arrive at a conclusion—presumably a mathematical algorithm.

- The assistant clearly relied on a network of information, since the "bill assistant" had some way to assess the reliability of the journals it checked on, and in turn that assessment was based on other assessments that weren't mentioned in the description. This suggests the exploitation of the *network effect*, in which the value of a network increases rapidly as the number of interconnected nodes increases.

- The human user is given recommendations by a software component.

Notice that there is no hint of reliance on a centralized authoritarian hierarchy, unlike the typical authentication supplied by PKI (discussed in section 10.2.4).

The key ingredients underlying this scenario are the subject of active research. In general terms, you look for ratings of the degree of confidence one person has in another. These ratings can be considered a kind of virtual network linking the people (see, for example, [Golbeck, Parsia, and Hendler 2003]). Of course, the mutual ratings may change over time and influence each other. The ratings are often self ratings, but they could also be implied by links between web pages or discovered by other means.

Next, you look for a good way to combine the network ratings. The aim is to arrive at a way to assess what confidence one person would (or should) have in a statement by another (see, for instance, [Richardson, Agrawal, and Domingos 2003]. This assessment could become the basis for an automated recommendation of the type we saw above.

This process is somewhat reminiscent of Google's PageRank approach to rating web pages (see chapter 5). Google basically uses the popularity of a page as a strong indicator of its worth for the purpose of responding to a search query. Google in effect builds a virtual network based on the degree of linking between pages. Thus Google's success is seen by some as a proof of principle, or at least as encouragement (see, for example, [Reagle 2002]). The process of obtaining confidence data by analyzing a network of person-oriented links fits nicely into what we call *social analysis* in chapter 5.

There are other hints that such social analysis can be effective. The Internet auction site, eBay, maintains ratings of the sellers given by those who have bought goods from them in the past. Amazon publishes customer reviews of books and other goods that it sells, and many customers are apparently influenced by these reviews. The Epinions web site has collected millions of consumer reviews. It attempts to discover which reviewers a user trusts the most, using a system of ratings, and it also establishes what it calls Advisors and Top Reviewers that are considered to be the most reliable. The intent is to connect a user with the reviews that both the user and Epinions consider to be especially reliable. Golbeck et al report on a research system called TrustBot (Gobeck, Parsia, and Hendler 2003), which provides trust recommendations to people chatting using IRC (Internet Relay Chat) by means of an analysis of trust networks. FOAF, the Friend of a Friend network discussed in the case study in the appendix, could form the basis for (or an exemplar of) a network of self-ratings for trust assessments.

Another school of thought advocates digitally signing as many Semantic Web statements as possible. Doing so would at least authenticate the source of the statements. By comparing a series of related statements issued over a period of time, it might be possible to form a good idea as to whether a given unsigned claim had really been made by the alleged author. See Reagle (2002) for an interesting discussion.

Once a system is in place for assessing the reliability of the source of information, we need a way to fit it in with existing stored information, with due regard to the reliability assessments. As mentioned earlier, RDF has no standard ways to capture such rating information, but a number of possibilities have been proposed. Not all of them require extensions to RDF itself. In addition, the logical basis for working with information of varying reliability isn't agreed on.

As a final complication, you may have a high degree of trust in someone and assess a statement by that person as reliable, yet still not entertain much belief in it. This is more about you and less about your trust in the other source, but the situation must be reflected somehow in your collection of information.

10.4 Agents and the Web of Trust

Intelligent, distributed software agents will pose a great challenge when it comes to determining what transactions are authorized (agents are discussed in chapter 9). Everything we've discussed so far will come into play, and more. In a way, agents are like bureaucrats: They tend to be removed from immediate responsibility for the final outcome. However, they have a much lower degree of common sense than human bureaucrats.

To illustrate, suppose I wish to travel to a foreign country on vacation. My personal digital assistant is supposed to handle my arrangements. It asks an airline travel agent (a software agent) to check schedules. Then it asks a booking agent to reserve the seats and purchase the tickets. Next it contacts a passport agent and uses the tickets as proof that a trip has been arranged, and it supplies a certificate as proof of my identity.

Now, by what authority can my assistant be authorized to pay for the tickets? The agent purchasing the tickets has to contact a ticket broker agent, which removes one ticket from a pool and in turn contacts a purchasing agent, passing it—what? My credit card? I never authorized the last agent to use my card. Why should my credit card company allow the transaction? Clearly, some kind of authorization must be combined with evidence of my identity, and each agent along the line has to be colored by that information. However, those agents can't be given authorization to use my credit card for just any purpose, but only for that one-time transaction. When the transaction has occurred, then back along the line, every agent must be disallowed from authorizing any more use of my card and prevented from reserving any more travel for me.

In addition, the agent for the State Department, when contacted to check the status of my passport—once the authority of the passport agent to act on my behalf has been established (passed on from my personal agent)—needs to somehow be sure that the ticket reservations have been made for me and authorized by me.

These are complicated sequences. It would seem that some kind of non-counterfeitable token of authorization will have to be passed from one agent to another and then returned as each transaction is completed. At each step of the way, the next agent will presumably have to use any or all of the means of the Web of Trust to make sure the token is authorized—and authorized for the claimed party. But the token will be a string of digital bits that can be copied, unlike a physical token. A form of digital signing will obviously be a necessary part of the solution.

We're a long way from having this capability today, but at least we can see its shape in outline.

10.5 *Summary*

As you've seen, when we have to take into account the inconsistent nature of information on the Web and the identities and trustworthiness of the players, many difficult issues arise. The Web of Trust must involve a well-defined and trusted infrastructure like PKI, so that identities and signatures can be authenticated, together with a network of information organized so as to permit a large degree of social analysis. The Semantic Web layer cake will contain support for much of this, once it's fleshed out with working specifications and software. Proof of principle for the social analysis may exist in the form of Google, Epinions, and FOAF, among others. Achieving agents that have the capabilities of the fictitious ones in our example scenarios will obviously take more doing, and presumably they will be the last to become fully evolved.

We've used the term *Web of Trust* for the PKI infrastructure, and also much more broadly, so that it includes all the areas of identity, authentication, and belief we've been examining. Fortunately, this Web of Trust will be able to evolve little by little as the various parts develop. It would be hopeless if its functionalities had to arrive all at once.

A great deal of research, development, and experimentation is obviously needed to support the more advanced scenarios for the Semantic Web. It's fascinating and encouraging that the primary approaches for resolving these difficult issues rely on the nature of the Semantic Web itself.

11 *Putting it all together*

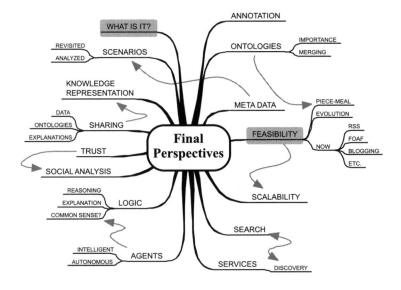

"Found WHAT?" said the Duck.

"Found IT," the Mouse replied rather crossly: "of course you know what 'it' means."

"I know what 'it' means well enough, when I find a thing," said the Duck: "it's generally a frog or a worm. The question is, what did the archbishop find?"

—Lewis Carroll, *Alice's Adventures in Wonderland*

Now that you have explored the terrain covered by this *Explorer's Guide*, you may be asking, like the Duck, "What did the archbishop find?" Indeed, there is no one road through this landscape, but rather a network of highways and byways that sometimes loop back and crisscross. This is altogether fitting for book with *Web* in its title. But what is "IT"? And can "IT" work?

Here in the last chapter, we pick up the various threads covered in the book and talk about how they can work together. Finally, we'll come back to the largest question of all: Can it really happen, or is the Semantic Web just an impractical vision?

11.1 *Just what is the Semantic Web?*

We start where chapter 1 started. The question has almost as many answers as there are people to give them. There is the "everything is meta data" view, the "it's all about smart services" view, the "Web as a giant database" view, and the "smart agents as servants" view. The W3C has it this way in (W3C 2003):

> The goal of the Semantic Web initiative is as broad as that of the Web: to be a universal medium for the exchange of data. It's envisaged to smoothly interconnect personal information management, enterprise application integration, and the global sharing of commercial, scientific and cultural data.

With all the different notions of the nature of the Semantic Web, there seems to be a persistent commonality: In all versions, computers will make much more use of the data that is accessible over the Internet, and with much less human intervention, than they can now. Loosely speaking, we can say that computers will "understand" all this information with little help from people. Of course, the word *understand* has a restricted meaning when used this way; it means that computers can accept the data, find out about its structure, and do something appropriate with it.

Basically, then, we can expect the Semantic Web to be characterized by these features:

- Data will be far more accessible to computers than it is now.

- Computers will weave together data from many different sources much more effectively than they do now.

- The data may be published anywhere on the Web.

- Computers will use that data to do useful tasks for people.

- Data will be described by and often will describe concepts as well as facts.

- Chunks of data will be interconnected by a widespread network of inter-connections and hyperlinks, much as web pages are today.

- Computer systems will be able to act with more autonomy than they do today, so that finding, understanding, and using data will happen with much less human supervision than is currently required.

- In the course of their work, computers and software agents will sometimes be able to infer facts that aren't explicitly recorded anywhere, using logical reasoning based on information that is known to them.

You could take the current Web, where most of the activity takes place or is at least initiated by people, and imagine that the same kinds of things continue to get done, but the people no longer have to be at their browsers and terminals to make it happen. People, in this view, have better things to do than attend to all the mechanical details needed for a day's affairs. Let computers handle them.

As an illustration, figure 11.1 depicts one view of the Semantic Web (www.semanticweb.org/about.html#bigpicture); this view emphasizes meta data, ontologies, and agents.

11.2 Scenarios redux

To put the Semantic Web's issues, technologies, and challenges into perspective, let's revisit the two scenarios we set forth in chapter 1. This time, though, we'll discuss how the technologies and disciplines discussed in the book fit into the capabilities envisioned by those scenarios.

11.2.1 The first scenario

During her stay at Honolulu, Clara ran into several interesting people with whom she exchanged vCards. When time to rest came in the evening, she had a look at her digital assistant summarizing the events of the day and recalling the events to come (and especially her keynote talk of the next day).

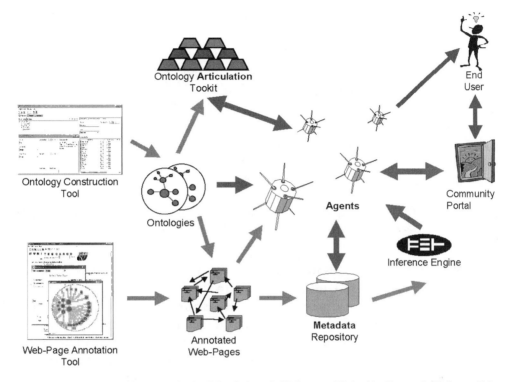

Figure 11.1 A view of the operations of the Semantic Web, as published by SemanticWeb.org. This view emphasizes autonomous software agents and the infrastructure of ontology and meta data that would support their operations.

The review of the day's events and those to come indicates some kind of calendar ability. A standard exists for exchanging calendar information on the Web: iCal. It's a plain text format rather than XML markup, but it's used for sharing schedule and planning information. An RDF format for iCal information is being experimented with. Clearly its use by a digital personal assistant is very plausible.

Clara's assistant automatically recorded each vCard (virtual business card) and performed some analysis on it. RDF formats for vCards have been proposed, and it's easy to picture the vCard exchange taking place quietly and automatically over a wireless connection. This is another piece that could be done with current technology plus a bit of standardization.

The assistant would probably have time-stamped the vCard data to show when it was received. It would be simple to integrate that information into the day's events, especially if both calendar and vCard used RDF. Presumably the assistant is scriptable, so it could be programmed to perform such an integration.

The part about summarizing the day's events is tantalizing. What would it mean to summarize the events? Perhaps the merged calendar of the conference and the vCards is to be displayed—but maybe there is more to it. Perhaps Clara entered notes into the assistant from time to time. Maybe people she met gave her copies of papers, which of course went right into her assistant. If so, the assistant could produce summaries, either crudely by showing the first few sentences (as some RSS news generators do today) or in a more sophisticated way using semantic analysis. It's possible that the result of such analysis would be stored as RDF or topic map data. Again, this would be feasible today or in the near future.

> The assistant popped up a note with a link to a vCard that reads: "This guy's profile seems to match the position advertisement that Bill put on our intranet. Can I notify Bill's assistant?"

Here, the assistant has to know that it should be looking for possible matches to a job opening. How would it know to do this? Is this even a matter for the Semantic Web? It might be. The assistant could be scripted to periodically update its store of job openings, which it would compare with the concepts in some ontology also obtained over the Web (probably from a Human Resources server). It could be scripted to check each new vCard against the skill sets called for. This much seems straightforward. Or, the assistant could be programmed to look up how to execute a task—in this case, the task of checking skill sets—specified in a semantic process language like DAML-S or its OWL-based successor.

To do the comparison of skills, the assistant would have to match terms in the vCard with terms in the job posting. With luck—or by specification—the vCard would identify the ontology it used, and there would be a known mapping between the two. You've seen that OWL is designed to piece together different ontologies and that it can declare two terms to be equivalent. So, this part would be harder, but it would still be possible. Today, the principle could be demonstrated with known, well-controlled vocabularies, but this would be a proof of principle rather than a real-world capability.

Once the ontology matter is dealt with, there remains the problem of assessing how well the skill sets match. Typically the match would be incomplete, and evaluating the degree of match would take special techniques. The evaluation might use so-called fuzzy logic, or perhaps Bayesian analysis, in making the analysis. Suitable analysis techniques exist; the issue so far as the Semantic Web is concerned would be for the software to understand the descriptions of the skills (and their assessments, as discussed shortly) well enough to be able apply them.

> Clara hit the "explain!" button. "I used his company directory for finding his DAML enhanced vita: he's got the required skills as a statistician who led the data mining group of the database department at Montana U. for the requirement of a researcher who worked on machine learning."

Chapter 6 mentions that the ability to explain a chain of reasoning will probably become important for the Semantic Web. This part of the scenario illustrates why. Explanations like this allow a person to intervene, rather than be blindly stuck with the computer's conclusions.

The reasoning here is rather sophisticated. The assistant has to know to look for a vita, how to use one, and how to find one. It has to know that leading a data-mining group is a relevant experience for a researcher in the field. It's unlikely that Clara would have pre-programmed this exact behavior; rather, the assistant would be expected to act in appropriate ways for a multitude of situations. Whatever the details of the methods used by the assistant, they would clearly depend on the integration of multiple ontologies. Sufficiently well-designed ontologies would provide links between, for example, machine learning and statistics, between statistics and statisticians, and between statistics and both data mining and databases.

Even with an adequate degree of support from ontologies—to be found by Semantic Web–enhanced search methods, no doubt—this part of the scenario would remain challenging.

> Clara hit then the "evidence!" button. The assistant started displaying "I checked his affiliation with university of Montana, he is cited several times in their web pages: reasonably trusted; I checked his publication records from publishers' DAML sources and asked bill assistant a rating of the journals: highly trusted. More details?"

This part makes extensive use of what we have called *social analysis*, and illustrates the so-called *Web of Trust* in action. But how did the assistant know what sources to check? And why would the bill assistant's rating of journals be useful with respect to someone's academic record, as opposed to the financial soundness of the journals? Here too, the real issue isn't how this particular case could be solved, but rather how the assistant can be designed to act appropriately in a wide range of situations that are only generally similar. This is the territory of intelligent agents, probably the most technically challenging area of all those covered in this book. In this scenario, at least two agents are interacting: Clara's assistant and the bill assistant (which may exist in Clara's personal assistant but clearly can act with some degree of autonomy).

In this scenario, you can see threads from all the areas discussed in this book, except services. Notice how assistant's abilities can be built out of parts and components, which would be integrated by means of a common knowledge representation like RDF and by selected ontologies that the assistant may need to discover via the Semantic Web. Thus the assistant could deal with calendars and summaries without being able to evaluate the quality of someone's research reputation. The latter ability would, however, be built on the same foundation as the former.

11.2.2 *The second scenario*

> Bill's and Peter's assistants arranged a meeting in Paris, just before ISWC in Sardinia. Thanks to Peter's assistant knowing he was vegetarian, they avoided a faux pas.

The concept of *vegetarian* would be in an ontology, and it's easy to see that a restaurant's information could be tagged with the categories of cuisine that it serves. The assistant could probably combine the two ontologies if necessary. But how did it know that Peter's status as a vegetarian would be of any interest or that special action would need to be taken? This would seem to require a degree of common sense or complex pre-programmed rules, and thus would be another difficult problem. On the other hand, perhaps the human principals worked out the issue themselves.

> Bill was surprised that Peter was able to cope with French (his assistant was not authorized to unveil that he married a woman from Québec). Bill and Peter had a fruitful meeting and Bill will certainly be able to send Peter an offer before he came back to the US.

This bit demonstrates a certain fine-grained security capability. Apparently certain classes of facts are tagged as being personal. This tagging would probably be done in the ontology rather than by annotating each individual fact. The system would infer the security restrictions of a particular fact from the restrictions in the ontology. The system would have to look up the class of each fact in the ontology to discover its security status. RDF + OWL systems are likely to perform lookups of class-specific constraints frequently, and so this kind of operation needs to be made very efficient.

> Before dinner, Peter investigated a point that bothered him: Bill used the term "Service" in an unusual way. He wrote: "Acme computing will run the trust rating service for semanticweb.org" (a sentence from Bill). His assistant found no

problem so he hit: "service," the assistant displayed "service in {database} equivalent To: infrastructure." Peter asked for "metainfo," which raised "Updated today by negotiating with Bill's assistant."

Several interesting things are going on here. The simplest point is that the same term is used with different meanings in two different ontologies. In OWL and RDF, terms are qualified according to their source, so they can be distinguished easily (and Topic Maps can distinguish them as well). However, the English text in the scenario is ambiguous about which meaning is intended to be applied. You'd think that a "trust rating service" would be a kind of web service and thus use the {web} ontology. The paragraph seems to indicate that this isn't the intent, but not clearly.

In any event, how would the assistant know which sense Peter intended? Either sense of the word would work. This particular task may be too challenging to be handled by Semantic Web agents, unless there is other information not described in the scenario. Another unanswered question is how the two assistants decided that there was something to negotiate in the first place. What kind of processing surfaced the discrepancy?

Peter again asked for "Arguments!": "Service in {database} conflicts with service in {web}." "Explain!" "In operating system and database, the term services covers features like fault-tolerance, cache, security, that we are used to putting in the infrastructure. More evidence?"

Here we see a new element, epitomized by the phrase "that we are used to putting in the infrastructure." This suggests that the assistant has a high degree of awareness of its environment (and that of its owner) and a considerable amount of common sense. Both of these characteristics have historically been difficult to achieve outside of limited environments. This kind of capability isn't likely to be available in the near future and perhaps not even in the intermediate future.

Peter was glad he had not to search the whole web for an explanation of this. The two assistants detected the issue and negotiated silently a solution to this problem.

The two assistants took some actions that could have consequences for the humans, and they did so without telling the humans first. This is certainly a vision of autonomous agents on the Web.

He had some time left before getting to the théatre de la ville. His assistant made the miracle to book him a place for a rare show of Anne-Theresa De Keermaeker's troupe in Paris. It had to resort to a particular web service that it found through a dance-related common interest pool of assistants.

Here, presumably, the term *service* is used in its {web} sense and not its {database} sense. The key issue in this bit is the discovery of the service on the Web, which must have required a semantically enhanced search to find the "dance-related" pool of assistants. After this, the web service would have had to be able to describe to the assistant how to purchase tickets. We see the confluence of search, discovery, services, and autonomous agents in this last part of the scenario.

11.2.3 *The scenarios in perspective*

It should be clear why we chose these two scenarios for chapter 1: Between them, they exercise most of the kinds of technologies that will probably play major roles in the Semantic Web. You see that there are certain common themes:

- The importance of ontologies to these advanced capabilities, and especially the ability to merge ontologies from several sources and to find equivalent terms in each
- The need for flexible ways to represent information, together with interchange formats that all parties can understand
- The need for enhanced ability to discover sources of information—ontologies, other agents, services, and so on.

You also saw that issues of trust and social analysis wound their way through the other activities.

No one knows if the full power described in these scenarios can be realized. Clearly, some parts (especially in the first scenario) could be implemented now or in the near future. Just as clearly, others are so advanced that they may not come to pass for a long time, if ever. This leaves a middle ground for the near to mid future.

11.3 *Some Key Issues*

Throughout this book, several issues and unanswered questions have made themselves known. They cover a wide range, from the identity of resources and ideas to the sharing of ontologies to the role of web services to the kinds of logic that will be needed. Here we look again at a small but strategic selection of issues from the viewpoint of how they work with or fit into the Semantic Web.

11.3.1 *Scalability*

Many technologies work well until they expand too much in size or activity. Beyond a certain level, they can no longer scale up. At this point, another design or another technology is called for. To take one example, a small network of 10 computers, where each computer talks to each other computer, may work well. But if you connect another 1,000 nodes into the network, communications will slow to a near standstill. Point-to-point communications, where any node can talk to any other, don't scale well, because the number of possible connections increases as the square of the number of nodes. Increasing the number of nodes by a factor of 1,000 increases the number of possible connections by 1,000,000. The demands of all those computers overwhelm the individual computers that must respond, and the network that was fine for 10 nodes can't handle all the new traffic, including network management overhead.

The size and scope of the Web are staggering. It would be easy to overwhelm a system with too much information. Many logical reasoning tasks are sensitive to the size of the data set they must sift through. It's important to minimize the size of the data and the complexity of the reasoning tasks, yet to get the intended value from the Semantic Web, where both size and complexity may become large. In particular, it isn't known how large and complex a system needs to be to allow intelligent autonomous agents to behave with what, in humans, we would call common sense, and it isn't known whether such a system can be made to perform with acceptable speed. Alternatively, there may be clever ways to get the same kind of results with far fewer resources, but that isn't known either.

Questions of scalability can affect Semantic Web technologies in many areas. Thus, central repositories of information are sometimes proposed. These might contain large standard ontologies, comprehensive data about web services, and so on. On a large scale, the role of central repositories tends to be questionable. Also, a central repository implies centralized control, which is likely to work against flexibility and open access to information. Fortunately most, if not all, Semantic Web technologies have the ability to integrate diverse collections of information. Therefore, distributed, decentralized alternatives can and should be made to work.

11.3.2 *Ontologies—universal or piecework*

If the goal is universal interchange of information, it's often thought that a universal vocabulary will be necessary. However, a universal ontology would suffer from all the problems of a centralized repository and more—presuming that such a thing could be developed. Experience shows that global agreement on a large vocabulary is next to impossible in computer disciplines and in business, just as with natural languages.

The next step down from a universal ontology would be a basic set of concepts that would be used by all ontologies, sometimes called a Standard Upper Ontology (SUO). It's far from certain whether one SUO, general enough for all applications and adaptable enough to be extended for any and all uses, is feasible. It isn't even known whether people function that way; that is, do people come with an SUO built in? Several efforts are in progress to develop SUOs. A few are available now, but it will probably be years before SUOs stabilize and become generally accepted (if this should ever happen).

At the other end of the range are relatively small-scale, special-purpose ontologies. That is essentially the situation today: Hundreds and thousands of special, incompatible vocabularies are in use around the world. Semantic Web technologies ought to make it possible to integrate separate ontologies when they're needed for particular tasks.

11.3.3 *Identity*

We've discussed the issue of identity in a number of places in this book. Most current Semantic Web technologies use URIs as identifiers for things and concepts of interest; but as you've seen, there are some unresolved problems with their use. Aside from the possibility of ambiguity (as when in RDF a URI might refer to a web page or to the subject the web page is discussing), there is the question of where to find the intended meaning of a given URI. If you encounter the URI

```
http://www.example.com/affairs/blankenstein
```

where should you go to learn what it's supposed to mean (recall that a URI doesn't have to point to an actual place on the Web)? What if you find two different explanations in two different places? How then should you use that URI? And what should your processor do if it finds that someone uses the URI in what seems to be the wrong way?

There have been many arguments about the way to deal with such questions. Definite possibilities exist, but so far none have surfaced as clear winners. Sooner or later, these issues will have to be resolved. In the meantime, people are going full speed ahead anyway.

You've seen that a thing's identity can sometimes be established by its relations with other things. When this is possible, potential problems with the use of URIs as identifiers become moot. The use of digital keys and digital signatures to establish the identity of a person or organization is a different, though related, matter and is brought up again in section 11.3.7.

11.3.4 *Strong AI and the role of logical reasoning*

Chapter 9 discussed logic-based agents and their relation to Artificial Intelligence (AI). *Strong AI* denoted an approach whereby a system's behavior was established primarily by logical reasoning, usually based on a set of rules. The problem turned out to be that the rules could never cover all situations, and the reasoning was too rigid. As a result, the classic approach to AI was discredited, at least in the opinion of many.

With the huge increase of computer power in recent years, the field of logical reasoning has seen a resurgence of sorts. Many researchers involved in developing RDF, OWL, and similar technologies talk about the Semantic Web as if it will be nothing more than a massive exercise in logical reasoning—based on established ontologies that supply logical relationships and possibly on extensive sets of rules—that gets applied to the vast storehouse of data scattered across the Web. People who remain skeptical of this view sometimes talk about it as being a resurgence of strong AI (the implication is usually rather negative).

The truth is, no one knows how important classical logical reasoning will be for the Semantic Web, and no one knows how practical its large-scale application will be. Research in automated reasoners has been active, and the discipline advanced considerably in the last decade or two. In comparison, the scope of Semantic Web applications will tend to be much larger than projects of the past. The outcome remains to be seen.

11.3.5 *Embedded semantic markup*

The most obvious way to semantically enhance information would seem to be to embed the enhancements in the data—for instance, to insert RDF into web pages. Historically this technique hasn't worked well, and it's questionable whether the practice will become widespread. It often turns out to be difficult and expensive to add meta data; even when it would be otherwise, the majority of information producers aren't interested in spending the time and effort after creating the work in the first place. In addition, self-embedded meta data can be inaccurate, and sometimes it's an outright falsehood.

Thus a place exists for marking up Web resources with embedded semantic meta data, but there will always be a large quantity of information that isn't so blessed. We don't want to ignore all these sources of information, but the question is what to do about them. There are various possibilities and no single answer.

You've seen how meta data can be applied to any desired resource—for example, by making the appropriate statements in RDF. Of course, this can't be done until the meta-data values are discovered, but that's why we want the meta data to be embedded in the first place.

In some cases, meta data of interest can be extracted by automated processing. In addition, the structure of a document can imply certain meta data (this approach can be very effective when it's possible). In other cases, it's possible to apply natural language processing (NLP) to textual documents with varying success.

The art of adding meta data to data sources, and extracting or deducing implicit meta data, is one that invites—and is receiving—a great deal of ingenuity.

11.3.6 *Web services and the Semantic Web*

You've seen that the current mainline approach to web services has little or nothing to do with the Semantic Web. At the same time, the description, discovery, and use of services is an important part of many people's vision of the Semantic Web. Why we have such a divergence of views is an interesting question in itself. More to the point, what role will the Semantic Web play in services on the Web?

In the short term, probably a very small one. In the longer term, it's clear that Semantic Web technologies *could* play a significant role, but it's far from clear whether they *will*. In the world of electronic commerce, dozens of specifications for all kinds of aspects of services have been and are being developed. This work carries its own inertia and may well get locked in before Semantic Web–style services become sufficiently developed. It's more likely that Semantic Web alternatives for, say, discovery of services may come into use and slowly be integrated into the mainstream. However, this prediction is very speculative.

11.3.7 *Trust, belief, and confidence*

The Semantic Web will have many activities in which some degree of confidence must be established. This might be confidence in the identity of a person who orders a diamond necklace, confidence that the credit account will pay the bill for the necklace … you can make up your own scenarios. In chapter 10, we split the issues into two categories: trust and belief. Trust must necessarily come in degrees, and belief is separate from trust—I may trust my daughter but still not believe that her daydream actually happened.

These areas may be the most difficult and elusive to solve. Those who think that strong AI is the right approach to the Semantic Web would have you believe that, given enough facts, you can compute the trustworthiness or authenticity of a source of information (which might be the credit card number to be applied to the purchase of that diamond necklace). Digital signatures would presumably be part of this chain of proof. But with the Semantic Web, especially if autonomous agents turn out to play important roles, the problem is transformed because other computers or agents start to gain the authorization and trust that used to belong only to people. How do we manage the assignment of critical authority to a chain of agents when they don't all belong to the original person seeking services (perhaps you) and don't all have the same agenda? This is strange and difficult territory. We are far, very far, from knowing how to navigate it.

There are also no well-accepted ways to record (let alone compute) degrees of belief in data, or to place data into appropriate contexts, especially for computer consumption. We don't know how to tell a machine to be suspicious of an offered Super Bowl ticket because it seems likely to have been stolen. We can't easily record that information along with the reasons it came to be suspicious. For any one such situation, we can come up with a range of solutions; but the problem is to come up with solutions that work without much (preferably with no) human intervention, that will work with other Semantic Web technologies, that will adapt to a wide range of tasks and environments, and that will scale up to the size of the Web.

Fortunately, much Semantic Web technology will be useful and practical long before many of these issues are solved.

11.4 *How semantic will it be?*

Pure mathematics, of which formal logic is commonly considered a branch, deals entirely in symbols and rules for combining them and manipulating them. Geometry, which for most of us is mainly about diagrams, can be done without using geometric diagrams at all, just by using rules and symbols. Computers do little except to manipulate symbols. *Semantics*, on the other hand, is usually taken to refer to the "meaning" of language.

If we consider that there's a distinction between symbol manipulation and meaning, then the Semantic Web could be said to be a web of symbols rather than a web of meaning. The computers and software agents will only be manipulating symbols. The Semantic Web, its computers and agents, will manipulate the symbols using formal techniques, and only the people will understand their meaning. For a good summary of this kind of view, see Butler (2003).

But in another sense, from an operational point of view, the system could be said to understand the meaning of its data and instructions. If a person or machine takes action appropriate to its environment and internal state, it can be said to understand its situation. This is especially the case when no clear, direct, cause-and-effect relationship exists between the stimulus, the environment, and the result. (It's true that this criterion would apply to an ant making a detour around an obstacle, which normally isn't considered to require much understanding, but the point remains.)

Goal-seeking activity comes primarily from the response to feedback signals that indicate how far the current state is from the desired one. An ordinary room thermostat attempts to maintain a constant room temperature, a simple form of goal-seeking behavior. When the goal, internal behavior, and environment are all complex, then the organism or machine seems to be self-directed, regardless of whether this perception is an illusion. If the goals and rules that affect behavior can change during the activity, and change because of that activity, then the illusion of intelligent behavior becomes more compelling. In this sense, the Semantic Web may deserve its name after all.

11.5 *Can it really come about?*

This may be the biggest question lurking behind the chapters in this book. By now it should be clear that the question can't be answered with any confidence. Difficult technical issues exist, and complex social and political concerns will make themselves known.

11.5.1 *The technology front*

One of the interesting things about the development of technologies for the Semantic Web is that all of them can be useful in other settings—situations that have nothing to do with the Semantic Web. RDF and topic maps can be used in small, local systems as a kind of flexible database system. OWL can be used to describe ontologies for use within a single project, one that never communicates with any other. Factories can and are using agents that will never integrate any data from other sources during their entire existence. Effective methods for the discovery and use of services can be put into place on restricted private networks that never use a URI. These technologies are likely to continue to evolve even if the Semantic Web doesn't.

The technical challenge lies in adapting technologies for widespread use on the Web or on some successor to the Web. Logic programming, schemas, and ontologies have been around for a long time. In previous incarnations, they weren't suitable for working with any resource anywhere on a huge network or in an open and possibly self-contradictory environment where connectivity wasn't always assured. Hyperlink technology existed for years that was more elegant than what we now have on the Web; yet the Web prospered, and the others faded out of the picture. The technologies have to be made sufficiently accessible to enough people, and their benefits must be clear enough, or it will be a challenge for them to be adopted and put to widespread use.

Some of the core technologies covered in this book exist already and are starting to spread. Toolkits are becoming available for RDF, topic maps, and some ontology languages, as well as for XML web services and even agents, although the current agent toolkits don't really help you create intelligent distributed agents. More companies, large and small, are starting to use RDF in everyday work. This is how the Semantic Web can grow and evolve: little by little, area by area, capability by capability. The trick for everyone involved will be to keep fostering interoperable languages and software, for without interoperability there can be no Semantic Web.

Such evolution has a precedent: The Web itself grew that way. More recently, XML-RPC started out small and is now appearing in more and more applications (it even fostered SOAP, which is in many ways XML-RPC–Second Generation). Web logging seems to be following the same path as FOAF (the informal Friend of a Friend language) and RSS (the news summary language), but more quickly. These efforts show that much can be achieved with simple means.

11.5.2 *Plugging in*

It's natural to wonder whether you can make any use of Semantic Web technologies today, or if you can or should do anything that might help promote the Semantic Web's growth. It's hard to give specific advice in a general book like this, yet there are a few useful guidelines. They arise from experience with simple network-like systems like FOAF and RSS, from successes using RDF and Topic Map technologies within companies' boundaries, and from the utility of certain non–Semantic Web data formats like the iCal calendar format. Adopting any of the approaches outlined in the next several sections will increase the possibility that your information and your systems will keep and increase their value over time as Semantic Web technologies become more widespread. At the same time, they will probably be helpful (or at least not unhelpful) for many projects right now. To go beyond these suggestions is certainly possible, but at the time of this writing would require substantially more learning and development effort.

The idea of the first group of guidelines is to get more utility for a low degree of extra investment and risk, while at the same time increasing the potential value of your data in the future.

RDF compatibility

If you need to devise a new data format for exchanging or storing data in XML form, consider making the format RDF compatible. Often this can be done with little effort—the so-called *striped* format discussed in section 2.6.1 is an example, as is the XML Package format (XPackage, not discussed in this book; see www.globalmentor.com/reference/specifications/xpackage/default.jsp). You don't have to use all of RDF's many optional syntax features, just a small subset. You can usually design a format that can be processed by standard XML methods and also by RDF-aware software.

This approach minimizes the amount of new technology you have to learn—basically, you make small adjustments to a format you would have developed anyway. The thinking required to turn your XML ideas into simple, valid, sensible RDF generally improves the quality of your work as a side benefit, since you come to understand better what you really intended to accomplish. If you don't quite like the results of this exercise, then at least design your format so that it's simple to transform into RDF. Either way, RDF will make it easier to combine your data with other kinds of data if you use RDF-aware processors to do the combining. This approach offers good potential for the future with no disadvantage for the present.

Self-describing networks

Favor self-describing networks, like FOAF networks, over centrally organized and repository-based systems where possible. By *network*, in this paragraph we mean an interconnected set of links rather than an electronic network like the Internet. You could have a network of, say, hobby clubs and suppliers. Each one could create a simple RDF page on its web site that describes itself and points to the RDF pages of other members that it knows about. It's simple to extract the data in such a file and make it into a human-readable web page, which is often useful.

See the FOAF case study in the appendix for an example of a self-describing network. This approach will decrease complexity and administration effort, while increasing flexibility and possibilities for future expansion.

Published Subject Indicators

If you need to publish definitions of certain concepts and terms, consider publishing them as Published Subject Indicators (PSIs, as discussed in chapter 3). Each PSI is denoted by a URI; the PSI will be usable by Topic Map processors, and RDF and OWL systems can use the URIs too. Human-readable descriptions located at the URIs will be useful to developers and anyone else you had in mind when you decided to publish them.

URI descriptions

If you make up a URI to denote a particular resource, concept, and so on, as you often will when you use RDF and OWL, consider making the URI point to a real web page that contains a description of the item indicated by the URI. In theory, these URIs don't have to point to a real location; but if you follow this convention, it will be easier for everyone to discover what you mean by the URI.

RSS feeds

If you frequently send updated summaries of information to customers, consider providing an RSS feed for the information. Doing so will make it easier for them to notice changes and new items they're interested in, and an RSS feed is simple to implement. Some bug-tracking systems, for instance, now automatically publish new and changed bugs using RSS. RSS is proving to be easy to mine for useful meta data, which is another advantage.

Next let's examine a group of suggestions that require more time and development but that are feasible (in a non-research environment) at the time of this writing. They're intended to make your data more sharable, more navigable, and more adaptable when the patterns of use change, as they are likely to.

Data availability

Make your data—data you're interested in sharing—available over the Web, perhaps with the help of topic maps or RDF. As far as possible, make the data addressable by URIs, because doing so will make it usable by more users in more flexible ways. Of course, you'll have to take security issues into consideration, as you would for any other web project.

Storing data as RDF or topic maps

If you need to aggregate large numbers of individual facts, and especially if the kinds and numbers of these facts may vary a lot for different subjects, consider storing the data as RDF or topic maps. RDF will probably be preferable, because it's especially suited for collecting many small bits of unstructured data (or meta data). This approach will work best when the data won't be changed often, because the tools currently available haven't yet evolved to support frequent updates or transactions.

Designing with topic maps and RDF

If you need to integrate data from a wide range of data sources, consider topic maps or RDF as part of the design. You can either create wrappers to make the data sources look like (say) topic maps, or you can translate the data as it comes from the databases. These technologies are effective in this kind of application, although they aren't yet developed enough to be used for extremely large data sets. Topic maps are probably preferable to RDF for integrating relational data, but either would be a good choice.

Ontologies and OWL

If you need to develop an ontology (a vocabulary or set of terms), especially when the classes and terms are related by constraints, consider defining it with OWL or with a tool whose output can be transformed to OWL. Some amount of mental retraining is needed to get used to the OWL way of modeling things, but if you aren't already using a particular system for doing the job, you might as well pick OWL. It's fully compatible with RDF, and an increasing number of ontology tools know how to work with it.

Topic maps would be equally capable of defining an ontology, but a standard language corresponding to OWL doesn't yet exist. Even using OWL, your work will be valuable to more potential users if you publish the URIs as PSIs as described earlier in "Published Subject Indicators."

A topic map–based approach

If you need to provide many different views into your data and many ways to navigate it, consider using a topic map–based approach. The data itself need not be stored in the topic map (although that would be possible). You should also publish your subject types as PSIs so that others can use them. The point is to build on a well-developed standard rather than to create your own each time.

Methods for accessing topic maps (and RDF) over the Web aren't yet standardized, so for the time being you'll have to develop your own methods or use the proprietary methods of the software you adopt. This situation is regrettable, but it will change.

11.5.3 Growing the Semantic Web

Ultimately, many complicated developments will have to be in place for the full Semantic Web, as some envision it, to exist. The big question is how the full Semantic Web can evolve from much simpler projects, or even whether the evolution is possible.

A few things are clear. If there is to be a Semantic Web, it will grow as a patchwork, and there will be an incessant conflict between the need for size and financial resources—because Web-wide systems are very expensive—and the desires of innovative individuals and small groups to have the freedom to create new and useful software. The nature of the Semantic Web will make it easier than ever to allow both views to coexist, because the technologies will help different kinds of systems adapt to each other. An example would be adapting WSDL to RDF (see chapter 8). Those who find it valuable to use RDF to describe services will be able to do so, and it will be easy to convert to the WSDL formats when needed. Another, more advanced, example would be an agent specialized for wrapping access to UDDI repositories with a FIPA-compatible wrapper (see chapter 9) so that other agents could gain access to them.

As the late Stephen Jay Gould made so clear,[1] evolution of all varieties proceeds in unpredictable ways—contingent, in Gould's phrase, on historical accidents. It will be the same for the Semantic Web.

---

[1] The contingent nature of both history and evolution is a major theme running through much of his published work, such as Gould (1989) and Gould (1993).

Appendix: Case studies

This appendix presents two case studies. Between them, they touch many of the threads that weave throughout this book, including searching, annotating, the organization of information, shared vocabularies, distributed data, and the benefits of standard formats for the interchange of data. These case studies are designed around small-scale applications to supply a certain immediacy, a sense of personal involvement, that may bring some of the abstractions of the Semantic Web to life. The appendix ends with some reflections on similarities between the two case studies and on the value of simple approaches.

A.1 *FOAF: Friend of a Friend*

In chapters 2 and 3, you saw how information can be modeled and shared using universal identifiers and a representation system like RDF or Topic Maps. In this case study, we'll look at an actual distributed database that uses RDF. It's called *Friend of a Friend* (FOAF).

FOAF is interesting for several reasons. For one thing, it's a grass-roots development that was started by two people, Libby Miller and Dan Brickley. For another, it's very simple, yet it can be extended almost at will. Ingenious people are constantly devising new things to do with FOAF data. FOAF illustrates one way that data can be linked over the Web.

A.1.1 *Sharing a bit of yourself*

The idea of FOAF is to share information about yourself and to say who you know, if you want to share that. Someone might decide to share the following, for example:

> Bob Smith has the email address bs@example.com, he is married to Liza Smith, lives in Groton, CT, likes music, graduated from Boston University, and knows Rob Corner and Marilyn James.

Each of these small facts can be stated in the RDF way as a triple (subject, property, value). Bob Smith can put an XML version of the RDF statements on his web site. Anyone who knows about it, or finds it through a search engine, can learn about Bob. FOAF has a standard vocabulary for stating these basic facts, and Bob can also use terms from other vocabularies if he wants to.

This isn't all that interesting so far, but a small refinement turns out to make a big difference: Bob's FOAF file can include links to the FOAF pages of other people he knows. They can link to his FOAF page too, if they choose. With the help of these links, a person, or a piece of software similar to the spiders used by search engines, can start forming a map or graph of who knows whom. The data in this map can be mined: You could find out who in the community knows Finnish, or who is friends with so-and-so's children, or any number of other things. FOAF files can contain information about chat connections, which could be useful for people who want to chat on line with others in their FOAF community.

A.1.2 A FOAF example

Let's look at an example of a FOAF file, to see how simple it is; then we'll examine some other things that can be done with the FOAF distributed data. The following example of RDF—FOAF data is always published in RDF—was created using the FOAF-a-matic web site (www.ldodds.com/foaf/foaf-a-matic.html). FOAF-a-matic makes it simple to create a starter FOAF page. (You may want to refer back to chapter 2 for more about RDF.)

The example in listing A.1 contains some of the data Bob Smith decided to share; it starts with a declaration that it's an RDF document and then lists the namespaces—in effect, the vocabularies—it will use. The file is in the standard RDF/XML format for interchanging RDF data. (Note that some lines have been wrapped at unnatural places to fit on the printed page.)

Listing A.1 An example of a FOAF file

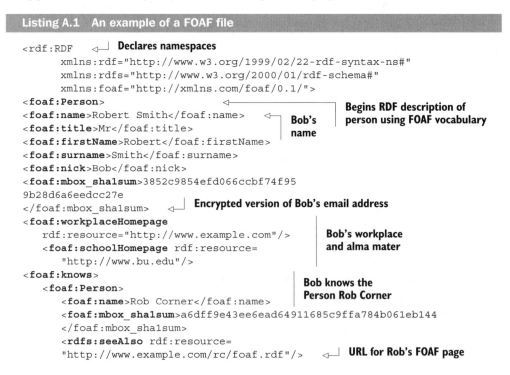

```
<rdf:RDF        ⟵ Declares namespaces
      xmlns:rdf="http://www.w3.org/1999/02/22-rdf-syntax-ns#"
      xmlns:rdfs="http://www.w3.org/2000/01/rdf-schema#"
      xmlns:foaf="http://xmlns.com/foaf/0.1/">
<foaf:Person>                              ⟵  Begins RDF description of
<foaf:name>Robert Smith</foaf:name>   ⟵ Bob's   person using FOAF vocabulary
<foaf:title>Mr</foaf:title>                  name
<foaf:firstName>Robert</foaf:firstName>
<foaf:surname>Smith</foaf:surname>
<foaf:nick>Bob</foaf:nick>
<foaf:mbox_sha1sum>3852c9854efd066ccbf74f95
9b28d6a6eedcc27e
</foaf:mbox_sha1sum>    ⟵ Encrypted version of Bob's email address
<foaf:workplaceHomepage
    rdf:resource="http://www.example.com"/>    Bob's workplace
      <foaf:schoolHomepage rdf:resource=         and alma mater
        "http://www.bu.edu"/>
<foaf:knows>
    <foaf:Person>                          Bob knows the
      <foaf:name>Rob Corner</foaf:name>    Person Rob Corner
      <foaf:mbox_sha1sum>a6dff9e43ee6ead64911685c9ffa784b061eb144
      </foaf:mbox_sha1sum>
      <rdfs:seeAlso rdf:resource=
      "http://www.example.com/rc/foaf.rdf"/>   ⟵ URL for Rob's FOAF page
```

```
    </foaf:Person></foaf:knows>
<foaf:knows>
  <foaf:Person>
    <foaf:name>Marilyn James</foaf:name>
    <foaf:mbox_sha1sum>cf23e89b9cb64cdf9d1322a4da483aaef1f14962
    </foaf:mbox_sha1sum>
    <rdfs:seeAlso rdf:resource="http://www.example.com/marij/foaf.rdf"/>
  </foaf:Person></foaf:knows>
</foaf:Person>
</rdf:RDF>
```

One point that isn't obvious is the encryption of Bob's email address. This particular encryption method is called *Secure Hash Algorithm* (SHA), which is why its element name is `foaf:mbox_sha1sum`. The ability to encrypt this identifying information is an optional feature of FOAF. If you prefer, you can give your email address in the normal, readable form. In FOAF, an email address is one of the basic ways to identify a person, under the assumption that only one person ever has a particular email address. Using the encrypted version allows a person to be identified reliably without exposing their personal email address.

A.1.3 *Identification without universal IDs*

FOAF is like the famous "six degrees of separation:" One person links to another, and after enough links, you can get to a lot of other people worldwide. But there is no universal way to identify people, so how can a computer know that different FOAF files contain information about the same person? It can sometimes do so by noticing what people, places, and interests a person is linked to. Dan Brickley has described the method well (http://rdfweb.org/mt/foaflog/archives/000039.html):

> Basically, off the shelf RDF tools can still do a lot to help us, but we have to help them. FOAF, as an application that focuses on the distributed, decentralized, *almost* out of control use of RDF 'in the wild,' ran into this problem after we had about half a dozen FOAF files. There are now hundreds, soon thousands, of FOAF documents. Most of them talk about people, quite successfully, despite the absence of a global person-id registry. This sounds like a recipe for chaos, yet somehow many of our FOAF aggregation tools are quite happy with this situation. They can often figure out when two files are about the self-same thing, without much help from the authors of those documents. We do this using what might be called "reference by description." Instead of saying, "this page was created by urn:global-person-registry:person-n22314151," we say "this page was

created by the person whose (some-property...) is (some-value...)," taking care to use an unambiguous property such as foaf:homepage or foaf:mbox_ sha1sum.

Dan goes on to explain more fully:

I am related to those things that are my homepages; FOAF's name for that relationship is 'foaf:homepage'.

I am related to those things that are my personal mailboxes by a relationship FOAF calls 'foaf:mbox'.

I am related to the strings that you get from feeding my mailbox identifiers to the SHA1 mathematical function by a relationship FOAF calls 'foaf:mbox_sha1sum'.

I am related to a myers briggs personality classification; FOAF calls that relationship 'foaf:myersBriggs'.

I am related to my workplace homepage (http://www.w3.org/) by a relationship called—you guessed it—'foaf:workplaceHomepage'.

I am related to my name, 'Dan Brickley,' by the 'foaf:name' relationship.

I am related to my AIM chat identifier by a relationship FOAF calls 'foaf:aimChatID'.

And so on. Other RDF vocabularies can define additional relationships (see the FoafVocab entry in our wiki for pointers). They all relate things to other things in named ways. A FOAF document, like any RDF document, is simply a collection of these simple claims about how things in the world relate.

The use of identification by description is also discussed in chapter 5 on searching. For it to work, some properties must be unique, or nearly unique, to one person. Brown hair is fairly common, so it wouldn't normally be useful for identification. But given enough matching non-identifying information, the chance of getting a good match can increase. If you have brown hair and live in a particular town and are of a certain height and have a 10-year-old boy named Julius and are married to a woman named Betty Lou—well, there can't be too many other people who match all these properties. Add a few more, and the match gets better still.

A.1.4 *Board of a board*

There is a web site, www.theyrule.net, that depicts the interconnecting relationships between companies that arise because some members of the board of directors of one company also sit on the board of directors of another. According to the site, Warren E. Buffet sits on the boards of both Coca-Cola and Berkshire Hathaway (at least, when the data were collected). This interconnectedness is the kind of thing that FOAF can capture. Although TheyRule wasn't done in FOAF (and isn't open and extensible), some of its data has been translated to FOAF.

FOAF can refer to photographs of the people being described, and several web sites let you find pictures of people in the FOAF network. A variation is to search for pictures that show two or more specific people in the same picture. The FOAFNaut site (http://foafnaut.org) has a whimsical, interactive, graphical display. Figure A.1 is an image from FOAFNaut. You can click the icons for different people and keep expanding the network.

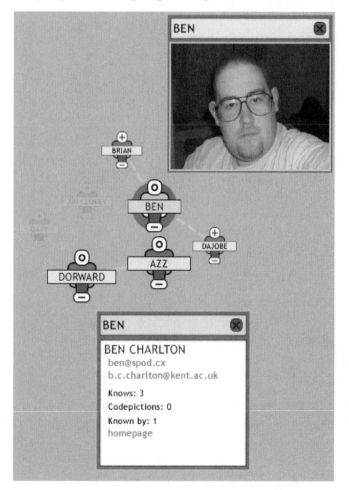

Figure A.1
Example display from the FOAFNaut web site. This application reads FOAF files and follows their internal links to construct a network of who knows whom. It also displays some of the personal information embedded in the FOAF files.

FOAFMap (http://jibbering.com/2002/8/foaf-people-map.svg) puts FOAF community members onto an interactive world map. Clicking on a person's marker brings up a FOAFNaut page for that person.

A.1.5 *Lessons*

FOAF is an interesting toy, but it has more significance than that: It's a test bed for integrating data without using a complex data standard or centralized repository. It has demonstrated that distributed data can be harvested in practice, and that RDF together with RDF processors work well for this purpose. FOAF may serve as an entertaining but useful laboratory and demonstration project, proof that a surprising amount can be accomplished with fairly simple means. That's how the World Wide Web got its own start.

A.2 *Browser bookmarks*

Browser bookmarks are usually organized into folders and a hierarchical list of individual bookmarks. Folders can contain both subfolders and bookmarks. My own set of bookmarks, just to use them as an example, includes about 1,000 folders and about 2,500 bookmarks. The main purpose of bookmarks is to let you return to information (in the form of web pages) that you've discovered. For this to work, you must be able to find the right bookmarks. This task involves the themes of information organization and searching. Information organization plays a prominent role in chapters 2, 3, and 7; searching is the subject of chapter 5, and chapter 3 (on Topic Maps) also relates closely to navigating through the space of information.

I try to name the folders in my set of bookmarks so that they help me find subjects I'm interested in. Here are some of my folder names:

- Agents
- Food
- Semantic Web
- Semantic Networks
- Topic Maps
- XML

I've created an apparently hierarchical vocabulary, as does everyone who puts bookmarks into folders. The names are highly individual—mine aren't much like yours, I'm sure; my vocabulary isn't necessarily consistent or well thought out. Vocabularies, their organization, description, and rules, form the subject of chapter 7 and also play important roles in chapters 2, 3, 7, and 8.

I often find that I want to include a particular bookmark in more than one folder, because it relates to several subjects. The only way to do this with a hierarchical list is to copy the bookmark into several places, but doing so is annoying when you want to annotate or update a duplicated bookmark. Also, the fact that the same bookmark has been placed into several folders means that those folders are related somehow, but ordinary bookmark managers don't discern that a relationship exists.

Another thing I'd like to do with my bookmarks is annotate them—add comments and notes. Annotation is the subject of chapter 4, and both Topic Maps and RDF can give you ways to annotate your bookmarks.

So the apparently simple, mundane subject of browser bookmarks touches perhaps half the material in this book. That makes it suitable as a case study. This isn't just an abstract discussion: I wrote an application based on the results reported here, and it has become indispensable in daily use.[1]

A.2.1 *Goals for the case study*

For the purposes of this case study, here are some goals for bookmark management:

1   Help find web pages otherwise lost in the maze of bookmarks.

2   Remind users what information they've seen before.

3   Comment and otherwise annotate bookmarks.

4   Share bookmarks with others.

5   Combine bookmarks from several browsers.

We might also hope that the bookmark manager will help us make unexpected connections between related bookmarks filed away in different places and forgotten. In the material to follow, you'll see some deficiencies of conventional bookmark managers. Then you'll see how a simple data model, using the Topic Maps approach, can capture the essence of a collection of bookmarks. We also discuss the ease with which the approach can adapt to the inevitable changes in the collection.

A.2.2 *Conventional bookmark managers*

Many bookmark managers are available. Some of them store your bookmarks on a web site so you can get at them when you're away from your computer, and some of those allow other people to use your bookmarks. A few insist on storing

---

[1]   The modeling and application described in this case study have been published as Passin (2003).

all your bookmarks in one flat space, with no folders to divide them; these rely on searching for bookmarks by title and by URL, and sometimes by keywords. This kind of search capability is useful, but it doesn't work well with a large collection. In addition, managing keywords becomes difficult as their number increases.

I've tried several bookmark products over the years. One of the better ones let me categorize any bookmark with as many keywords as I liked, and it could filter on keywords so that I didn't have to sort through all the bookmarks and categories. That application worked pretty well, but here is what I learned:

- *My ability to organize the keywords was limited.* After I had created many categories, I started to forget which keywords should be applied to a given topic. Also, sometimes I still had to put a copy of a bookmark into several categories.

- *A proprietary storage format is a problem.* The company stopped making the in-computer application and went to a system of storing bookmarks on its web site, and then it started charging for storage. The bookmarks that had been stored on my computer became worthless, because they were in a proprietary binary data format that I couldn't use with any other software. Now the company has given up its original bookmark business and maintains a directory of business links.

So, let's add another goal to the list from the previous section:

6 Use a standard data format for interchange of bookmarks.

We'll avoid the proprietary storage format problem by using a standard one—in this case, Topic Maps. If we aren't going to rely on keywords, and we aren't going to get rid of folders, how should we model the bookmark collection?

A.2.3 *Modeling the bookmark collection*

Representing a set of bookmarks involves several design issues. Since the list of folders looks like a real hierarchy and also looks like an organized vocabulary, it's tempting to try to define an ontology that reproduces the folder structure. However, this approach fails for several reasons.

First, the folders don't really form a hierarchy. This is clear because the same bookmark sometimes has to be put into several folders. Besides that, in many cases the folder order could be reversed. For example, if

```
Python
    Programming
```

were to be replaced by

```
Programming
    Python
```

the result would be perfectly sensible and understandable (Python is a computer programming language). But if the order of the nested folders isn't that important, then once again they can't form a true hierarchy.

The folders don't form a structured vocabulary, either. In the previous example, *Programming* isn't a subclass or kind of *Python*, nor is *Python* a kind of *Programming*. What, then, shall we do with the folder names? Obviously they mean something to the person who created them. In fact, they contain a lot of semantic content, but it's irregular and of a very mixed nature.

Folder structure

It's clear that the folder structure into which a bookmark is filed has importance. Say we have the following folders:

```
Python
    Articles
Java
    Articles
```

Obviously, there is some difference between the two *Articles* folders, even though they have the same name.

The key insight here can be seen by writing the folder structures as *path statements*, like this:

```
Java/Articles
Python/Articles
Software/Languages/Java
XML/Schemas/Relax-NG/Tools
```

It's easy to see that the whole path expresses the context for bookmarks located in the right-most folder. These path expressions are reminiscent of *subject language* expressions used by library science to catalog publications. There are many different subject languages; in some of them, the separate terms are ordered hierarchically, and in others they aren't hierarchical but represent different *facets*, or properties of interest. A book might be cataloged according to this non-hierarchical plan: *Location*:: *History*:: *Culture*:: *Economy*. Our bookmark folders are put together in a similar way, except that they aren't as consistent as a subject language that a library would use.

Compound and atomic terms

Next, we can split up the path expressions, since the higher-level folders in turn form the context for the lower-level folders. We split each path into a left-hand and a right-hand part, so that *Software/Languages/Java* spawns *Software/Languages* and *Java*. These two terms are related to each other, because the full subject term (the one before it's split up) is formed from the combination. So, we create a three-way relationship between the two parts and the whole. The right-hand fragment may have no bookmarks of its own, but it forms a link between other paths that share it. The left-hand fragment, which represents a high-level folder, may also have bookmarks filed in it. Figure A.2 illustrates this process of splitting and relating the terms.

We continue by splitting *Software/Languages* into *Software* and *Languages*. If these terms don't already exist in the system, we create them. These two terms are *atomic*, because they aren't compound terms and can't be split any further.

Often, a compound term like *Java* is related to more than one other compound term. My collection of bookmarks includes the compound term *Databases/*

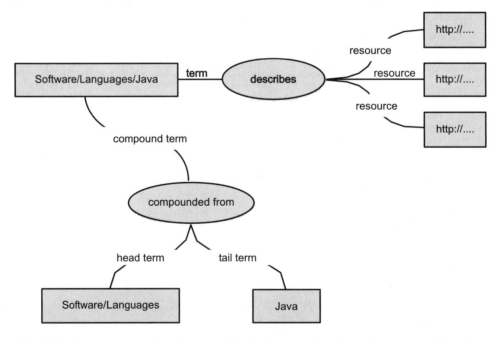

Figure A.2   A compound subject term is split into two parts, forming a three-way relationship between the original term and the two parts. The phrases *compound term*, *head term*, and *tail term* label the roles that the three terms play in the relationship. Here the structure of the bookmark folders is modeled in the style of a topic map (see chapter 3).

Products/Relational/Java. The terms *Databases/Products/Relational* and *Software/Languages* are related through *Java*. Figure A.3 is a screen capture taken from my bookmark manager application,[2] which I designed using these principles.

By means of these relationships between the terms—remember, they came from path statements, which are a condensed way to write the folder structure—it's easy to move around the collection from one area to another related area, even when those areas are far apart in the ordinary tree display that a browser presents. In my collection, I constantly rediscover filing places and related bookmarks that I had completely forgotten about.

With this system, searching is still a helpful tool, but now it tends to lead me on voyages of discovery. Even when I search through the titles of bookmarked

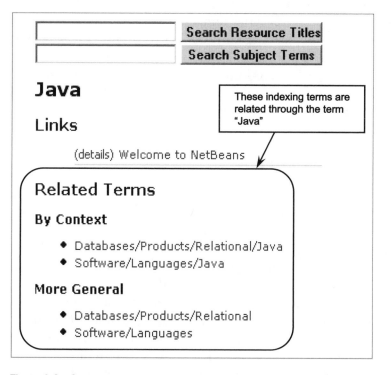

Figure A.3   Screen capture showing all terms related to *Java* compound-term relationships. Conventional bookmark managers don't help you discover forgotten relationships like these.

---

[2] The bookmark manager is included in the TM4Jscript package, located at http://tm4jscript.sourceforge.net.

web pages (using the Search Resource Titles function shown in figure A.3), I find these kind of linkages. They often prove to be more valuable than the specific title I was searching for.

Using this model, it's easy to attach notes and annotations to bookmarks. It would be possible for people to share and combine their bookmark collections over the Internet, simply by sharing the underlying topic maps.

A.2.4 *Simple means*

The analysis presented in this case study is simple and rather mechanical in its application. The computer system knows nothing about the semantics of any of the folder names, except that their relationships are significant.[3] Of course, any other semantic information that the system could discover would serve to improve its ability to help the user, but what is remarkable is how useful the system is with only this simple means of analysis. This simplicity is important in an unexpected way, as well: Over time, the bookmark collection continues to evolve. It's normal for the folder structure to change—bookmarks are re-filed, whole subsections are condensed, new folders with new names are created, and old folders are renamed. The collection is dynamic, and the design is invaluable for letting the system adapt and grow with the bookmark collection.

A.3 *Reflections on the case studies*

Parallels exist between this case study and the FOAF case study. Both of them use simple means. Each of them uses a standard knowledge representation system: FOAF uses RDF, and the bookmark system uses Topic Maps.[4] So it's easy to exchange data between computers and easy to use the data in ways the original designers didn't anticipate. The data will outlive the demise of any of the applications that use it, because it is available in standard formats.

In a word, both case studies demonstrate that a surprising amount of value can be obtained from simple means. This is worth bearing in mind when you're reading the rest of the book, because sometimes it seems that the Semantic Web must be extremely complex to have a hope of working. These case studies give us hope that relatively simple Semantic Web projects can evolve into realistically useful systems.

---

[3] The application also performs a few other simple enhancements that are similarly mechanical. It would take us too far afield to cover them here.

[4] My application uses a topic map, but the model could have been implemented in RDF or even in a relational database.

references

(American Heritage 2001). *The American Heritage Dictionary*, 4th ed. New York: Delta Book.

(Amitay 2000) Amitay, Einat. 2001. InCommonSense: Rethinking Web Search Results. IEEE International Conference on Multimedia and Expo. ICME 2000. http://citeseer.nj.nec.com/cache/papers/cs/14426/http:zSzzSzwww.ics.mq.edu.auzSz~einatzSzpublicationszSzieee_multimedia2000.pdf/amitay00incommonsense.pdf.

(Ankolekar et al 2001) Ankolekar, Anupriya et al. 2001. DAML-S: Semantic Markup for Web Services. SWWS'01: The First Semantic Web Working Symposium. http://www.semanticweb.org/SWWS/program/full/paper57.pdf.

(Anutariya et al 2001) Anutariya, Chutiporn, et al. 2001. Semantic Web Modeling and Programming with XDD. SWWS'01: The First Semantic Web Working Symposium. http://www.semanticweb.org/SWWS/program/full/paper17.pdf.

(Berners-Lee 2000) Berners-Lee, Tim. 2000. *Weaving the Web: The Original Design and Ultimate Destiny of the World Wide Web by Its Inventor.* New York: HarperCollins.

(Berners-Lee, Hendler, and Lassila 2001) Berners-Lee, Tim, James Hendler, and Ora Lassila. 2001. The Semantic Web. *Scientific American*, May. www.sciam.com/article.cfm?articleID=00048144-10D2-1C70-84A9809EC588EF21.

(Blyth 1982) Blyth, R. H. *Haiku*, vol. 3, Summer. Tokyo: Autumn Hokuseido Press.

(Bratko 2001) Bratko, Ivan. 2001. *Prolog Programming for Artificial Intelligence*, 3d ed. Harlow, England; New York: Addison-Wesley.

(Bray 2003) Bray, Tim. 2003. On Search: Metadata. http://tbray.org/ongoing/When/200x/2003/07/29/SearchMeta.

(Broekstra and Kampman 2003) Broekstra, Jeen, and Arjan Kampman. 2003. Inferencing and Truth Maintenance in RDF Schema: Exploring a Naive Practical Approach. First International Workshop on Practical and Scalable Semantic Systems. http:// km.aifb.uni-karlsruhe.de/ws/psss03/proceedings/broekstra-et-al.pdf.

(Bryson et al 2002) Bryson, Joanna, et al. 2002. Agent-Based Composite Services in DAML-S: The Behavior-Oriented Design of an Intelligent Semantic Web. www.cs. bath.ac.uk/~jjb/ftp/springer-daml.pdf.

(Butler 2003) Butler, Mark. 2003. Is the Semantic Web Hype? www-uk.hpl.hp.com/people/ marbut/isTheSemanticWebHype.pdf.

(Cost et al 2001) Cost, R. Scott, et al. 2001. ITTALKS: A Case Study in the Semantic Web and DAML. SWWS'01: The First Semantic Web Working Symposium. http://www. semanticweb.org/SWWS/program/full/paper41.pdf.

(Cranefield 2001) Cranefield, Stephen. 2001. UML and the Semantic Web. SWWS'01: The First Semantic Web Working Symposium. http://www.semanticweb.org/SWWS/ program/full/paper1.pdf.

(De Roure 2003) De Roure, David. 2003. W3C Tracking—OWL. Global Grid Forum 7. www.semanticgrid.org/presentations/ggf7/ggfowl.ppt.

(Degler and Battle 2003) Degler, Duane, and Lisa Battle. 2003. Can Topic Maps Describe Context for Enterprise-Wide Applications? Extreme Markup Languages 2003. www. mulberrytech.com/Extreme/Proceedings/html/2003/Degler01/EML2003Degler01-toc.html.

(Description Logics) Description Logics. http://dl.kr.org.

(Desmontils and Jaquin 2001) Desmontils, E., and C. Jaquin. 2001. Indexing a Web Site with a Terminology Oriented Ontology. SWWS'01: The First Semantic Web Working Symposium. http://www.semanticweb.org/SWWS/program/full/paper5.pdf.

(Doctorow 2001) Doctorow, Cory. 2001. Metacrap: Putting the Torch to Seven Straw-Men of the Meta-Utopia. www.well.com/~doctorow/metacrap.htm.

(Dornfest 2000) Dornfest, Rael. 2000. Writing RSS 1.0. www.oreillynet.com/pub/a/network/ 2000/08/25/magazine/rss_tut.html?page=1.

(Enderton 2001) Enderton, Herbert. 2001. *A Mathematical Introduction to Logic*. San Diego: Harcourt/Academic Press.

(Euzenat 2001) Euzenat, Jerome. 2001. An Infrastructure for Formally Ensuring Interoperability in a Heterogeneous Semantic Web. SWWS'01: The First Semantic Web Working Symposium. http://www.semanticweb.org/SWWS/program/full/paper16.pdf.

(Extreme) Extreme Markup Languages. www.mulberrytech.com/Extreme/index.html.

(Finkelstein et al 2001) Finkelstein, Lev, et al. 2001. Placing Search in Context: The Concept Revisited. *ACM Transactions on Information Systems* 20:116–131. http://portal.acm.org/ citation.cfm?doid=503104.503110.

(FIPA) Foundation for Intelligent Physical Agents. www.fipa.org.

(FIPA-OS) FIPA-OS open source project. www.emorphia.com/research/about.htm.

(FOLDOC) Free On-line Dictionary of Computing. http://wombat.doc.ic.ac.uk/foldoc/contents.html.

(Foster, Kesselman, and Tuecke 2001) Foster, Ian, Carl Kesselman, and Steven Tuecke. 2001. The Anatomy of the Grid: Enabling Scalable Virtual Organizations. *International J. Supercomputer Applications* 15. http://www.globus.org/research/papers/anatomy.pdf.

(Freese 2003) Freese, Eric. 2003. Taking Topic Maps to the Nth dimension. Extreme Markup Languages 2003. www.mulberrytech.com/Extreme/Proceedings/html/2003/Freese01/EML2003Freese01-toc.html.

(Garcia and Delgado 2001) 2001. Garcia, Roberto, and Jaime Delgado. Brokerage of Intellectual Property Rights in the Semantic Web. SWWS'01: The First Semantic Web Working Symposium. http://www.semanticweb.org/SWWS/program/full/paper5.pdf.

(Golbeck, Parsia, and Hendler 2003) Golbeck, Jennifer, Bijan Parsia, and James Hendler. 2003. Trust Networks on the Semantic Web. Cooperative Intelligent Agents 2003. www.mindswap.org/papers/Trust.pdf.

(Gould 1989) Gould, Stephen Jay. 1989. *Wonderful Life: The Burgess Shale and the Nature of History.* New York: Norton.

(Gould 1993) ———. 1993. *Eight Little Piggies: Reflections in Natural History.* New York: Norton.

(Guha and McCool) Guha, R. V., and Rob McCool. TAP: Towards a Web of Data. http://tap.stanford.edu/j1.html.

(Horrocks 2002) Horrocks, Ian. 2002. Description Logic: Axioms and Rules. European Conference on Artificial Intelligence 2002. www.cs.man.ac.uk/~horrocks/Slides/dagstuhlS070202.pdf.

(Hoschek 2002) Hoschek, Wolfgang. 2002. The Web Service Discovery Architecture. IEEE/ACM Supercomputing Conference. http://edms.cern.ch/file/342747/1/wsda2002-1.pdf.

(IBM and Microsoft 2001) IBM and Microsoft. 2001. Web Services Framework. W3C Workshop on Web Services. www.w3.org/2001/03/WSWS-popa/paper51.

(Joseph 2002) Joseph, Sister Miriam. 2002. *The Trivium: The Liberal Arts of Logic, Grammar, and Rhetoric.* Philadelphia: Paul Dry Books.

(Keil 1979) Keil, Frank 1979. *Semantic and Conceptual Development: An Ontological Perspective.* Cambridge, MA: Harvard University Press.

(Klein and Bernstein 2001) Klein, Mark and Abraham Bernstein. Searching for Services on the Semantic Web Using Process Ontologies. SWWS'01: The First Semantic Web Working Symposium. http://www.semanticweb.org/SWWS/program/full/paper2.pdf.

(Lakoff and Johnson 1999) Lakoff, George, and Mark Johnson. 1999. *Philosophy in the Flesh: The Embodied Mind and Its Challenge to Western Thought.* New York: Basic Books.

(McGrath and Murray 2003) McGrath, Sean, and Fergal Murray. 2003. Principles of Service Oriented Integration. www.propylon.com/products/whitepapers/principles_of_soi.pdf.

(Nardi and Brachman 2003) Nardi, Daniele, and Ronald Brachman. 2003. An Introduction to Description Logics. In *The Description Logic Handbook*. Cambridge: Cambridge University Press. www.cs.man.ac.uk/~franconi/dl/course/dlhb/dlhb-01.pdf.

(Ogbuji 2002) Ogbuji, Uche. 2002. Using RDF with SOAP: Beyond Remote Procedure Calls. www-106.ibm.com/developerworks/webservices/library/ws-soaprdf/.

(Park and Hunting 2002) Park, Jack, and Sam Hunting. 2002. *XML Topic Maps: Creating and Using Topic Maps for the Web*. Boston: Addison-Wesley.

(Passin 2003) Passin, Thomas. 2003. Browser Bookmark Management with Topic Maps. Extreme Markup Languages 2003. www.mulberrytech.com/Extreme/Proceedings/xslfo-pdf/2003/Passin01/EML2003Passin01.pdf.

(Patel-Schneider et al 1998) Patel-Schneider, Peter, et al. 1998. NeoClassic User's Guide Version 1.0. www.bell-labs.com/project/classic/papers/NeoGuide.

(Patel-Schneider et al 1998a) ———. 1998. Introduction. NeoClassic User's Guide Version 1.0. www.bell-labs.com/project/classic/papers/NeoGuide/node1.html.

(RAPPID) RAPPID (Responsible Agents for Product-Process Integrated Design). www.erim.org/cec/rappid/rappid.htm.

(Reagle 2002) Reagle, Joseph M. Jr. 2002. Finding Bacon's Key: Does Google Show How the Semantic Web Could Replace Public Key Infrastructure? www.w3.org/2002/03/key-free-trust.html.

(Reynolds et al 2002) Reynolds, Dave, et al. 2002. SWAD-Europe Deliverable 12.1.1: Semantic Web Applications—Analysis and Selection. www.w3.org/2001/sw/Europe/reports/open_demonstrators/hp-applications-selection.html.

(Richardson, Agrawal, and Domingos 2003) Richardson, Matthew, Rakesh Agrawal, and Pedro Domingos. Trust Management for the Semantic Web. Second International Semantic Web Conference. www.cs.washington.edu/homes/mattr/doc/iswc2003/iswc2003.pdf.

(Salz 2003) Salz, Rich. 2003. Vox Populi: Web Services from the Grassroots. http://webservices.xml.com/pub/a/ws/2003/07/08/salz.html.

(Seidl 2001) Seidl, F. Andy. 2001. Elmer Preview: A Standards-Based Architecture for Creating a Unified Information Space. XML 2001. www.idealliance.org/papers/xml2001papers/slides/Seidl/Elmer%20Preview%20-%20XML%202001%20Conference%20-%20Orlando.ppt.

(Shabajee, Miller, and Dingley 2002) Shabajee, Paul, Libby Miller, and Andy Dingley. 2002. Adding Value to Large Multimedia Collections through Annotation Technologies and Tools: Serving Communities of Interest. Museums and the Web 2002. www.archimuse.com/mw2002/papers/shabajee/shabajee.html.

(Sokvitne 2000) Sokvitne, Lloyd. 2000. Understanding Metadata. www.servicetasma-nia.tas.gov.au/papers/understanding_metadata.asp.

(Sowa 2000) Sowa, John. 2000. *Knowledge Representation: Logical, Philosophical, and Compu-tational Foundations*. Pacific Grove: Brooks/Cole.

(St. Laurent 2003) St. Laurent, Simon. 2003. There Is No Cheap Metadata. www.oreilly-net.com/pub/wlg/3584.

(Svenonius 2000) Svenonius, Elaine. 2000. *The Intellectual Foundation of Information Orga-nization*. Cambridge, MA: MIT Press.

(SWAD-E) Semantic Web Advanced Development for Europe. http://www.w3.org/2001/sw/Europe/.

(SWWS) Semantic Web Working Symposium. www.semanticweb.org/SWWS.

(TAGA) Travel Agent Game in Agentcities. http://taga.umbc.edu/taga.

(Tallis, Goldman, and Balzer 2001) Tallis, Marcello, Neil Goldman, and Robert Balzer. The Briefing Associate: A Role for COTS Applications in the Semantic Web. SWWS'01: The First Semantic Web Working Symposium. http://www.semanticweb.org/SWWS/program/full/paper54.pdf.

(TM4Jscript) Topic Maps for JavaScript. http://sourceforge.net/projects/tm4jscript.

(Tuecke et al 2002) Tuecke, S., et al. 2002. Grid Service Specification. www.gridforum.org/ogsi-wg/drafts/draft-ggf-ogsi-gridservice-04_2002-10-04.pdf.

(Tuttle et al 2001) Tuttle, Mark, et al. The Semantic Web as "Perfection Seeking:" A View from Drug Terminology. SWWS'01: The First Semantic Web Working Symposium. http://www.semanticweb.org/SWWS/program/full/paper49.pdf.

(Utah) Proposed State of Utah Web Metadata Element Set Standard. http://gils.utah.gov/standardsutah.htm.

(W3C 1999) W3C. 1999. Resource Description Framework (RDF) Model and Syntax Specification. www.w3.org/TR/1999/REC-rdf-syntax-19990222.[1]

(W3C 2000) ———. 2000. Semantic Web Development: Technical Proposal. www.w3.org/2000/01/sw/DevelopmentProposal.

(W3C 2003) ———. 2003. Semantic Web Activity Statement. www.w3.org/2001/sw/Activity.

(W3C 2003a) ———. 2003. SOAP Version 1.2 Part 0: Primer. www.w3.org/TR/soap12-part0/.

---

[1] The original RDF Recommendation was published by the W3C in 1999, but work has continued both on RDF and on related subjects, such as RDF Schemas (covered in chapter 7) and the theoretical basis of RDF. The newer version of the RDF Recommendation, found at www.w3.org/TR/rdf-syntax-grammar, together with a suite of related documents, have now been released as final Recommendations. The material in chapter 2 by and large follows the 1999 Recommendation, but the changes that the new versions have brought are small as far as this chapter is concerned.

(W3C 2003b) ———. 2003. Web Services Architecture. www.w3.org/TR/2003/WD-ws-arch-20030514.

(W3C 2004) ———. 2004. Entailment. Resource Description Framework (RDF): Concepts and Abstract Syntax. www.w3.org/TR/rdf-concepts/#section-Entailment.

(W3C 2004a) ———. 2004. RDF Semantics. www.w3.org/TR/rdf-mt.

(W3C 2004b) ———. 2004. RDF Vocabulary Description Language 1.0: RDF Schema. www.w3.org/TR/rdf-schema/.

(W3C 2004c) ———. 2004. Resource Description Framework (RDF): Concepts and Abstract Syntax. www.w3.org/TR/rdf-concepts.

(Weiss 2000) Weiss, Gerhard, ed. 2000. *Multiagent Systems: A Modern Approach to Distributed Artificial Intelligence*. Cambridge, MA: MIT Press.

(Weisstein) Weisstein, Eric. Graph. From *MathWorld*—A Wolfram Web Resource. http://mathworld.wolfram.com/Graph.html.

(WordNet) WordNet. www.cogsci.princeton.edu/~wn/.

(Zamir and Etzioni 1998) Zemir, Oren, and Oren Etzioni. 1998. Web Document Clustering: A Feasibility Demonstration. http://citeseer.nj.nec.com/zamir98web.html.

index